*The Remaking of Pittsburgh*

SUNY Series in American Social History
CHARLES STEPHENSON AND ELIZABETH PLECK, EDITORS

FRANCIS G. COUVARES

*Amherst College*

# The Remaking of Pittsburgh

## CLASS AND CULTURE IN AN INDUSTRIALIZING CITY, 1877–1919

*The State University of New York Press*

ALBANY

Published by
State University of New York Press, Albany

© 1984 State University of New York

All rights reserved

Printed in the United States of America

For information, address State University of New York
Press, State University Plaza, Albany, N.Y., 12246


**Library of Congress Cataloging in Publication Data**

Couvares, Francis G., 1948–
  The remaking of Pittsburgh.

  (SUNY series in American social history)
  Bibliography: p. 162
  Includes index.
  1. Pittsburgh (Pa.)—Social conditions. 2. Pittsburgh (Pa.)—Industries. 3.
Labor and laboring classes—Pennsylvania—Pittsburgh. 4. Pittsburgh (Pa.)—
Popular culture. I. Title. II. Series.
HN80.P6C68 1984       306′.09748′86       83-5044
ISBN 0-87395-778-4
ISBN 0-87395-779-2 (pbk.)

10  9  8  7

# Contents

# List of Tables

# Acknowledgments

I could not have carried out the research for this book without the help of several institutions and persons. I thank the Horace H. Rackham School of Graduate Studies, University of Michigan, for a grant that helped finance the early stages of research. For research assistance I thank the staffs of the University of Michigan Graduate Library; the Robert Hutchings Goddard Library, Clark University, especially Jean Perkins, Mary Powers, and Mary Hartman; the Historical Society of Western Pennsylvania; the Archives of Industrial Society, University of Pittsburgh, especially Frank Zabrosky; and the Carnegie Library of Pittsburgh, Pennsylvania Division, especially Ann M. Loyd, who located sources, found the illustration that graces the cover of this book, and supplied some of the old maps on which the map in this book is based. Tim Fast and the staff of the Clark University Cartography laboratory drafted the map expertly and quickly. Terry Reynolds, Rene Baril, and Roxanne Rawson ushered the manuscript through several stages of revision, and Trudy Powers provided "emergency" typing help. Dr. Susan Suarez of SUNY Press has been a helpful and patient editor.

For encouragement, inspiration, and critical insight, I thank first of all Gerald F. Linderman. He devoted himself to the health of this project and this scholar for many years, first as graduate mentor, then as friend and colleague. I intend to repay him in the only way he would accept—by becoming a better writer and teacher of history.

Elizabeth Pleck, Charles Tilly, David Montgomery, and David Hollinger helped nurture the dissertation from which this book evolved and offered sound advice on revisions, although I took it probably less often than I should have.

In recent years, versions of several portions of this book have benefitted from the critical attention of friends and scholars. In particular, I thank Bruce Laurie for some of the best criticism and all of the best jokes. In a sense, he is responsible for this book. In my first history course as an undergraduate at the University of Pittsburgh, Bruce served as teaching fellow in a way that made me want to emulate him. After years of distant, although fond, friendship, it is my good luck now to have him as a neighbor; from this new vantage, I intend to exploit his energy and practical wisdom even more methodically than I have in the past.

I also thank Charles Stephenson, David Brody, Herbert Gutman, David Wilkins, Leon Fink, Bruce McConachie, and Richard Oestreicher for helpful comments along the way. Most recently, an article drawn from Chapters 7 and 8 was expertly shaped and edited by Michael Frisch and Daniel Walkowitz, who included it in their *Working-Class America: Essays on Labor, Community, and American Society* (1982). I acknowledge my debt to them and to the University of Illinois Press, which published it.

In the last stages of revision, my former colleagues at Clark University, George Billias, Douglas Little, John Conron, and Ronald Formisano supplied useful comment and encouragement. For a longer period of time, although at a greater distance, I have benefitted from the advice and good cheer of David Lux and Harold Cook. I am grateful to these friends and scholars.

Finally, my debt to Betty, my wife, and Peter, my son, can be acknowledged, but never repaid. Their disinterested support made the research and writing of this book possible. They contributed nothing to scholarship, but everything to one scholar. I dedicate the book to them.

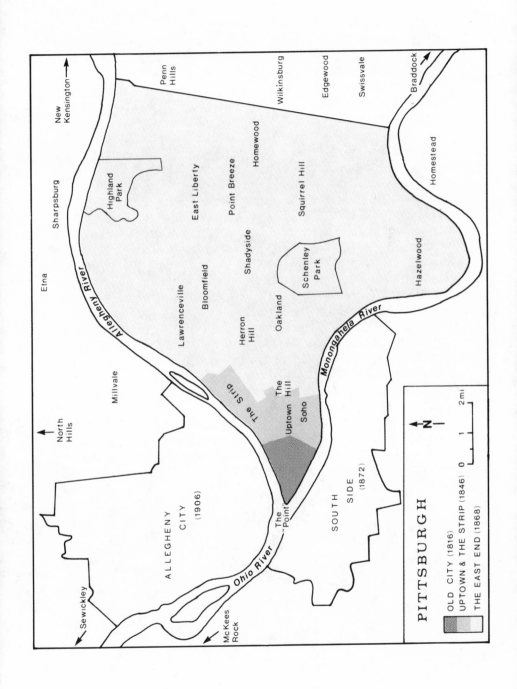

PITTSBURGH

OLD CITY (1816)

UPTOWN & THE STRIP (1846)

THE EAST END (1868)

0    1    2 mi

N

Sewickley

North
Hills

Etna

Sharpsburg

New
Kensington

Penn
Hills

Wilkinsburg

Edgewood

Swissvale

Braddock

Highland
Park

East Liberty

Point Breeze

Homewood

Squirrel Hill

Homestead

Millvale

Allegheny River

Lawrenceville

Bloomfield

Shadyside

Schenley
Park

Hazelwood

Herron
Hill

Oakland

Monongahela River

The Strip

Uptown

The Hill

Soho

McKees
Rock

Ohio River

The
"Point"

ALLEGHENY
CITY
(1906)

SOUTH
SIDE
(1872)

# Introduction

To know Pittsburg thoroughly is a liberal education in "the kind of culture demanded by modern times."

—James Parton, 1868

This study explores the cultural dimensions of industrialization in one American city. Pittsburgh recommends itself as the subject of such a study because, as Parton[1] and many subsequent observers noted, it was so preeminent and exemplary a site of industrialization in America, indeed, in the world. Surprisingly, however, it has received from historians little attention compared to other great cities such as Chicago and Philadelphia, and even compared to smaller industrial cities such as Lowell and Lynn. Given this historiographical oversight, I have in this study relied less on a body of secondary sources devoted to Pittsburgh itself than on the suggestive work of social historians engaged in the study of other times and places.

My study of Pittsburgh took shape initially in response to my observation of a sharp contrast between earlier and later stages in the history of that industrializing city, particularly of its working class. This contrast generated a question: How did the city that embraced the labor struggle of 1877 turn into the city which so fiercely repudiated the labor struggle of 1919? What forces transformed a plebeian community, in which industrial workers and other petty citizens exercised a real measure of power over their lives, into a grim metropolis whose inhabitants were decisively mastered by Big Steel?

*1*

In pursuing the question I have assumed that an answer can best be approached along the lines of the "new social history," which insists that the cultural and political dimensions of the industrializing process were as important as the economic ones. At the present time it is hardly necessary to delineate the pedigree of a study conducted along such lines. Other young historians—e.g., Paul Faler, Alan Dawley, Bruce Laurie, John Cumbler, Leon Fink—have already explored similar questions and, in so doing, have acknowledged their debt to two scholars, E.P. Thompson and Herbert Gutman.

In *The Making of the English Working Class,* Thompson revealed, with extraordinary detail, the profound links between class and culture in industrializing Britain and, in the process, released a generation of social historians from the grip of a narrowly economic analysis of social change. Taking a cue from Thompson, Gutman showed, in a series of articles published in the 1960s, the ways in which republican ideology, religion, popular culture, and local community shaped class consciousness and action in nineteenth-century America. His work made it possible for me to inquire into, among other things, the role of temperance, leisure, and local political culture in shaping the values and actions of plebeian Pittsburghers.

Another historian influenced by Thompson, Gareth Stedman Jones, suggested a way to extend the themes explored by Gutman into the early twentieth century. His "Working-Class Culture and Working-Class Politics in London, 1870–1900," led me to explore the extent to which the emergence of mass culture remade, perhaps coopted, working-class consciousness and action in the twentieth century.

The work of other historians sensitive to the cultural dimensions of social change provided more general inspiration for my enterprise. Some, like Natalie Davis, William Sewell, Raymond Williams, Asa Briggs, Brian Harrison, and Peter Burke, in studies of European society and culture, were influenced to varying degrees by Marxist social theory and by the methods of cultural anthropology. Others, like John Higham, Thomas Bender, Robert Sklar, and John Kasson, worked within the more familar historiographical context of American studies and intellectual history. All encouraged me to read in popular culture the imprint of class and other kinds of social experience and, conversely, to recognize the ways in which belief, custom, and ritual shape responses to the socioeconomic order.

Finally, several other historians influenced this study. David Brody and David Montgomery have gone beyond the old labor history's "institutional" approach, with its focus on workplace and labor union, without repudiating its commitment to the study of the economic constituents of class power. Brody's pathbreaking *Steelworkers in America: The Nonunion Era* and Montgomery's essays in *Workers' Control in America* laid the groundwork for my interpretation of the "craftsmen's empire" and, more generally, for my analysis of the impact of work upon working-class culture. In a different, although related, way, the urban historian Sam Bass Warner alerted me to the ways in which the functional reorganization of urban space in the late nineteenth century reinforced the class differences generated by industrial capitalism. From these historians I hope I have learned to discipline my fascination with the milieu of working-class life, and to remain cognizant of the structural foundations of that milieu.

Given this historiographical context, I shaped my study of Pittsburgh around another, more specific question: What were the sources of conflict and solidarity within the working class and within the wider community? The first and larger part of the text addresses that question within the period between the 1860s and 1880s. It describes the craftsmen's empire in the mills and shows how plebeian culture and local politics reinforced working-class power and communal solidarity in Pittsburgh. It also reveals some of the tensions among different kinds of workers and between them and other social groups in the city, and investigates the way in which local politics and the temperance movement both reflected and sought to resolve those tensions. The second part shows how new immigration and the proletarianization of work in the steel mills combined with the reorganization of urban space to shatter that local community within which workers had exercised significant power. It also describes the emergence of a more assertive elite culture, and details the earnest, but unsuccessful, efforts of reformers to "civilize" the increasingly alien masses. And, finally, it outlines the emergence of a new mass culture which, on the one hand, confirmed the demise of the plebeian city, and on the other, laid the ground for a new cultural consolidation, which would be realized in the context of the industrial nation rather than the industrial city.

A final note. "Writing an introduction," quipped a colleague of mine recently, "is like trying to draw the bull's-eye around a dozen arrows you've just shot at a wall." I have tried here to offer a target for the chapters that follow. However, because my topical arrows have been drawn from several quivers—most obviously, from labor history, urban history, and the history of popular culture—the target is broader, perhaps more misshapen, and certainly less densely occupied than it might have been had I exploited a single quiver more systematically. Nevertheless, as a consequence both of personal inclination and of the limitations of primary and secondary sources, I have chosen to write a series of essays on discrete, although interrelated, topics. In so doing, I hope I have made a suggestive contribution to that community of discourse known as social history. At the very least, in any case, I will be satisfied if readers simply come away from the text with a richer knowledge of the life of a great city and of the struggle of its people to resist and accommodate to the experience of industrialization.

# CHAPTER 1

# 1877

On July 19, 1877, trainmen in Pittsburgh unhooked their engines and went on strike. Four days later most of the property of the Pennsylvania Railroad within the city limits lay in smoking ruins; most industrial workers in the city and surrounding towns had also joined the protest in the streets of Pittsburgh; and most of the city's opinion-makers and respectable citizens concurred in ascribing responsibility for the violence and arson that accompanied the strike to the railroad and its allies and not to the working class of the Iron City.[1]

These events were neither entirely unique nor unprecedented. In 1873, at the start of a severe economic depression, similarly spontaneous or loosely organized strikes had shaken the railroads and mobilized much public support. The latest trouble, occurring in the fourth year of that sustained slump, involved trainmen throughout the country. Events of the next few days in other town and cities in America resembled those in Pittsburgh. But Pittsburgh's upheaval surpassed all others in intensity and breadth. More than anywhere else, in the upheaval and in the response to it, Pittsburghers reaffirmed the sturdy, if not seamless, character of their community.

Within hours of the trainmen's walkout, thousands of Pittsburghers had come to embrace a protest not simply against an employer, but against "monopoly." Although they offered no systematic definition of the term, what they meant was clear. They meant the Pennsylvania Railroad, with its immense resources, its dominance of markets, its arrogant treatment of distant customers, its political influence, and its militarized command structure, which turned employees into mere foot soldiers and sometimes into mutineers.

In the years immediately preceding the strike, the railroad had won especially harsh criticism from Pittsburgh newspaper and politicians. William C. McCarthy, pressman, labor leader, and spokesman for small property owners in the old city, had been elected mayor a few years earlier on a platform denouncing the city's assumption of a huge railroad debt. As the small property owners of the old wards were taxed most heavily to pay off the city's bonded debt, McCarthy linked all the forces calling for the extension of city services to the suburbs with the forces of monopoly epitomized by the Pennsylvania Railroad. Supplementing the mayor's coalition of workers and small property holders was the influence of businesssmen who resented the high-handed practices and discriminatory rate structure of the railroad and had for years tried to generate competition. Most recently, Pittsburgh men and money had reorganized the Pittsburgh and Lake Erie Railroad to compete for the seventy-mile run to Youngstown, Ohio. Editorials like that run by the *Pittsburgh Post* on July 6, entitled "Railroad Vultures," thus struck a common chord of indignation throughout the city.[2]

As soon as the strike began, other workers spontaneously associated their own grievances against employers with those of the trainmen. Before it became a riot, the strike had already begun to look like a general strike. Miners, hearing of the trouble, began heading for Pittsburgh on striker-run trains and on foot. At many iron plants, workers who had recently won strikes against wage reduction presented new demands. One special source of bitterness was the refusal of some managers to pay the "hot dollar" bonus for work during the traditional July-August break. At the Jones and Laughlin plant the effect was dramatic. Ironmaster B.F. Jones noted in his diary:

> Today tuesday the 24th nearly all the day hands about the mill have been in a state of excitement since coming to work this morning and now at 2 P.M. after holding an excitable meeting they have all (some 350 men) marched out of the mill saying they must have 25 cents per day added to their wages. . . .

These were dollar-a-day men, laborers whose wages had sunk during the depression and who were trying to recover their losses. Having no intention of submitting to the laborers' demands, Jones put them off with meetings, but he had also to deal with "the forge hands" and the "cinder boys," and, more important, with the highly skilled puddlers. Although bound by contract to stay at work, the puddlers made it clear they were "with the strikers."[3]

The general strike turned into a riot only after the railroad introduced outside force. Although strikers and their allies had already damaged some railroad property, for the most part their activities remained orderly. They concentrated on shutting down commercial operations while making an effort to deliver mail and provide some commuter service. However, the corporation convinced the governor of Pennsylvania to use state militia to reopen the line. After a Pittsburgh militia unit refused to oppose the strikers, a Philadelphia militia company arrived to a hostile reception. Met by a huge crown of taunting men, women, and children, the nervous militiamen fired, killing and wounding dozens of people, and were furiously chased out of the city.

Even a flintly ironmaster like B.F. Jones lamented the killing of "citizens" and noted. "This started the riot and workingmen throughout the country and city took it up. . . ."[4] From that moment, the property of the Pennsylvania Railroad was doomed. Nearly every depot, rail, car, and engine within reach of the crowds went up in flames or was otherwise destroyed.

From their homes nearby, middle-class citizens looked upon the flames and anxiously hoped for order. But few possessed either the means or the clearly fashioned desire to crush a community in revolt. Few voices rose to defend the railroad or to elevate the crisis to the status of a revolution against property in general. Respectable citizens directed their indignation less toward the strikers and rioters than toward the unscrupulous policies of the railroad and its allies, who had gone over the head of the mayor in soliciting troops.

Thus, when Mayor McCarthy called on citizens to contain the violence and protect property, he insisted that his effort was not directed against the strike. Similarly, when steelmaster James Park, Jr. and banker John R. McCune rallied a crowd of people leaving church on Sunday, July 23, they made it clear they had no intention of opposing the strike, but only of returning the conflict to its local context. "We do not want any more military here, God knows!" In its first public statement, the committee of safety organized by McCarthy:

Resolved, that in making this effort, we pledge our faith to the workmen. We have no purpose to assist in the introduction of armed force from a distance but look solely to the protection of the rights and interests of all by amicable means.

The committee enlisted labor leaders in the cause. Joseph Bishop of the Amalgamated Association of Iron and Steel Workers, John M. Davis of the Knights of Labor, Andrew Burtt, local teacher and champion of labor, and Thomas A. Armstrong, editor of the *National Labor Tribune,* served on the committee along with businessmen, shopkeepers, clergymen, and others. The committee sought to protect residents and retailers from the spreading threats of fire and looting. John M. Davis coauthored the proclamation calling upon "industrious workmen" to oppose the "thieves and similar classes of population, with whom our working classes have no affiliation." At the Oliver Brothers factory in Allegheny, members of the Amalgamated lodge took up the call and stood guard around the plant for the remainder of the disturbance. Miles Humphreys, the leader of the iron puddlers, who had just been nominated by the Republicans to succeed McCarthy as mayor, made a speech at the depot denouncing violence and looting.[5]

In all these efforts, however, no attempt was made to associate disorder with a specific occupational or ethnic group. As one student of the upheaval has shown,[6] those arrested during the disturbances represented an almost perfect cross-section of Pittsburgh's ethnic and occupational structure, including many skilled craftsmen. Although angered and frustrated by the excesses of the crowd, neither craftsmen, politicians, nor other respectable citizens anathematized the rioters as an alien or incomprehensible mob. On the contrary, they saw the rioters as fellow citizens driven to extremes by outsiders.

Why did a strike of unskilled trainmen turn into a community revolt against monopoly? The next several chapters will attempt to answer this question. Chapter Two will discuss the power of skilled craftsmen at the workplace and in the public life of the Iron City. Chapter Three will describe plebeian culture, which reinforced the values of craft autonomy, republican equality, and local solidarity. Chapters Four and Five will indicate the extent to which the ideological heritage of anti-monopoly republicanism and the loosely organized character of local politics permitted plebeian citizens to balance, and sometimes overmatch, the power of the industrial elite. In brief, these chapters will show that the events of 1877 represented not a sharp departure from the social norm in Pittsburgh, but rather a spectacular dramatization of that norm.

# CHAPTER 2

# The Craftsmen's Empire

In the years between 1860 and 1920 Pittsburgh was an industrial city. Until about 1890, however, methods and relations of work that might appear "pre-industrial"—and would be inconceivable in later years—emerged in that thoroughly industrial setting. In particular, in each factory a "craftsmen's empire" limited the power of employers and set the stage for a broader labor movement that would contend with capital for the future of the industrial order.

Coal, iron, and glass laid the foundation of Pittsburgh's economy. The entire southwestern Pennsylvania region was built, literally, on coal. Outcroppings six to fifteen feet thick stared from the sides of hills. Throughout the nineteenth century, inhabitants of the region took advantage of that cheap fuel to heat their homes and run their workshops. The immense "Pittsburgh seam" made a major contribution to the region's economic growth, especially to the growth of the iron and steel industry in the latter decades of the century. But its impact was limited until the 1850s, when low-sulphur coking coal was discovered in Connelsville and other sites to the south and west of Pittsburgh. Well before then—when iron mills still relied on charcoal or on anthracite imported from eastern mines—Pittsburgh had already emerged as a manufacturing center.[1] What fueled its growth was not coal but location. Pittsburgh was perfectly placed to supply manufactured goods to the booming trans-Allegheny West.

By the 1830s, Pittsburgh had already begun to meet the growing western demand for glass, especially window glass. Because of its fragility, glass could not easily be transported across the mountains, and so, from its vantage at the head of the Ohio River, Pittsburgh quickly became the glass capital of America. Immediately following the Civil War, the demand upon glass works of every kind was so great that many ran "21 months without stopping," an unusual practice in the trade which customarily observed a two-month break in the heat of summer. By 1880 Allegheny County was producing nearly 27 percent of all glass manufactured in the United States. Its nearest rival, Philadelphia, turned out 7.7 percent. Throughout the period, glass making accounted for about one-tenth of all industrial employment in Allegheny County.[2]

The iron and steel industry was Pittsburgh's largest, and growing larger.[3] The biggest employer, the producer of the greatest value, the most heavily capitalized—by every economic measure, iron and steel led the way. The early discovery of iron ore in western Pennsylvania, the unlimited supply of wood and later mineral fuel, the rivers which afforded ready transport for immense tonnages, all contributed to Pittsburgh's ascendance in the iron industry. Moreover, the Civil War lent massive impetus to that growth. The sudden, staggering demand for all manner of hardware, especially for rails, cars, ordnance, and textile machinery, presented Pittsburgh's ironmasters a challenge they met with relish. While industrial employment in Allegheny County doubled in the 1860s—as it did in coal and glass—it nearly tripled in iron and steel. While capital investment nearly tripled and value of product more than tripled in Allegheny County in these years, they rose in iron and steel by a staggering 330 percent and 532 percent, respectively.

By 1880, Allegheny County was producing about one-eighth of all iron and steel tonnage in the United States. The value of this product—more than $46 million—represented fully one-sixth of the entire value of iron and steel production in the nation. Iron and steel dominated Allegheny County, accounting for nearly half of the industrial employment, investment, and productive value. If to the total of rolling mills, blast furnaces, and assorted nut, bolt, and pipe firms is added the host of smaller machine shops and foundries and the associated metal-working and hardware firms, the significance of iron and steel to the life of city and region becomes even more apparent.

The industrial boom generated great fortunes for manufacturers and investors in Pittsburgh, especially in the iron business. But despite their wealth, the iron barons did not exercise an iron grip upon their fellow citizens or their workers. The nature of the iron trade and the internal organization of the typical iron mill account for the limited power of the iron barons.

First, the iron industry was highly competitive.[4] No effective trade association regulated producers, and primitive pooling efforts fell apart under the pressure of strong price competition. Moreover, the expansion of rail transportation, which greatly increased the demand for iron and steel, also helped to create a more competitive national market. As Peter Temin has noted, in the post–Civil War years "the cheapening of transport reduced the extent of local monopolies and increased the competition between producers of various regions."[5]

Second, firms were numerous and relatively modest in size. Personal management by an individual owner or a few partners was the norm. Integration—either backward to raw material supplies or forward to finishing—was distinctly limited until the 1880s and 1890s.[6] It is true that blast furnaces and rolling mills were among the largest establishments of their time, and growing larger. But in 1860, the average iron mill employed fewer than two hundred workers, the average blast furnace fewer than a hundred. While the average number of employers per establishment increased to three hundred and fifty in 1880, it was not until around 1890 that integrated steel mills replaced the smaller and more numerous iron mills as the dominant employers of labor in the Pittsburgh area.[7]

Finally, even plants employing many hundreds were really congeries of individual workshops, and each of those workshops was run by a relatively autonomous, highly skilled craftsman. Given the "fragmented, decentralized organization" of the typical iron mill, managers were in no real sense in charge of production. In fact, "all the boss did was to buy the equipment and raw materials and sell the finished product."[8] He knew little about the techniques of production and had limited contact with workers in day-to-day operations. Not the boss but the craftsman was the indispensible man in the factory, the crucial link in the productive process. As in glass blowing and many other industrial crafts of the time, the key processes of iron making—especially puddling and rolling—could not be broken down into subordinate tasks. Each required the involvement of a single person from beginning to end. To such men the managers related as to subcontractors whose skills and inclinations had to be respected.

The keystone of the craftsman's autonomy was his skill. That skill took a long time to develop, and the craftsman guarded it jealously. To get a better understanding of the character of that skill and its implications for the relationship between employer and employee, it is useful to describe the kind of work performed in Pittsburgh factories in these years. Among the most vivid accounts of the process which transformed pig iron into wrought iron is that penned in 1871 by the British journalistic team of Keeler and Fenn.[9]

> The pig-iron is put into a puddling-furnace presided over by a puddler and a helper. The helper attends to the firing and does the first part of the puddling—that is, stirring the iron at the consistency of water. The skill is to know just the boiling-point, and then to separate the metal in the furnace into exactly three parts. This the puddler does by the eye and with his three tools called puddling-irons. With these he deftly kneads the three separate masses as so much dough. As soon as a mass is worked to the satisfaction of the puddler it is drawn forth, placed on a species of two-wheeled cart called a buggy, and put into the squeezer. . . . A shapeless mass of metal goes into the squeezer and comes out in a plug half the original size. If during the revolution of the wheel of the squeezer the mass breaks, it is a sure test that the metal has not been sufficiently puddled, and much to the disgust of the puddler, it is returned to the buggy and the furnace, and must be worked over again. Should the roll go through the squeezer unbroken, it is passed on to the rollers, which have grooves of various depths, and finally comes out in beautiful square strips. Most of the puddlers, in their anxiety, follow the buggies that carry their work till it has passed the squeezer. Noticing a great brawny fellow who did not leave his furnace at this anxious moment, we asked him why he did not follow his buggy too. "O," said he, with a proud swagger, "my iron never breaks," and it never did.

Similarly, Keeler and Fenn describe the process of window-glass making, with the same attention to the craftsman's skill.

> From the great pots in which the glass is melted the "gatherer" or assistant takes upon the end of a blow-pipe a piece of the molten glass weighing from sixteen to twenty-five pounds and hands the blow-pipe to the glassblower. The latter places the mass on a concave block, turning it rapidly as he blows it, while his helper pours water over it. The mass gradually assumes a globular shape ten or twelve inches in diameter, with the greater portion of the glass on the lower side. The blower next places the globe in the opening of the furnace, resting his blow-pipe upon an upright rod with a groove in it, and turning it round begins to blow the imperfect globe into a cylinder. He continues to blow until the convex end of the cylinder—which extends into the furnace some distance—is perforated, when it is withdrawn and the blower steps down from his platform to the floor and deposits his cylinder on a form; he then touches the end toward him with a cold iron, and that portion of the glass adhering to his blow-pipe, cracks off leaving a ragged edge. Picking up a piece of molten metal with a pair of pincers, he pulls it out into a thin thread, draws the latter around the jagged end of the cylinder, touches it with a cold iron or a drop of water, and the glass cracks off leaving the edge perfectly even. A workman then approaches with a long iron rod, heated to a red heat,

and presses it from one end of the cylinder to the other, lets fall a drop of water on the iron, and the cylinder cracks in a perfectly straight line from end to end. The cylinder is now passed on to the flattening oven, where by light pressure and gradual heat, it becomes a sheet of glass. At the end of forty-eight hours it is taken to the cutting-room. The cutter lays the broad sheet of glass upon his table and cuts it into the number of pieces required. . . .

Here is the "aristocracy of the mills" at work. According to a contemporary, the glassblower "challenges admiration" precisely because, with his simple tools, he "defies machinery."[10] That ability to do what no machine could do was what made the craftsman so respected and so deeply committed to his craft. James J. Davis, a puddler who went on to become Secretary of Labor under Warren G. Harding, was "proud of the 'batting eye' that enables an iron puddler to shape the balls to the exact weight required. . . . The artist and the sculptor," he asserted, "must have this same sense of proportion."[11]

In neither iron nor glass making had technology allowed managers to dispense with the crucially skilled craftsman. In iron making, the bottleneck remained the puddling process. To get wrought iron from pig, a furnace commanded by a puddler and his helper remained the *sine qua non.* Expanding output meant simply increasing the number of furnaces and puddlers in order to keep up with the speedy rolls. Likewise in the window-glass industry until the turn of the century, the irreducible component of production remained the blower and his "pot." "In this phase of glass-making," noted one observer in 1880, "there has been little or no advance in half a century. . . . A straight blow-pipe and a bench are the workman's appliances."[12]

The possession of irreplaceable skill gave the industrial craftsmen of Pittsburgh considerable freedom from bossing and regimentation at work. Although they worked a long day, craftsmen flexibly determined the schedule of work for themselves and their assistants according to craft custom. Managers did not contract with craftsmen for a specified number of hours of labor, nor did they direct them as to the proper sequence or delegation of tasks. Rather, managers contracted for a specified number of boxes of glass or "heats" of iron. That is, they bought production, not time, from the craftsmen.

In 1883, John Jarrett, president of the Amalgamated Association of Iron and Steel Workers, explained to a Senate committee why movements to restrict the length of the workday little appealed to his comrades:

*13*

There [is] no stipulated number of hours. That is not the way in our
business. Our men simply turn out so much weight in iron per day.[13]

Paid on a "sliding scale" pegged to the selling price of iron, the
craftsman determined the amount produced, and hence indirectly
his own wage. Operating without punch clock or stop watch, the
puddlers "fired their furnaces between three and four o'clock in the
morning" and "seldom quit before sunset." When, in the 1880s, the
union managed to reduce the number of heats from six to five per
day, the puddlers' workday was shortened from twelve or more hours
to about ten hours, with slightly longer hours for finishers. It is
important to note that the impulse here for reduction in hours was
part of an attempt to limit production and not a response to demands
for a shorter day. Ironworkers never championed the eight-hour
movement, even after affilliating with the American Federation of
Labor in the late 1880s. It was impossible to fit five heats into eight
hours, so a day of three eight-hour turns was out of the question.
Even if it had not been, however, ironworkers would have been
skeptical of a three-turn schedule that might have generated over-
production and a surplus of skilled men. Furthermore, ironworkers
simply refused to be rushed. "The puddler has always been accustomed to arrange for himself the time for starting and quitting,"
noted an early twentieth-century student of the craft. "He objects
to being hurried in order to produce a reasonable output."[14]

Such a schedule allowed craftsmen to participate in the kind of
scene recalled by John Fritz, a businessman who had risen from the
ranks of the skilled workers he described.[15]

In the evening, between heats, while they were smoking their pipes,
. . . I would sit down on a charge of pig iron and listen to them
describing their mills in England and Wales, and their methods of
working.

Fritz no doubt romanticized the golden age of skilled ironwork, but
his nostalgic reminiscence illustrates both the workers' habits of rest
and the respect which managers paid to "their methods of working."

These habits and methods shaped not only the workday but the
entire calendar of work in the industry. Thus, skilled ironworkers
might choose to meet a sudden large demand by working through
the weekend, although their custom was to work five and a half
days, the Saturday half-day often reserved for repairs. Until the mid-
1880s, when Bessemer steel production began to impose its more
relentless schedule on increasing numbers of men, the Amalgamated

Association never even considered the contractual guarantee of Sunday and holiday rest. Instead it preferred to leave the matter to custom and "to local agreement." Similarly, the window-glass workers flexibly determined their holiday work schedule. "During holidays, such as Christmas," their 1886 Convention noted, "blowers and gatherers are in the habit of calling a meeting to decide whether they shall work or not." Even local conformity was not imposed, however, and individual craftsmen sometimes determined for themselves whether or not to work on holidays.[16]

One of the strictest conventions of both iron and glass trades was the summer break. For at least a month the iron works closed down and the workers escaped the already overheated mills. While such holidays were first guaranteed by custom rather than by contract, they were observed as law. The window-glass workers were even more jealous of their summer holiday, which extended for two or even three months. When the firm of Albertson, Peck and Company petitioned the Window Glass Workers Association, requesting "the privilege" of starting its works early in the 1884 season, the union promptly rejected the request, even though the company pleaded that a breakdown had robbed it of a month's production earlier that year. Whether in summer or at other times, therefore, it was by "mutual conference" or even by individual inclination that glassworkers determined their work schedule. "The same is true with respect to workingmen in many occupations," noted the Pennsylvania Bureau of Industrial Statistics. "They prefer to stop every now and then for a day or longer period."[17]

As the foregoing has demonstrated, entrepreneurs in Pittsburgh's leading industries lacked real control over production. The craftsmen who exercised that power consequently demanded and received a high price for their services. Sufficient evidence exists to substantiate the impression given one contemporary that "the wages are extraordinary."[18]

In an era when common labor earned little more than a dollar a day, Pittsburgh craftsmen earned two to ten times that amount. The highest paid craftsmen were the iron rollers. The chief roller at one bar mill, "considered the best situation in the mill," was paid the extraordinary sum of $5,707 in 1887, a year in which the mill operated for 261 days. At $21.86 per day, the roller's wages far exceeded those of anyone else in the plant. Almost certainly, this man had ceased to work as a craftsman and had crossed the line into management, a phenomenon which will be discussed further below. But other craftsmen in the same plant were all well paid, receiving wages ranging from the roughers' $3.01 per day to the rollers' average of $10.69 per day (see table 1). The incomes of iron craftsmen usually equalled or exceeded those of foremen, clerks, and other skilled men in the mill. The same was true in the glass industry, where blowers, flatteners, and cutters usually made more than foremen, with gatherers and teazers not far behind (see table 2.)[19]

Comparing iron craftsmen with miners and common laborers, Robert Layton, an officer in the Knights of Labor, told the U.S. Senate that, while in Pittsburgh's tight housing market craftsmen were generally renters, they nevertheless had

Table 1. Average Daily Wage in Rolling Mills, 1874–1887

| Occupation | 1874 | 1876 | 1880 | 1887 |
|---|---|---|---|---|
| Roller | 5.78 | 4.00 | — | 10.69 |
| Heater | 4.73 | 4.00 | — | 6.11 |
| Puddler | 3.70 | 3.00 | 3.50 | 3.50 |
| Rougher | 2.82 | — | — | 3.01 |
| Catcher | 2.68 | 2.25 | — | 5.61 |
| Roll Hand | 1.50–2.50 | — | 1.65 | 2.77 |
| Laborer | 1.53 | 1.25 | 1.24 | 1.40 |
| Boy | .68 | .35–1.00 | 1.24 | 1.40 |
| Machinist | 3.80 | 2.75 | — | 2.70 |
| Foreman/Supervisor | 5.09 | 4.00 | 3.44 | — |

SOURCES: Pa. Statistics 1874–1875, p. 530 (one iron and steel works in Pittsburgh; daily wage derived by dividing average wage for 54-hour week by 5.5); Pa. Statistics 1876–1877, p. 683 (Juniata Iron Works, Pittsburgh); Pa. Statistics 1879–1880, pp. 208–210 (averages for all Allegheny County rolling mills; no finishing crafts); Pa. Statistics 1887, pp. C.12–28 (one unnamed firm employing 2,324).

Table 2. Average Daily Wages in Glass Factories, 1874–1880

| Occupation | 1874 | 1876 | | 1880 |
|---|---|---|---|---|
| Blower | 3.00 | 5.80 | 3.50 | 3.91–5.30–8.30 |
| Gatherer | — | 3.00 | 2.00 | 2.12–2.90–3.74 |
| Flattener | — | 5.80 | — | 6.95 |
| Cutter | — | 4.00 | 2.50 | 4.50 |
| Teazer | 2.50 | 3.57 | 2.30 | — |
| Batch-mixer | 1.05 | 1.75 | 2.25 | — |
| Boy | .60 | .70 | 1.00 | — |
| Foreman | 3.33 | — | — | 4.67 |

SOURCES: Pa. Statistics 1874–1875, p. 531 (one Pittsburgh firm); Pa. Statistics 1876–1877, pp. 686–687 (two Pittsburgh firms); Pa. Statistics 1879–1880, pp. 214–216 (county averages; figures for blowers and gatherers represent separate averages for three kinds of firm, each of which produced glass of different quality and price).

more home comforts, more of the little things that go to make a home comfortable and pleasant. The iron-worker has usually more room and better furniture, carpets, and so on, and his children are bettered clothed. . . . They eat more fresh beef as a general thing.

As for the rollers, they "often occupy an entire house themselves and . . . they will in many instances have a piano in the house."[20] Throughout the years between 1860 and 1890, the income of iron and glass craftsmen remained high, despite the fact that wages declined, or increased only slightly, in the mid-decade depressions of the 1870s and 1880s. The sizeable drop in the cost of living kept real earnings generally, and among iron and steel craftsmen especially, at a high level.[21] Moreover, because cheap fuel gave Pittsburgh iron a cost advantage over that of eastern firms, local wages for puddlers and other skilled men exceeded those of their eastern counterparts by thirty to fifty percent throughout the 1870s and 1880s.[22]

If craftsmen comprised an elite, however, it was not a small one. There were, by any standard, a lot of skilled men in both iron and glass factories. In 1887, "one of the largest and most eminent iron and steel working establishments in the country" employed 2,324 men. Of these, fully 862 or 37 percent were skilled workmen, about half of them in the rolling mill, the other half in the nail works, forges, and fabrication shops, and in machine repair and maintenance. Adding to this total the better-paid roll hands and helpers, the portion of workers making $2.50 per day or better comes to more than 40 percent.[23]

Glass factories contained large numbers of skilled men, especially in window glass and tableware production. One Pittsburgh firm employed 119 workers of whom 47 were craftsmen, earning between $3.00 and $5.80 per day. Another employed 113, of whom 64 were skilled glassworkers earning from $2.00 to $3.50 per day.[24]

In not all iron and glass works were wages so high or skilled men so numerous. At blast furnaces, steel mills, and finishing plants, there were fewer craftsmen, wages were generally lower, and the range of earnings narrower than in iron rolling mills. Similarly, while window-glass making required the most skilled work and paid the highest wages, other sorts of glass making required less blowing, and hence fewer blowers, the elite of the glass industry. At the extreme of cheap pressed glass, skilled work was confined to various operations surrounding the molding process, with the bulk of the work done by boys and girls earning less than a dollar a day. Yet even a pressed-glass producer like Doyle and Company in 1876 retained 34 skilled workers, earning between $2.00 and $3.75 a day, out of a total of 80 employed.[25]

It should be noted that high daily earnings did not guarantee high yearly earnings. Slumps and seasonal slowdowns could drive the annual income of craftsmen to the subsistence level. Indeed, as will become clearer below, a chief motive of craft unionization in these years was the desire to stabilize employment. Nevertheless, even during less than robust times, Pittsburgh's craftsmen suffered less and rebounded more quickly from economic slumps than did other kinds of workers. And at all times they exercised greater control over their working lives than did most of their contemporaries.

Despite their location within an industrial setting, therefore, Pittsburgh's iron and glass craftsmen surprisingly resembled artisans of the handicraft era. Although employed in large factories, they worked in smaller shop-like units where "custom and expediency determined the method and flow of work."[26] Although they worked with immense machinery that had to be purchased by others, they possessed and guarded skills that made them indispensible to those wishing to acquire their product. Their complex pay scales, pegged to the market price of the finished product, were in this sense elaborate translations into the industrial setting of the independent artisan's right to name his own price.

That the craftsmen won a high price and considerable autonomy was not only a consequence of their productive skills. For, like artisans, industrial craftsmen retained a significant managerial responsibility: the organization and direction of a team of workmen of differing skills, all of whose coordinated effort was needed to manufacturer a finished product. In Pittsburgh's iron and glass factories, labor was organized by means of a "contract" or "helper" system, whereby employers bought the services of craftsmen who supervised and even hired and paid the work teams.[27] Each factory can be seen, therefore, not simply as the arena in which craftsmen performed their admirable art, but as the craftsmen's empire.

From the melting of raw material to the trimming of the finished product, both iron and glass making required close and careful teamwork. For the glass blower, the safety of his workers and his fragile product could not be assured unless "all engaged in the 'team' work get into a harmonious swing." The entire team had a stake in maintaining the smooth and rhythmic flow of work and the good humor of the team leader. The blower set the pace of work and, therefore, the rate of pay for the whole team. The "intimate relation of these helpers to the blowers" implied no equality between them.

*18*

The mysterious skill of blowing glass resided in a demanding, sometimes personally distant, craftsman who kept a close watch on his trade and close control over its apprenticeship system.[28]

In the iron mill, two poles of authority governed the work process. The puddler was the most highly skilled worker in the plant. Without his "batting eye" and his smooth provision of worked iron, nothing went through the rolls. He always had one helper, on some occasions two; he also directed the several workers in charge of cleaninng and refueling his furnace.

But the roller exercised even greater authority. Besides possessing considerable skill, he supervised many more workers than did the puddler, as many as two or three dozen. Once the wrought iron balls left the jurisdiction of the puddler, the roller took charge. He supervised the muck rollers' initial squeezing of the iron, and determined whether it was of a quality which permitted it to proceed to the next stage. He supervised the hookers who guided the iron through the train of rolls by means of long hooks suspended from pulleys. He supervised the catchers and roughers who handled the iron as it went through the rolls and returned it for another pass. He supervised the assistant rollers who readjusted the rolls for greater compression at the next pass, and he often performed the adjustment himself. He determined the precise moment at which the cooling iron needed to be turned over to the heater for reheating.

The heater had authority over his furnace and his helpers. His skill at maintaining his fire and in determining the length of reheating necessary for a particular ingot made him the second-highest paid man in the mill. Nonetheless, his job comprised a step in the process for which the roller had prior and subsequent responsibility.

Throughout this difficult process of repassing, reheating, and readjusting, the roller was in charge of a host of roll hands and miscellaneous workmen who were distinct from common laborers and whose customary titles described their different duties. Pilers, chargers, drag-outs, drag-downs, straighteners, shearmen, lever men, poke-ins, scrapers—the list goes on. At a large bar mill in Pittsburgh, one head roller supervised an assistant, six heaters, two catchers, eight roughers, and sixteen roll hands. At another, five rollers and five assistants set the pace for ten heaters, twenty roughers, and a horde of roll hands and helpers.[29]

While methods of payment varied, most skilled men paid their own help. Throughout these years, for example, the tonnage rate brought a puddler the equivalent of between $5.00 and $5.50 a day, out of which he paid his helper "one third plus five per cent," or about $2.00. While puddlers were the most numerous of the skilled workers in the plant, their paymaster responsibilities were limited to one, perhaps two, helpers each. There were far fewer rollers, but their payrolls could be very large, as the size of their work teams suggests. It is not surprising that such men might aspire to become "boss rollers" and foremen or that, as they strove to perfect the organization of rolling work and increase productivity, they might become more secretive about their incomes and more distant from their colleagues and subordinates.[30]

Opportunities for self-promotion could spark conflict among craftsmen and between them and less skilled workers.[31] However, if differences in skill and in opportunities for advancement divided workers, two sources of solidarity helped counteract these differences. The first was a product of long experience. Imbedded in craft custom and idealized by generations of craftsmen, a "mutualistic ethic"[32] guided relations among workers. That ethic bound masters of a craft to one another. Like preindustrial guild artisans, industrial craftsmen banded together to guard their skills, limit access to the craft, and nurture camaraderie. Fellowship extended beyond the workplace and into the taverns, boat clubs, firehouses, and other places where they socialized and exchanged news. In just such a place, iron puddlers in Pittsburgh founded their first formal union. The very name they gave that tavern—"Our House"—and that union—the Sons of Vulcan—suggested that familial values shaped their collective identity. The Vulcans saw themselves as inheritors and bequeathers of a legacy of skill and practical wisdom. Although their mutalistic ethic might be seen simply as a means to "pure and simple" ends or even as a nostalgic defense of exclusive craft privilege, it was always more than that. It was, plainly put, an ideal and as such it shaped as well as reflected a way of life.

The character of that ideal was best revealed in practice. For example, one puddler[33] described the way he and his fellow craftsmen pulled together in hard times:

> Those who had jobs divided their time with their needy comrades. A man with hungry children would be given a furnace for a few days to earn enough to ward off starvation.

This description suggests that the ethic of mutualism extended beyond brothers in the craft. Indeed, a species of paternalism marked relations between craftsmen and their helpers. In part this reflected the not uncommon experience of fathers hiring their sons as helpers. While one observer attributed the prevalence of father-son teams in the iron mills to the high representation of supposedly clannish Germans, there is no reason to believe that Welsh, Irish, or Anglo-American craftsmen were less likely to try to pass their skills on to their children. James J. Davis believed that every puddler wanted to hand "his" furnace down to his son. The same seems to have been true of window-glass workers.[34]

Mutualism may also have been reinforced by the fact that craftsmen shared with subordinate workers a common experience of strenuous labor. However privileged in terms of income and autonomy, industrial craftsmen enjoyed no special dispensation from exhausting and dangerous work. These were, after all, men who sang of themselves as "noble sons of labor" who produced the nation's wealth not only with "brain" but with "bone" and "fibre" as well. Certainly, iron craftsmen exerted bone and fibre in their daily work. As James J. Davis recalled, the puddler's "charge" of pig iron weighed about 600 pounds, making each of the balls kneaded and lifted about 200 pounds each. Not surprisingly, such men took pride in being conventionally described as "brawny." Similarly, glass blowers were characterized as stocky, barrel-chested types, "strong of muscle and stronger of lung."[35]

The terrific heat of the furnace took its toll on iron and glass craftsmen. It was blamed for the "legacy of rheumatism" and respiratory disease among ironworkers, as well as for their prodigious thirst. In crucible steel making the problem of heat was even worse. There, in order to approach the fire, workers swathed themselves in old bags and coffee sacks soaked with water. Robert Layton, reported in 1883 that "it is a very common thing to pick up the paper and to read of five or six men having been overcome by the heat in a single day." Glassworkers also suffered from the heat. The typical glass blower ate salt and drank "from thirty to thirty-five cups of water in the nine hours he is on duty." In addition, when facing directly into the fire, glassworkers wore wooden masks, "kept in place by a projecting bit of wood which the masker holds in his mouth" and, when released, hung by a string around his neck.[36]

The work of the craft team was not only hot and heavy, it was fast. Particularly in iron making, the skilled craftsman worked with a fury that startled outsiders. That commitment to speed no doubt reflected the craftsman's expectation that, especially in periods of high demand, increased production meant a greater reward for him and his team.[37] Still, no less than his subordinates, the craftsman was a manual worker, subject to heat, noxious fumes, and the strain of great physical exertion at high speeds.

For a variety of reasons, therefore, craftsmen and other workers in Pittsburgh were accustomed to thinking and acting collectively. The power of their mutualistic values need not be exaggerated, however. Conflict within the major crafts in iron and glass remained a recurrent motif throughout the decades of intense labor organization. And, despite professions to the contrary, craftsmen actually admitted very few less-skilled workers to their amalgamated unions, though they often lent material aid to organization of the unskilled. The centripetal pull of mutalism certainly encouraged and shaped the post–Civil War drive for organizational solidarity in Pittsburgh, but it did not in itself generate that drive. When Pittsburgh workers mobilized their resources—both moral and material—they did so in an act of collective self-defense against a series of external threats from employers.

The first threat was felt most sharply by craftsmen. Although technology did not revolutionize the glass or iron industries in these years, craftsmen could not be oblivious to the specter of skill degradation. When in the late 1870s the patent crimper reduced the number and the power of blowers in the chimney-glass factories, even the secure window-glass blowers shuddered. In the 1880s, new steel-wire drawing and cutting machines made wrought iron nails—and the nailers who produced them—suddenly obsolete. As the now semiskilled nailers struggled to survive, the ironworkers' union cut them loose, but not without a painful internal debate.[38]

Furthermore, even though manufacturers failed to find technological alternatives to the major crafts in rolling mills and blast furnaces, they did not stop trying. Nor did they mask their devout wish someday to destroy "the abominable English system, imported with the skilled labor, of 'working to fool the master' . . . ."[39] In the meantime they continued to improve and expand other machinery, to mechanize hauling and loading, and to better integrate the flow of work in the mills. And some of them began looking with more interest at the growing steel industry, which, although still small, underwent continuous technological evolution, each stage of which eliminated more traditional craft skills.

Even more important than the threat of skill degradation in shaping craft solidarity was the response of manufacturers to the sharply cyclical nature of the iron and steel trade.[40] In the last half of the nineteenth century, business boomed around the turn of each decade and slumped in the middle. Rapidly expanding markets promised immense profits but also subjected manufacturers to greater competition and more volatile fluctuations in demand. To insure the biggest return on their increasingly large investments, manufacturers needed to maximize profits in good times and spread their losses in bad. In boom times, when they could ill afford a stoppage that might limit their share of growing markets, ironmasters' efforts to increase output and cut wage costs met stiff resistance from their indispensible craftsmen. But in hard times employers applied the pressure. Layoffs and reduced hours created a pool of unemployed and underemployed craftsmen more willing than usual to work for less and to violate craft custom in order to get work. Even after full production resumed, the experience of poverty and of damaged solidarity could make craftsmen more tractable for a while.

Not surprisingly, the strategy of craftsmen in some large part reflected this pattern. They fought to survive in hard times and pushed for more formal controls over production in good times. Indeed, the history of unionization in Pittsburgh and other iron centers is a chronicle of worker resistance to cyclical, as well as seasonal, insecurity. Although they sought higher wages and other "bread and butter" rewards, craftsmen created their sliding scales and the unions that defended them principally to stabilize employment and to limit the extent to which they had to bear the hardships of slumping markets.[41]

It was in the process of forging those mechanisms of control that iron and glass craftsmen developed an organizational solidarity whose logic went well beyond the familial values rooted in craft custom and teamwork and produced "the most powerful labor unions of the manufacturing sector."[42] In spearheading the organizational drive, craftsmen sought to bolster their immediate interests, but neither they nor anyone else in the Iron City doubted that they were indeed building a broad movement. Precisely because it built upon the craftsmen's empire, the labor movement in Pittsburgh was able to go beyond it. Whether in trade unions or Knights of Labor assemblies, in central labor bodies or political associations, craftsmen and other workers endeavored to realize ever-broader ties of solidarity among "laboring classes" and "citizens." By the time of the great riots of 1877, the labor movement had become a real presence in Pittsburgh. Behind the relatively spontaneous events of that week in July, therefore, lay a decade of organization.

More than any other event, the Civil War, which produced both price inflation and labor shortage, gave renewed impetus to the scattered organizational efforts of craftsmen in Pittsburgh. And more than any other group, the iron puddlers responded to that impetus and directed it forward. Having lapsed soon after its founding during the recession of the late 1850s, the Sons of Vulcan revived under the leadership of Miles Humphreys at the onset of war. Demand for skilled workers so exceeded supply that, even with the importation of metal workers from England, the Vulcans needed only strike or threaten to strike to win their point quickly. In 1863, for example, puddlers at Everson, Preston and Company easily won the exceptional rate of $6 per ton after only a few days out. Similarly, window-glass workers, miners, butchers, copper workers, and others found the exigencies of war a spur to higher wages and successful organization.[43]

At war's end, craftsmen sought to consolidate the gains of the war years in the face of recession and stiffened opposition from employers. In 1867, when the recession had begun to lift, both puddlers and glassblowers engaged in major and successful strikes which established their unions as enduring institutions. For the puddlers especially, the 1867 strike was a stunning victory. They imposed for the first time formal restrictions on output and confirmed once and for all their right to negotiate a yearly sliding scale as the basis of wages for the craft. Within a few years the union doubled in size, claiming as members the great majority of puddlers in Pittsburgh.[44]

Indeed, 1867 marked the beginning of the first important stage in the labor history of Pittsburgh, during which the organization of many individual crafts became an established fact. It was at this stage that craftsmen moved "beyond functional autonomy to the next higher level of craft control, the enactment and enforcement of union work rules. In one respect, union rules simply codified the autonomy."[45] If formal unity within the craft tended to restrict individual autonomy—as it did, for example, in disciplining crafts-men who exceeded production quotas—its goal remained the pro-tection of the very character of autonomous work. In the first instance craftsmen strove to conserve a way of work—even a way of life—and not to forge a new way.

Puddlers took the lead in pushing the principle of craft unionism. Joined by other highly skilled workers—glassworkers and pressmen in particular—they made Pittsburgh a nationally recognized center of union activity. In 1867, the city hosted two conventions, one of Vulcans, the other of Labor Reformers from around the country, both of which broadcast the message of organization. William C. McCarthy, in his first term as mayor, opened the Vulcan convention with a welcoming speech. Also welcoming the Vulcans was the *Workman's and Soldier's Advocate,* a newspaper just founded by

Thomas A. Armstrong and "practically adopted as the official organ of the union."[46]

Though the *Advocate* failed after a few months, Armstrong remained in contact with craft unionists and with local Radical Republicans, many of whom were organized into politically conscious veterans' groups. With Humphreys, McCarthy, and others, Armstrong helped translate labor militance into political action. Already in 1865, when the Republican Party gave in to demands for a city primary and McCarthy was nominated for mayor, the power of labor in politics was becoming a fact. When the party abandoned the primary two years later, depriving McCarthy of renomination, workingmen of both parties convened, nominated a Democratic judge for mayor on a "workingmen's" ticket, and subsequently elected him by a landslide. Labor politics had arrived. Later in the year, Miles Humphreys was elected as a Republican to the first of his three terms in the state legislature, and Andrew Burtt, a school teacher and former glassworker, ran a surprisingly strong campaign for state senator. Running on a new Labor Reform ticket, Burtt swept the iron and glass wards of the south side and, although unsuccessful, gave the Republican Party a scare.[47]

The second important period in the labor history of Pittsburgh began with the Panic of 1873. Two themes emerge from a study of the years following that event. First, although hard-pressed by depression, most craft unions survived, and new unions of skilled and unskilled workers came into being. Second, workers pushed for ideological and organizational solidarity beyond individual unions. By the end of the depression they had achieved a great deal: amalgamated craft unions in iron and glass, a city-wide labor council, a large Knights of Labor District Assembly, a mature labor press, and an expanded political coalition. The first year of depression was a tumultuous one in Pittsburgh. Layoffs, wage cuts, and defensive strikes hit the railway, mining, iron, glass, and printing trades, among others. Not all these strikes succeeded, and for some workers defeat in long and bitter struggles nearly wiped out their fledgling union. But most survived in some form and proceeded to work toward amalgamation.[48]

The iron puddlers, having managed to defeat an employer lockout, spurred the cause of inter-craft unity in the iron trade. The fruit of that effort was the establishment in 1876 of the Amalgamated Association, a union of the Vulcans, the Brotherhood of Heaters, Rollers, and Roughers, and the Roll Hands Union. At their founding convention in Pittsburgh, delegates clearly reiterated the lesson which

*25*

ten years of organization had taught. James Penney, a roller from the south side, put it simply: "Men should drop their petty jealousies and go to the Lodge as an Iron or Steel Worker, and not as a Boiler, Heater, Roller, etc." Experience had proven to David Reese, a puddler from Wheeling, the "necessity of one head, one convention." Reese was willing to accept the radical implications of this line of thought. In choosing leadership, he said, the craftsmen should turn to "the best talent of the Lodge . . . , even it it was a laborer." The aristocracy of the mills may have come to such conclusions grudgingly, and they certainly never admitted many unskilled workers to their union. On the other hand, they repeatedly aided the Knights of Labor and others in the effort to organize unskilled workers. In the city labor council and in local politics, moreover, they showed that the values which spurred their "passion for extension and completeness of organization" within and among the crafts, could also provide a rationale for broader solidarity.[49]

The first purpose of amalgamation, however, was to secure the interests of the major crafts. The Amalgamated Association extended the Vulcans' sliding scale to all the iron crafts and fought to maintain and improve base rates of pay. In this respect, it was eminently successful. Until 1882, each yearly conference of employers and union representatives resulted in acceptance of the union's scale demands. In 1879, for example, when employers threatened a lockout rather than continue the scale of the previous year, the union president reported that "the men of all departments of their mills ceased work. Such a movement," he continued, "was never known before . . . . In less than twenty-four hours the manufacturers were ready to negotiate for peace . . . ." Amalgamation permitted craftsmen to win not only better pay scales but also a voice in determining "card rates," i.e., the schedule of selling prices for various kinds of iron. Along with output restrictions, this measure regulated the excesses of competitive pricing and represented a significant step toward the craftsmen's goal of stabilizing production in the industry.[50]

Comprehensive craft organization brought success at the bargaining table, and success further stimulated growth in membership. Especially powerful in the Pittsburgh area, the Amalgamated controlled about three-fourths of all iron mills in the United States. Having begun with a membership of 3,700, it claimed 16,000 members in 1882. Although membership dipped sharply during the mid-1880s depression, by 1890 it had rebounded to 24,000.[51]

Organization in the iron industry was accompanied by similar tendencies in the glass industry. After losing a bitter and protracted strike in 1874, glassblowers nursed their battered craft association through the bleak years of depression, awaiting the opportunity to reorganize. That opportunity came in 1877 when Knights of Labor organizers encouraged them to join with glass gatherers in forming District Assembly 8. Within two years they reorganized as Local Assembly 300, amalgamated with cutters and flatteners, and became a force to be reckoned with. Indeed, L.A. 300 won pay scales and a level of control over production that exceeded even that of the ironworkers. It eventually joined manufacturers in a "bilateral monopoly" which implemented "a rigid, detailed, and all-inclusive system of regulation of window glass production that lasted into the early years of the twentieth century." As co-custodians of the trade, craftsmen and manufacturers successfully lobbied for tariff protection, restricted output, and, in annual conference, set wages and prices for the industry as a whole. In the mid-1880s, L.A. 300 even organized a Universal Federation of Window Glass Workers, which for a time regulated the flow of workers from Belgium, England, France, Italy, and Germany, and took some steps to rationalize international glass markets. Given final shape after two strikes in the early 1880s, the bilateral monopoly was never seriously disturbed until introduction of the Owens glass-drawing machine at the turn of the century. Though L.A. 300 became increasingly exclusive in the late 1880s, it nonetheless actively supported the struggles of workers in Pittsburgh and elsewhere for more than a decade. As its creation had depended on aid from the Knights, so it helped finance strikes and organizing drives, becoming a key force in the Knights' national organization.[52]

The Knights of Labor tapped a wave of worker militance that went well beyond the glassworkers. The mid-1870s marked the beginning of the Knights' rise to prominence in the American labor movement, and Pittsburgh was its most active center of organization. One organizer among western Pennsylvania miners remembered that, "in the winter of 1875 and 1876, such was the excitement in the Pittsburgh district, along the rivers and railways, that a man must have been dull indeed not to know that some kind of secret organization was being organized." Led at first by the ubiquitous and indefatigable John M. Davis, thousands of workers, skilled and unskilled, in an enormous variety of occupations from steelworker and construction laborer to journalist and retail clerk, joined the movement. Though many formed trade assemblies that operated like trade unions, others joined mixed local assemblies, and all sent representatives to the District Assembly, which brought mutual aid and coordination to the movement. By 1876, District Assembly 3 had grown to more than 100 locals. Organization was so rapid and so loosely planned that, throughout the decade, no one could have declared exactly how many thousands of Knights there were in Pittsburgh, or who they were.[53]

The development of a mature labor press strengthened solidarity within the working class and among a wider plebeian citizenry. Although the glassworkers' weekly, the *Commoner* (begun in 1877), and the Knights' national organ, the *Journal of United Labor* (published in Pittsburgh between 1880 and 1882), contributed to that solidarity, the *National Labor Tribune* played the greatest part. During the strike wave of 1874, a number of pressman, including Thomas A. Armstrong, had begun a *Printers Tribune* as a strike journal. After the pressman's strike, John M. Davis took the lead in establishing this publishing experiment as a permanent labor journal, and the *National Labor Tribune* was born. Davis soon moved on to continue organizing for the Knights, and within the year Armstrong had become editor, a post he retained until his death in 1887. Based on the organized power of Pittsburgh's craftsmen and expressing their point of view, the *Tribune* went beyond the narrower concerns of craft, continually reminding working people that they shared a common fate. When a resentful official of the Waverly Coal Company called the *Tribune* "the mortar with which the bricks of these labor organizations [are] cemented together," he spoke with precision. By alerting workers to the problems faced by different groups among them, by rallying strike support, by putting forward and organizing support for "workingmen's" candidates to local office, the *Tribune* promoted working-class consciousness and helped turn discrete organizing efforts into a labor movement.[54]

The *Tribune* cemented workingmen to more than just one another. It certified the unity of all citizens who rose to defend free labor against the threat of monopoly. Armstrong always insisted that, as citizens of the community and the nation, workingmen appropriate the symbols and the rhetoric of American republicanism to their cause. On a practical level, Armstrong, a Civil War hero and member of several veterans groups, brought together organized veterans and organized labor in local politics. With fellow veterans Isaac Cline of the glassworkers and Alexander Callow of the typographers, Armstrong forged a coalition that twice elected Callow mayor of Allegheny and William McCarthy mayor of Pittsburgh. In the 1870s, "Colonel" Armstrong and "Colonel" Cline mobilized Amalgamated men, miners, and Knights of Labor behind the Greenback-Labor Party, sometimes advertising political rallies as convocations of the "Soldiers and Sailors of Allegheny County."[55]

The Civil War rhetoric was most telling here. "Labor papers," declared the *Tribune,* "must drill our soldiers from the corporal's squad up to the division drill" in preparation for storming the "Vicksburgs of Labor's enemies." Those enemies, the railroads and other great corporations, threatened not only the welfare of employees but the very principles of liberty and the rule of law upon which the nation was founded. In the widest sense, then, the men who "carried the banners of Grant and Sherman" pursued a struggle which, having freed the slave, must proceed under "another Lincoln" to fulfill itself in the fight for "industrial independence."[56]

The Greenback movement showed that the mobilizing energies of Pittsburgh's workers could not be confined to workplace issues. It is true that the *Tribune* and other labor spokesmen sometimes cast a skeptical eye on "labor reform sop" intended to buy workers' votes on the cheap, and cautioned them not to scatter their energies too broadly.[57] Nevertheless, the same logic of organization that had led workers to consolidate their economic power led them to wield it politically. Usually they responded, as they did in the workplace, to the initiatives of their adversaries. Thus, the *Tribune* reminded workers, whenever parochial craft or ethnic considerations threatened to divide them, that they were too weak to survive in a world of expanded markets, corporations, and political systems. Only by building "a machinery to suit the times"[58] had they won a measure of security and self-respect at the workplace. They required a similar machinery in politics, especially since vast entities such as the Pennsylvania Railroad had stolen a march on the plebeian citizenry. During the depressed 1870s, in particular, the threat or use of public force to break strikes in the railway, coal, and other industries outraged workers and alerted them to the need for political vigilance. These years also taught them the need for state regulation of big businesses, for factory inspection, and for child-labor and maximum-hour legislation.

However, even without these spurs to action, the labor movement had been born, and would have remained, political.[59] In Pittsburgh, as in much of America, workingmen had for generations been voters and political actors. Even before the Civil War had sharpened consciousness of national politics, they had learned to build coalitions, to elevate and influence politicians, and to express their views on issues ranging from local taxes and schools to slavery, tariffs, and temperance. In short, for better or worse, the experience of citizenship inevitably shaped the evolution of working-class consciousness.

This was especially true on the local level. Perhaps more than in most other spheres of their lives, workers experienced in local politics something of the freedom and rough equality they believed central characteristics of American society. In the local context they identified themselves not simply as employees or union men but as neighbors, customers, clients, volunteer firemen, members of school boards, comrades in leisure—that is, as citizens of the republic, writ small. It is not surprising that such citizens interpreted the 1877 upheaval as a battle for "industrial independence" and even for the fate of the republic. Nor is it surprising that many other local citizens who did not labor for wages nevertheless responded in a similar fashion. For Pittsburgh was a plebeian city. Most of its residents shared not only a common republican discourse but a daily experience of community. That experience shaped the labor movement as much as did the craftsmen's empire. It assured workers that, in their city, they were neither strangers nor second-class citizens.

# CHAPTER 3

# Plebeian Culture

The success of labor organization in Pittsburgh in the post–Civil War years derived in part from the power wielded by autonomous craftsmen within the mills and factories, but it sprang as well from the sense of community which workers inherited as citizens of the Iron City. Beyond the mill gates, in the streets and playing fields, in saloons and theaters, "thousands of rival trades were brought together."[1] Indeed, plebeian culture was a broad, public inheritance that included citizens of all kinds—save, perhaps, for a small elite too genteel or too scrupulous to indulge in common leisure. Although inclusive, therefore, plebeian culture was also decidedly vernacular, putting working people and their social equals in the center stage of life in Pittsburgh. It was also intensely local. Although Pittsburgh welcomed the growing variety of sports and entertainments which riverboats and railroads had begun to deliver to the American hinterland, it was still a provincial city. Its industrial elite was both distant from the cosmopolitan centers of the East Coast and, for a time at least, disinclined to participate in bourgeois "high" culture. For all these reasons, the rich and varied repertoire of plebeian leisure and ritual set the tone for the Iron City.[2]

In the late nineteenth century, along with its economic boom, Pittsburgh experienced rapid population growth (see Table 3). Between 1860 and 1880, 177,000 people were added to the population of Allegheny County, most of them in the city. Immigration fueled the growth of population. In 1880, nearly seven out of ten Pittsburghers were of foreign parentage, nearly three of ten foreign-born.

Three-fourths of these immigrants came from Ireland and Germany, the rest chiefly from Great Britain.[3]

Notwithstanding this demographic boom, however, the Iron City of 1880 was still much the same kind of city it had been in 1860. The bulk of its industry and population were "curiously hemmed in"[4] by topography. Within the triangle created by the Allegheny and Monongahela rivers and the escarpment of hills that cut it off from the east, the old city comprised less than two square miles of terrain. Pressure for growth did force development beyond the triangle—northeast along the Allegheny River, to the flatland known as the Strip, and across the river to Allegheny, Pittsburgh's twin city; southeast along the Monongahela River to Soho, and across the river to the south side, the fastest growing area of all, incorporated into the city in 1872. Still, the developed zone remained limited to a few square miles. The twin cities alone accounted for two-thirds of the population and nearly nine-tenths of all industrial employment and investment in Allegheny County in 1880.[5]

It is true that in 1868 Pittsburgh annexed a vast terrain of eastern boroughs and townships which increased its physical size by more than a factor of ten. But the east end remained largely the site of agriculture and "rural retreat." As late as 1873, a successful hunt was organized to catch a fox that "had been troubling the chicken houses of the neighborhood"—this in Oakland, within a decade a center of industrial and residential development, within twenty-five years the site of the Carnegie Institute and the cultural center of the city. As late as 1886, hunters were being sued for trespass by farmers on Squirrel Hill, soon to be a thickly settled neighborhood of substantial residences. Thus, although its population density between 1860 and 1890 did increase from 2.25 to 7.59—a rate far exceeding that of the old city—the east end generally remained outside the zone of development. In the older wards clustered about the juncture of the three rivers, densities ranged from 40 to more than 120

Table 3. Population of Metropolitan Pittsburgh, 1860–1880 (to the Nearest 500)

|  | City* | Allegheny County |
|---|---|---|
| 1860 | 78,000 | 179,000 |
| 1870 | 139,500 | 262,000 |
| 1880 | 235,000 | 356,000 |

SOURCE: U.S. Census 1870, vol. 1, pt. 1, pp. 370–371, 374; U.S. Census 1920, vol. 1, pp. 85, 586–587.
* Combined figure for Pittsburgh and Allegheny City.

32

persons per acre.[6] It was this "walking city"[7] to which people referred when they uttered the name of Pittsburgh.

Considering the "helpless dinginess" of the city's environment, the limited extent of suburbanization needs explanation. Once again, topography played a key role. For Pittsburgh's rivers and hills not only bounded the old city, they also gave horses and primitive engines a hard time of it. Streetcars were not unknown, but it was not until the introduction of cable and electric cars in the late 1880s that a respectable transit system was possible in Pittsburgh.[8] Until that time, most of the elite lived in the midst of the city, near office, exchange, church, and theater.

Of course, some class differentiation marked the walking city. The south side and the Strip were overwhelmingly industrial and filled with the homes of workers. Allegheny City's Commons, surrounded by stately homes, was the favorite site of bourgeois residence, a haven in the industrial landscape. The river bottoms, especially the first ward at the Point, packed the poorest, usually Irish, workers in among the warehouses and factories, while just east of the commercial center the Irish middle class surrounded St. Paul's Cathedral with a few blocks of prosperous stores and fine houses. German neighborhoods, especially in Allegheny and on the south side, were cohesive and enduring. Yet despite the fact that wards were "relatively autonomous communities,"[9] with their own schools, aldermen, fire companies, watchmen, overseers of the poor, etc., they were not enclaves. Little distinguished one from another in terms of class. Laborers, craftsmen, merchants, and manufacturers lived close together, often on the same street. While ethnic separation may have been sharper, it should not be exaggerated. The typical pattern of Pittsburgh's older wards was the patchwork: a number of ethnic subcommunities, each no more than a block or two in extent, clustered about a mill.[10] Thus, if an Irishman prayed in his "own" church and drank in his "own" saloon, it was never very far out of sight or earshot of the Methodist chapel or the German beer hall.

The neighborhoods of the walking city were peopled not only by factory workers but by petty retailers and tradesmen who depended on a working-class clientele. Many of these were themselves former millmen or relatives of millmen. Their close identification with wage-earning neighbors led many retailers to endorse explicitly the cause of organized labor. Moreover, saloons, groceries, tobacco stores, and other small shops served as centers of information and communication, where local residents staged social events, shared news about jobs, sports, and politics, and sometimes organized unions and po-

*33*

litical associations.[11] Even the business and professional families who sustained the least intimate relations with wage-earning neighbors could not escape their daily presence in the streets and shops where all had to conduct the ordinary business of life. Save for the privileged few who retired to their suburban villas at the end of the day, most Pittsburghers worked, played, and resided within the same compact space. Few were allowed the privilege of exclusivity or of ignorance about conditions of life around them. All swam in a plebeian sea.

The structure of life in a small, integrated industrial city helps to explain the weakness of genteel or cosmopolitan culture in Pittsburgh. So does the dour provinciality of the iron elite, a fact which contemporary observers were quick to point out. In the words of one visitor in 1868, the ironmasters were

> mostly of the Scotch-Irish race, Presbyterians, keen and steady . . . , singularly devoid of the usual vanities and ostentations, proud to possess a solid and spacious factory, and to live in an insignificant house. There are no men of leisure in town . . . . The old men never think of "retiring," nor is there anything for them to retire to . . . . Until very recently, in Pittsburg, it would have boded ill for a man to build a handsome house a few miles out of the smoke; and to this day it is said that a Pittsburg man of business who should publish a poem would find his "paper" doubted at the bank. "A good man, sir, but not practical."[12]

Local commentators agreed that the ironmasters counted among themselves "fewer gentlemen of leisure, than in any city of the Union." No matter how hard the cosmopolitan might try to find it, no matter how hard the labor reformer might condemn it, luxury was a sin to which the ironmaster seldom had to confess. A deeply puritan and utilitarian sensibility made the fussier sublimations of Victorian respectability seem out of place in Pittsburgh. Neither home, nor manners, nor civic duty distracted the businessman from his business: the pursuit of wealth and family security.

The ironmaster lived in a small, provincial world. His factory was staffed by sons and nephews. His children usually married within the local elite and seldom went to finishing schools or to Ivy League colleges. If after public schooling his sons went to college at all, it was to Western University in Pittsburgh or to a technical school such as Lehigh.[13] To his children the ironmaster transmitted a dual message: Pursue wealth yet disdain its enjoyment. Thus, at a reunion of the Central High School class of 1880, a class spokesman recalled growing up in a community that measured progress "in tons of pig iron" and success "by mere accumulation." He and his classmates saw "the world of ideals" as a means either of civilizing or escaping from the "purely material" world of their fathers.[14]

Similarly, Elizabeth Moorhead, daughter of a leading transportation and iron magnate, remembered Pittsburgh as "a barren and unlovely place . . . dominated by our industries." With some emotion she recalled her and her friends' repeated efforts to legitimize their interest in drama in the face of strong disapproval. Their Shakespeare Reading Club was finally allowed to exist, though its performances were "strictly censored."[15] Even those, like the family of William G. Johnston, who little shared the Presbyterian prejudice against amusement, felt its disapproving weight upon the conscience. Sitting in his cheap seat at the theater, young Johnston suspected that "there was something ominous . . . in the name of the place in which I sat—the pit."[16] Young Moorehead and Johnston were both aware that some Presbyterians in Pittsburgh still pledged "to abstain from the opera, the theater, the circus, and card playing," and that Methodists condemned even more persistently "the frivolous and sometimes filthy thing which is to-day called . . . theater." Thus, when the Pittsburgh Opera House opened in 1871, its management saw to it that the son of a leading Presbyterian minister (with the impeccable name of Knox!) composed a verse oration in defense of the "Gods of Drama." Read during opening ceremonies, it presumably eased the transition to the melodrama *Ruy Blas,* though it won for its author "the condemnation of pulpit and church."[17]

The ironmasters demonstrated no inclination to participate in the forging of a distinctive bourgeois cultural order or to link themselves spiritually with their class.[18] Indeed they regularly frustrated those who called upon them to assume cultural responsibilities. Thus the *Gazette* lamented on 23 February 1850:

> Our city lacks, exceedingly, those more healthful and proper sources of amusement, which render other cities so attractive, such as galleries of pictures, museums, public institutes, and Libraries, &c.

For more than forty years such laments continued to sound and to elicit little response from the ironmasters. Until the 1890s, prosperous Pittsburghers who sought genteel recreation had little to choose from: an occasional concert organized by local talent, a church Christmas concert, a performance by one of the German singing societies. The Pittsburgh Female Academy and a few private teachers offered musical training to their children, but few musicians, music teachers or dealers survived long in Pittsburgh. Literary diversion was even scarcer: an almost bankrupt library association, an occasional lecture, and a small Philomathic Club which debated topics of moral and political concern.[19]

For those more physically inclined, a Gymnastic Association offered at its downtown gym exercises designed to relieve "the hurtful effects of sedentary occupation." Its spare facilities, however, attracted only a few young lawyers, clerks, and other white-collar employees. Wealthy Pittsburghers may have pursued private athletics, but there was not a single sporting goods store in Pittsburgh until 1880. One had to sent to Philadelphia or Boston to acquire cricket, archery, or gymnastic equipment.[20] There was a racing season at both Collins and Friendship Parks in East Liberty. Its sponsors, however, were not great merchants and manufacturers but men like John A. McKelvey, carriage-maker and liquor dealer. Respectable citizens may have patronized the track, but, if they did, it was in rough company and not among their own kind.[21]

The Pittsburgh elite did pursue passionately one form of recreation. Between 1872 and 1887 at least five hunting and fishing associations came into being. For a fee of twenty-five to fifty dollars a year, members had access to spacious woodland preserves and well-equipped lodges. Membership rolls were strictly limited and included such names as Carnegie, Mellon, Frick, Pitcairn, Moorhead, Phipps, Horne, Thaw, and Scaife—in short, the choice of the elite. For a few weeks each summer members went to the mountains to hunt, fish, and compete in shooting matches. At those specified times when spouses were invited, they also enjoyed fancy dinners and balls.[22] Thus, when the mills shut down in the summer, the ironmaster and his family shared the urge "to escape from the heated and dusty confines of the city and ruralize . . . ." Closer to home, fashionable resorts such as the Point Breeze Tavern in the east end and the Mount Emmet Hotel, overlooking the Ohio river west of Allegheny City, offered the "first families of the two cities" the opportunity to eat sumptuously, stroll the well-kept grounds, play ten-pins, and enjoy "social intercourse." Farther from home they took the water cure at Loretto Springs or Ohio White Sulphur Springs; rowed, bowled, and shot billiards in Mercer County; and swam at the Jersey shore.[23]

If the ironmaster and his peers allowed themselves to unbend during their summer retreat, they managed to content themselves with little or no leisure upon returning to the Iron City. Perhaps elite culture was not utterly austere, but neither was it full or free. With no museums or galleries, no orchestra or musical societies, no night life or club society, no literary or artistic circles, opportunities for establishing bonds of sociability and solidarity among the "natural kings of Pittsburg"[24] were severely limited. With neither the trappings of elegant culture nor the customary duty to serve as patrons of plebeian culture, they lacked local status commensurate with their wealth. With a few notable exceptions, Pittsburgh's leading industrialists remained simply rich men. The very ethic which bound them to hard work, self-discipline, and competitive individualism as marks of moral superiority prevented them from seizing upon the marks of cultural superiority which might have confirmed their class advantage. The Presbyterian elite was ill-suited to the role of patriciate.

However austere the cultural life of the upper classes, the bulk of Pittsburgh's citizens endured no such deprivation. On the contrary, plebeian culture was rich and relatively uninhibited. It was also public, reflecting the fact that most workers lived in cramped quarters and took to the courtyards and streets for leisure. Especially after the ironworks let out on Saturday afternoon, downtown Pittsburgh became the scene of "a decent carnival":

> The principal streets are given over completely to the workman and his wife and sturdy little ones, who sally forth in their washed-up best to make their purchases and amuse themselves.[25]

Noting the same scene, James Parton added some detail to the picture:

> They stroll about; they stand conversing in groups; they gather in semicircles, about every shop-window that has a picture in it, or any bright or curious object; especially do they haunt the news-stands, which provide a free picture-gallery for them of Illustrated News, Comic Monthlies, and Funny Fellows.[26]

In addition to the newsstands, a number of art shops served as public galleries of original art. Pittsburgh was the center of a rather lively regional art network whose most talented figure was David Blythe.[27] Blythe's genre renditions of local scenes—"humorous interiors and other kindred subjects"—appealed both to wealthy collectors and to the artist's cronies in the volunteer fire companies and the Sons of Vulcan. Despite his numerous drunken outrages, Blythe continued to receive private and public commissions until his death in 1865. His pictures regularly appeared in the window of J. J. Gillespie's art shop, where they became "the talk of the town and attracted such crowds that one could hardly get along the street." Similarly, Gillespie's announcement that "our fellow townsman W. C. Wall, Esq., has just completed a beautiful picture of Pack Saddle Gap" drew crowds to his window for days. The work and persons of at least two other painters, George Hetzel, a landscapist, and Trevor McClurg, a portrayer of historical subjects, were well known to ordinary Pittsburghers in the 1860s and 1870s.[28]

Beyond the art shops, the Pittsburgh Exposition displayed an entire hall of local paintings once a year, attracting large audiences. Moreover, ever-popular dioramas, panoramas, and cycloramas—painted scenes mounted on rolls or panels, usually portaying spectacular landscapes or historical events—filled halls for days at a time. Finally, at least one fire company maintained an art gallery open to the public.[29]

Music was as readily accessible as painting. Since the 1840s Pittsburgh had been "band-conscious." "Soirees" organized by fire and militia company bands were well-advertised and attended. On the banks of the Monongahela, rival steamboats played calliopes and offered brass band concerts. After 1860 the demand for band music was strong enough to support several professional bands. Some were hired for picnics, expositions, or Fourth of July celebrations, others for special subscription concerts or benefits.[30] The Great Western, probably Pittsburgh's most successful band, typified the organization of music in the city through the 1880s. Originally attached to the Duquesne Greys militia company, the Great Western prospered to such an extent that its director, Balthasar Weiss, who had been a barber in 1860 and a saloonkeeper in 1870, could by 1880 support himself as a musician and music teacher. By the late 1880s, Weiss's organization had grown to seventy-five men, making it the largest band in the city and the obvious choice for the biggest public celebrations.[31]

Like Weiss, other band leaders were men of humble origins, among them a glassblower, a woodturner, a jeweler, and a man who was successively tobacconist, foreman, and shoemaker. Joe Christy, leader of a string band and favorite figure-caller of the old Fifth Ward, worked as a common laborer for almost twenty years before being able to list himself as a musician in the 1890 directory.[32] Little is known about band musicians, but the participants in a fife and drum corps contest at the 1882 Exposition were a typically plebeian assortment. With the exception of one clerk who would rise to managerial rank in a few years, the musicians were all laborers, craftsmen, or shopkeepers.[33]

*38*

Although the trend was toward professionalization, most music-making remained amateur through the 1880s. Indeed, some kinds of amateur music-making, such as barbershop singing, grew in popularity as the century wore on. The "musical mascot," who wrote campaign songs for his political party and sang them throughout the city, lasted into the twentieth century.[34] Union balls, testimonials, and fund-raisers always included music. Their programs reveal a taste for traditional ballads, catches, and topical songs. On such occasions participant and spectator were often one and the same. Many members composed as well as sang, although some lodges had a special bard who turned out tunes on request. Some of these local songwriters and poets reached a wider audience through the newspapers, especially the *National Labor Tribune,* which regularly published poems and ballads written by and for workers.[35]

The local theater occupied a central place in Pittsburgh's plebeian culture into the 1880s. It was vernacular, full of variety, and responsive to local demand. In the midst of a welter of concern saloons, billiard halls, bowling alleys, and freak shows, the theater served as a source of common imagery and common experience for the city's plebs.[36]

The most striking feature of the theater was its audience: It was overwhelmingly working-class and masculine. One account of the Saturday night theater crowd emphasizes both its size—an "army of ten thousand men"—and its social composition—"these workers in iron and steel and glass." Parton's description is, as usual, full of detail:

> Not a woman was present. The place was packed with brawny men and noisy boys, all washed, all well-disposed, though half mad with joyous excitement. On the walls were posted such admonitions as these: "Hats off," "No hallooing or whistling allowed," "Applaud with your hands," . . . [but] the audience paid no heed to them whatever. The performances consisted of farces raised to the fiftieth power, comic songs, and legs. Never have we seen an audience so amusable. It often happened, during the performance of a farce, that the people would keep up such a roar of laughter, that for many seconds at a time not a word could be heard from the stage. We discovered here what the playbills mean when they speak of "roaring farces," and of farces that are 'screaming" . . . .[37]

At a price of twenty-five cents or less, the variety show was the staple of the Pittsburgh stage. Offered at the legitimate houses as well as at the varieties, it appealed to a mixed, although predominately lower-class, audience. Until the 1890s, no theater, legitimate or otherwise, could survive unless, as one manager explained, it drew regular support from "the working classes."[38] No theater in Pittsburgh catered exclusively to a refined audience. However, the manner in which the Pittsburgh *Post* anticipated a local performance of Gounod's *Faust* on the night of May 11, 1863, suggests the existence of a delicate and informal code which allowed the elite occasional use of the public theater:

> In Pittsburgh—without wishing to make any invidious comparisons between different classes—there is a class who understand and thoroughly appreciate the difficult music of the opera. Their tastes are cultivated and refined . . . .

As if on cue, a "large and fashionable audience" attended the following night. But such events were rare. Those distinguished citizens who chose to attend the theater had normally to sit alongside an audience of craftsmen, laborers, and "urchins" of all kinds.[39] And they had to take their Shakespeare—if that is what they sought—with a large dose of spectacle, melodrama, and farce.

Intended to provide something for everyone, theater programs were exceptionally varied. To compete with the caravans, circuses, and menageries which regularly came to town, the theater offered plenty of spectacle. To compete with the dioramas and panoramas it offered "historical tableux." To compete with the saloon it filled its bills with songs, comic skits, and farces, and opened its own bar at intermission. Finally, it offered what only the theater could provide, the staple of the nineteenth-century stage, melodrama.

There was some differentiation in programming between the varieties and the legitimates. At the former the emphasis was on the "low"—song and dance, farce, and the like of "M'lle Marie Zoe, the beautiful Cuban Sylph." At the latter, "high" drama appeared with some frequency, but even the most respectable houses varied the programs and filled them with the same sketches and mimes that dominated the variety show. A look at programming in the months of October and November 1882 reveals the variety and scope of entertainment in the legitimate theaters in Pittsburgh. Within that period Library Hall ran successively high-toned melodrama (including the inevitable *East Lynne*), comic opera, minstrels, and melodrama again. At the same time the Opera House went from Haverly's Consolidated Mastadon Minstrels to *King Lear,* with the usual assortment of varieties in between. In both these houses short comic skits and musical routines opened, closed, and punctuated the bills.

*40*

Mixed programs allowed them to compete with brasher enterprises such as Trimble's Varieties and Harry Williams' Academy of Music. Moreover, the legitimates made their melodramatic offerings as sensational as possible. Execrated by critics, those "cut-throat dramas" filled with "railroad collisions and steamboat collisions" and with "women in unmentionables" satisfied the plebeian taste for action and excitement. Special effects, animals, and numerous female extras bolstered the legitimates' appeal to audiences which might otherwise choose such amusement as that offered at Harris' Mammoth Museum. Opened in 1883, the Museum programmed an occasional melodrama or comic opera in a schedule packed with "Midgets," "YOUNG AJAX, the Boy Serpent," "MARVELLE, Prince of Magic," "Hurtt's Baby Quartette, "Charles Tripp, the armless wonder," and the like.

If the exotic and spectacular drew plebeian audiences, however, so did the homely and familiar. Indeed, among the more distinctive features of theatrical programming in the years between 1860 and 1890 was the extent to which melodrama and comedy were based on local and working-class themes. They were, like London music hall fare, "both escapist *and yet* strongly rooted in the realities of working-class life."[40]

"The pieces are local" was an advertisement most theaters counted on to draw an audience. Comedies like *Two Brides of Allegheny* and *Did You Ever Send Your Wife to Oakland?*, and melodramas like *Pittsburgh by Gaslight* successfully adapted well-known formulas to local tastes. Local playwrights such as Bartley Campbell and David Lowry portrayed the lives of millowners, craftsmen, and laborers. In so doing, they often provoked cries of recognition and delight from the gallery.[41]

Ethnic characterizations enjoyed wide appeal. Specialists in Irish and German types regularly presented their sympathetic, if sometimes ridiculous, portrayals at the legitimates, varieties, and saloons. In doing so they ratified the fact that these immigrants, who had faced nativist hostility as recently as the 1850s, had become better integrated into the city's skilled trades, commerce, and politics. Far less sympathetic was the treatment of Negro characters, although outside the minstrel show and with the notable exception of *Uncle Tom's Cabin,* any treatment of blacks was rare.[42]

In *The Story of a Coal Miner, The Workmen of Pittsburgh, The Molly Maguires, The Boss,* and *Our Boarding House,* Pittsburgh's working people saw familiar types in familiar settings. For example, *The Workmen of New York; or, The Curse of Drink,* retold the

*41*

familiar temperance story of ruin and resurrection with attention to the everyday details of industrial work. Indeed, as staged at the Pittsburgh Theater in 1865 its locus seems to have shifted to a nearby foundry

> in which are shown huge furnaces, glowing with heat, crowds of busy workmen, and the ponderous machinery . . . complete in all its details.

Such shows were not realistic—the light they cast on ordinary life was often absurdly sentimental. Nonetheless, for the materials with which to inhabit the moralistic formula and the romantic cliché, they turned not to antiquity or to exotic locales but to the recognizable milieu of factory and plebeian city.

That Pittsburgh theaters hewed so closely to the tastes of their plebeian audience was due in part to the nature of theatrical organization in the era before the rise of national syndicates. Managers such as William Henderson and John Ellsler were actor-entrepreneurs whose sole business was local or regional entertainment. They maintained resident stock companies whose stars claimed loyal followings and whose familiarity with the common life around them gave their skits and characterizations special appeal. Actors were well known about town and they often incorporated into their acts suggestions heard on street corners or in saloons and barber shops. Such managers and actors are perhaps best seen as craftsmen. They were capable of putting together topical shows, such as those dramatizing events of the Civil War, at a few days' notice. The distinction between manager, actor, and stagehand was slight or nonexistent. The Ellsler family, which dominated theatrical entertainment in Pittsburgh and Cleveland in the 1870s, performed at one time or another almost every function required of the company on and off stage. Members of Henderson's Pittsburgh Theater company did likewise.[43]

Nothing illustrates the character and function of the plebeian theater better than the 1878 production of Bartley Campbell's *The Lower Million*. In that play, the local author depicted events of the great riot of 1877. Its locus is a Pittsburgh iron mill. When the mill owner treats a workers' committee with contempt, the workers strike and join the growing crowd in the streets. The play's hero, Frank Farwell, is a mechanic and aspiring inventor who is loved—and whose inventions are financed—by the mill owner's daughter. The villain is one Gilbert, who wants to seize control of both the mill and the mill owner's daughter. These are stock characters, as are Gilhooley, the Irish worker, and Geister, the German. But their very simplicity and conventionality allowed men like Ellsler to set them in motion in such a way as to register, with extraordinary immediacy, the state of public opinion upon questions of great moment. Thus Farwell and his ethnic comrades "stand up for the workingmen's rights" at the same time that they expose Gilbert's plot and save the mill owner from ruin. In the end Farwell wins not only the mill owner's daughter but his respect and, not least, his concession to new terms in the mill. Among the numerous judgments made along the way one stands out: The skilled craftsman is the key to the industrial system in the Iron City; he is the link to all varieties of workingmen and the savior of honest management as well.[44]

*The Lower Million* was John Ellsler's major production of the 1878 season at the Fifth Avenue Lyceum and it was a big success. Elaborately staged, employing the full stock company and scores of extras (including, by one account, "veteran rioters from the strike"),[45] it was one of the fullest expressions of the plebeian theatrical taste which Pittsburgh's working class cultivated and helped shape in the post–Civil War years. It displayed many of those characteristics which made the theater so central a part of plebeian culture: an intimate acquaintance with local events and personalities; an idealization of the common man[46] and a sympathy for republican and craftsmanly values; and an inclusiveness and accessibility that made each theatrical event itself, regardless of content, an enactment of plebeian community.

Workingmen and their neighbors enjoyed a variety of traditional pastimes in addition to the theater. Horse racing, boxing, wrestling, cockfighting, and bowling were popular sports. Loosely organized and performed sporadically, they demanded no clear separation between professional and amateur. Participants competed on a part-time basis and remained part of the same milieu as that of their spectators. Most sports were linked with betting and saloon life, and were therefore less than respectable. Except for its strict Sabbatarianism, however, Pittsburgh gave narrow compass to the forces of Calvinist respectability. Indeed, betting was a passion easily and openly indulged. Contests of every sort—from foot races to fire engine trials to barber shop singing duels—were regularly advertised, and betting lines announced, in the daily press.[47]

This informal network of sporting activities was loosely organized by a string of fire houses, taverns, groceries, tobacco shops and other centers of plebeian sociability. There matches were arranged, bets placed, betting lines fixed, and contests analyzed and interpreted. At one of the most notable of these, Taylor's tobacco shop in the Strip district, sporting talk punctuated and lubricated the conversation of local newsmen, politicians, and other worthies, including Miles Humphreys of the Vulcans. "In such places," a chronicler has noted, "one could always find an open forum gathered around a common stove, discussing politics, war, boat races, and prize fights."[48]

Into this setting after the Civil War came two new sports which drew unprecedented crowds and attention. Baseball arrived with returning veterans who had learned the game in camp, and it quickly became the most popular participant sport in town. Dozens of amateur teams competed with local and regional rivals. While it is difficult to ascertain much about membership, many teams appear to have been recruited on the basis of neighborhood and work relationships. Some teams descended directly from military units, with former officers serving as patrons. Playing at Union Park in Allegheny and at Friendship and Collins Parks in the east end, amateur teams drew large crowds and much journalistic notice. Pittsburgh's first professional team, the Alleghenies, joined the International Association in 1876, but it made little impact on the local sporting scene. The professionals were poorly paid and undependable. Their level of talent was no higher than that of the amateurs with whom they continued to compete and from whom they apparently failed to distinguish themselves.[49]

For twenty years following the Civil War, enthusiasm for competitive rowing equaled or exceeded that for baseball in Pittsburgh. Part of a nationwide surge of interest in the sport, nearly twenty Pittsburgh-area clubs regularly competed on three different courses. Like fishing clubs, which were also popular at the time, boat clubs sometimes sponsored balls and picnics. Like fire companies, they were both centers of male sociability and organizers of spectacles for the public at large.[50]

The basis upon which clubs were organized varied. For example, the Juniata was named for an iron mill and was probably composed of mill men. Others, such as the Soho and Allegheny clubs, were clearly associated with sections of the city, as were a number of other clubs: the Clipper with the Strip, the McKee with the south side. Other clubs were named for past or present local worthies. Thus the Blackmore club was named for the Democratic judge who was elected mayor as a workingmen's fusion candidate in 1867.[51] Although any statement about the social composition of clubs must reflect the imprecision of membership data, it can be noted that oarsmen mentioned in Pittsburgh newspapers in the two decades following the Civil War are almost all industrial craftsmen, trades-men, clerks, and laborers.[52]

Boat races were immensely popular in Pittsburgh. On the Mon-ongahela and especially on the Allegheny, sculls and crews drew crowds estimated in the tens of thousands and purses in the thou-sands. Races among local clubs, against regional competitors, and sometimes against opponents from distant cities, were public sporting events of the highest note. In the winter of 1874, for example, the *National Labor Tribune* looked forward to a big spring race with keen anticipation:

> Nail City Boat Club, Wheeling, West Virginia, composed chiefly of mill men, are going to take the colors from the Pittsburgh spruces, if it is in the timber of their club.[53]

A hero of the sculls achieved wide celebrity in the city. Pittsburgh's first great oarsman, glassblower James Hamill, went from local vic-tories to nationwide notice after winning big races on the Schuylkill and Hudson rivers in the 1860s. After losing what was billed a championship race in 1867, he retired from competition and invested his purse and notoriety in the Constitution Saloon. In the 1870s Evan Morris, an iron heater, assumed local and national prominence as an oarsman, attracting big crowds and purses to the banks of the Allegheny. He further parlayed celebrity into prosperity by offering testimonials, regularly printed in the *National Labor Tribune,* to the curative ministrations of one Dr. Yates. "I attribute my success (in a measure)," Morris claimed, to the fact that Yates "treated me by electricity during my training." Like Hamill, Morris retired to the retail liquor trade.[54]

Among the best organized and most popular sportsmen in Pitts-burgh were the volunteer firemen. Until 1870 the volunteer com-panies performed at least two functions beyond that of firefighting. They were centers of masculine sociability within neighborhoods, and they provided entertainment and spectacle for the public at large. In the performance of those functions the fire companies typified the interpenetration of private and public spheres charac-teristic of plebeian culture.

Most volunteers were workingmen, shopkeepers, and clerks. While membership data are sketchy, it appears that skilled workers played a large part within the fire companies. In 1862, for example, half of the committee members and officers of the Vigilant Fire Company were either independent artisans or industrial craftsmen. Three businessmen, a tavern keeper, two white-collar workers, and a janitor completed the roll.[55] Seven of seventeen delegates to the city-wide Firemen's Association were skilled workers, while five were businessmen and four were white-collar or professional men. Some fire companies, like the south side Mechanics, contained no members above the social level of skilled worker. Earlier in the century some companies had been "largely composed of young businessmen, in high standing in the community," and volunteer service may have been considered part of the public responsibility of genteel young men. Although some companies still contained a number of such men in the 1860s, none possessed the character of an elite social club and all were dominated by plebeian majorities.[56]

The rise of "a rowdy element" intensified rivalries between fire companies. Fire engine races and water-throwing contests had always been a part of the competitive character of volunteer service. From the 1840s on, however, rivalries intensified and became more violent, a trend possibly abetted by the withdrawal of elite members. Inter-company fights drew increasing public condemnation in the 1850s. It was not uncommon for rival companies to allow a building to burn to the ground while they fought one another for priority at the scene. This competitiveness may have been whetted by the expectation of monetary bonuses which owners of threatened properties sometimes paid attending firemen. But the money incentive hardly seems capable of generating the degree of murderousness displayed in those brawls. With knives, guns, and axes firemen assaulted and sometimes murdered one another. On a number of occasions volunteers even set fires in order to lure their rivals into an ambush. Moreover, violence between companies did not require the occurrence of a fire. Fights erupted in the streets outside fire houses and saloons and at Fourth of July picnics.[57]

Because fire companies were neighborhood institutions, brawls sometimes took the form of ethnic territorial battles. The Strip district, for example, contained three companies, one of Irish Protestant Orangemen, one of Irish Catholic Fenians, and one composed of German Turners. The former two especially sustained a fierce rivalry. One indication of the strength of company loyalties is the fact that, at the outbreak of the Civil War, each company enlisted nearly en masse in a separate military unit; at war's end, many returning veterans rejoined their old fire companies.[58]

Ethnic solidarity appears to have shaped the behavior of other firemen, although evidence on this question is at best suggestive. Perhaps Protestant firemen in the Eagle and Relief companies, who bent before the winds of religious revival in 1858–1859, sought to develop a style of behavior distinct from that of the Catholic immigrants against whom they harbored hostility. Bible readings and YMCA-led prayer meetings may have sharpened the character of the firehouse as a base for assaults upon alien cultural symbols and institutions. When volunteers trained their hoses on the windows of unspecified but iniquitous "dens," chasing the occupants into the night, were they just sporting, or were they expressing the common moral judgment of their neighbors, who hoped to separate themselves from poorer, encroaching aliens? Company resolutions and revised constitutions of the late 1850s and 1860s, emphasizing temperance and orderliness within and without the firehouse, may have reflected a desire less to placate bourgeois dissatisfaction with company indiscipline than to generate a more distinctive, plebeian form of Protestant respectability.[59]

No doubt the simpler and more benign functions of the fire house— providing opportunities for drinking and card playing and "a place where mighty questions are discussed"—attracted and held members. The fire company provided edification and entertainment to members and non-members through its library, debate club, and art gallery. It also helped neighbors observe significant occasions, especially funerals and weddings. For example, the Mechanics company regularly performed a happy ritual suggestive of the village past of one south side borough:

> [W]henever any citizen of Birmingham, whether fireman or not, got married, the bridegroom was loaded upon the hose reel and hauled over the roughest streets possible, until he ordered up drinks for the party at the nearest saloon.[60]

As firemen identified with their neighborhood, so their neighbors supported them. When a fire company planned a fund-raising picnic or ball, it invariably chose as sponsors and managers of the event saloonkeepers and other small property owners in the ward. Such sponsorship reflected self-interest on the part of the property owners, to be sure. But it also represented a willingness to support a cultural institution that provided not only fire protection but musical, sporting, and other entertainments as well. When in order to finance a trip to the firemen's tournament in Sandusky, Ohio, the Relief company employed the usual method of fund raising—i.e., "canvassing the ward"—it was not simply playing on the fears of property owners. It was testing the neighborhood's level of support for its principal sportsmen.[61]

*47*

Despite such intense parochialism, however, the fire companies were always more than just neighborhood institutions. They had long been conscious of their role in elaborating a city-wide plebeian culture. Their "Soirees" attracted broad audiences and their concerts had made Pittsburgh a band-conscious city. More important, the fire companies were the indispensible element in any public celebration. The parade through the main streets of the city, with volunteers and horses in full regalia, engines gleaming and garlanded, little children in costume riding on the decorated floats, was the principal form of public ritual in the Iron City. Firemen took the lead in organizing the celebration of July Fourth and other occasions. To the fireman's plans and expectations, city officials and other citizens geared their own participation.

That the firemen were indeed conscious of their city-wide role is suggested by two widely spaced events. When John Quincy Adams visited Pittsburgh in 1843, the firemen ignored suggestions that the aged traveler might not be up to an elaborate welcome. With their comrades in the militia, firemen organized a large torchlight procession and other festivities designed to properly welcome a distinguished guest to their city. Twenty-one years later, when genteel organizers of the Sanitary Fair failed to invite their participation, the firemen showed up anyway. Accompanied by the Sons of Vulcan, the fire companies forced their way into the parade, thereby foiling the Fair committee's attempt to overturn local custom.[62]

The latter incident indicates that events of the 1860s accentuated the outward rather than the inward direction of fire company energies. Both Civil War mobilization and the activities of the ascendant craft union movement tended to overcome ethnic and other divisions among the plebs of Pittsburgh. Both reinforced the companies' role in cultivating and maintaining the values of plebeian localism, as opposed to neighborhood parochialism. The differential arrangements made to welcome returning veterans in 1863 demonstrated the extent to which firemen had assumed that role. As the locally recruited 123rd Regiment approached Pittsburgh, the fire companies issued the call for a big public welcome. They mobilized the mayor (himself a member of the Relief Fire Company), the Subsistence Committee, and numerous other citizens to participate in the parade and reception. Similarly, when the 136th Regiment, also recruited locally, arrived in Pittsburgh a few weeks later, firemen participated fully in the celebration. However, the arrival of two other regiments at about the same time elicited no response whatsoever from the firemen. To welcome the 134th Regiment, politicians and other prominent citizens managed to assemble a respectable, if unenthusiastic, crowd. Nothing marked the arrival shortly thereafter of the 137th Regiment except a two-sentence announcement in the newspaper. Both of these latter regiments were composed of men recruited from beyond Allegheny County. Neither, therefore, could expect to be welcomed back as local heroes.[63]

With their roots in the wards, with their prominence as performers of public ritual, and with their impressive ability to mobilize men and resources quickly, the fire companies held obvious attraction to politicians. Both B. C. Sawyer, Jr., and William C. McCarthy won mayoralty races in the 1860s while members of the fire companies. When McCarthy won the Republican primary in 1865, the Duquesne Engine Company rang bells and paraded through the streets in celebration. The prominence of saloonkeepers, aldermen, and justices of the peace in the sponsorship of fire company fund-raisers testified to the importance of the firemen as political forces in ward and city. In 1870 the city fire marshal was an alderman, the chief engineer was a member of the city common council, and the janitor and messenger of the Firemen's Association was also the messenger of the council.[64]

With the inauguration of professional municipal fire service in  1870, the volunteer companies disbanded. In a sense, this marked the beginning of a new era in which politics and public service were to become more professionalized and bureaucratized. Yet it was only a beginning. Even after reorganization, the fire companies retained many old members, recruited new ones from the same milieu, and continued to play their role in public ceremonies. Moreover, long after reorganization, the public culture which fire companies had helped to create retained its character.

For another fifteen years, for example, celebration of the Fourth of July gave symbolic expression to the centrality of the plebs in the Iron City. With craftsmen, merchants, newsmen, athletes, militiamen and entertainers, firemen assumed the task of organizing and performing the public ritual. Elite citizens played only secondary, ceremonial roles, in the performance of which they had to share a platform with men like Richard Realf, the poet who celebrated the ironworker, and J. N. Gotthold, popular actor and theater manager. Moreover, the heart of the celebration was never in the brief patriotic observance—the speech making and recitation of the Declaration of Independence—however important an element this remained. The plebeian Fourth sought less to define unity than to display diversity. It sought, on the one hand, simply to dazzle the public with spectacle:

boat regattas, balloon ascensions, chariot races, fire engine trials, etc. On the other hand it presented a procession of the city's nationalities, neighborhoods, and trades. In 1876, for example, hundreds of trades-men marched with their wagons in a seemingly endless line: cracker wagons, ice wagons, florist wagons, coal wagons, butcher wagons— even one with a "mammoth sausage chopper" in operation! These were followed by seven hundred butchers on horse and the entire work forces of two iron mills. Swiss, German, French, Scotch-Irish, Colored, and Bohemian associations and four Catholic Total Absti-nence societies marched along with scores of neighborhood, lodge, and professional bands, winding their way through the wards of the old city. Leading and marshaling the entire line of march were militiamen and firemen in full regalia. After formal ceremonies at parade's end, the crowd moved to the Allegheny River bank to see the day's premier event, the boat club regatta.[65]

The parade and its associated events were not the sole forms of celebration. For many citizens private picnics and neighborhood gatherings supplemented or even superseded the main celebrations. Moreover, commercial amusements attracted numerous customers who chose to enjoy in their own way a day free of labor.[66] None-theless, thousands of people did participate in the public ritual. The few voices heard to challenge the character of the celebration did so from a lonely, elitist position. Within more austere Presbyterian and Methodist circles, the very plebeian enthusiasm which marked the day invalidated its usefulness as a pious commemoration of national purpose.[67] For many years, however, such voices com-manded little attention in the Iron City.

The plebeian Fourth was an untidy event, but it was neither random nor formless. Its traditional format—parade, followed by platform ceremony, followed by spectacles and games—was designed to be inclusive and to display the diversity of social experience within the Iron City. Its broad banner of republicanism required no explicit ideological program to impose unity upon that diversity. Yet a certain coherence emerged simply as a result of the pervasiveness of plebeian types in the celebration. As militiamen, parade marshals, musicians, athletes, and sometimes as public officials and speakers, plebeian Pittsburghers dominated the day's events. The Fourth of July an-nounced that, in work and leisure, Pittsburgh was their city.

# CHAPTER 4

# Sober Citizens

On November 26, 1876, "the greatest temperance revival ever known" began in Pittsburgh when Francis Murphy, the apostle of Gospel Temperance, addressed eight thousand people at the Opera House. He created a sensation and was immediately hired by the Young Men's Temperance Union to launch a local crusade. Its success was spectacular. Within two months, thirty churches were holding temperance meetings, temperance clubs were set up throughout western Pennsylvania, and a movement newspaper had been founded. In February 1877, a national organization was launched with its headquarters in Pittsburgh. Forty thousand drinkers had signed the pledge. The glassworkers' union even reported a noticeable "falling off in the call for whiskey glasses and beer mugs."[1]

Interesting in itself, the Murphy revival also serves as a window on the ambivalent relationship between the labor movement and the plebeian milieu in Pittsburgh. Union leaders and Labor Reformers passionately supported Murphy. That they should have done so requires explanation, first, of the kind of temperance Murphy preached and, second, of the kind of men who heard and absorbed his message. In regard to the latter especially, the Murphy revival is most suggestive. For Murphy won his following among men who were pulled in different, but equally powerful directions. On the one hand, they were locals and traditionalists, wedded to the craftsmen's empire and the plebeian community; on the other, they were cosmopolitans and modernizers, builders of new formal organizations which required disciplined, organization men. Although they asserted the historic task of the "producing classes" to restore republican virtue to the

*51*

industrial community, they feared an enemy far closer to home and more deeply imbedded in working-class life than the "monopolists" and "money interests" who haunted their rhetoric. They worried that plebeian culture had the potential to subvert, as well as to nurture, the labor movement. As they strove for more perfect forms of organization, moreover, they also worried that, without a sense of community and an ideal of citizenship, organization might become an end in itself. For a time at least, temperance seemed to resolve these tensions. Sobriety could easily be understood as one of the traditional virtues of the self-respecting citizen and the autonomous craftsman. It could also be understood as a modern code of discipline for soldiers in the army of labor. Whether it restored men or remade them, however, working-class temperance was a call to collective and personal action.

Although it crowned a century of temperance agitation, the Prohibition crusade represented a particularly narrow and singleminded strain of the movement. Until the rise of the Anti-Saloon League in the 1890s, the enemies of Demon Rum held diverse and shifting opinions about the proper ends and means of the movement. For many, perhaps most, of its advocates, temperance still meant voluntary self-control. Even among total abstainers like the Murphyites and the earlier Washingtonians, the temperate individual claimed a responsibility to society more as a model than as a censor. He urged his fellows to "come out" of the Babylon of habitual drunkenness, not to raise an army against it. Nor did he generally idealize bourgeois life as a Jerusalem of sobriety. He appealed to urges less for respectability than for self-respect. He addressed anxieties about personal and family stability more than those about social status.[2]

It was this sort of temperance that Murphy preached in Pittsburgh in 1876 and 1877. Those who heard him credited his success to "geniality." His meetings were informal, marked by "free, impromptu outpourings of the heart," spontaneous testimonials, chatting and applause. Sometimes he invited such popular performers as the Stephen C. Foster Serenaders to entertain his flock. Richard Realf, the ironworkers' poet, recited at his meetings. Murphy never had a hard word for drunkards or saloonkeepers, whom he consistently addressed as "brothers" and "dear friends." Personal experience was his only text. An Irish immigrant whose descent into drunkenness had destroyed his family and his successful hotel and saloon business, Murphy put himself on an equal footing with his plebeian audiences. Refusing to badger or condemn his fellow-sinners, he invited them to identify with the mysterious workings of "the grace of God," "the

free and saving spirit" in his life. Men who seldom responded to
such appeals chose to identify with Murphy's story. He converted
some notorious drinkers: alderman Harry B. Smithson, police detective Joseph Cupples, saloonkeeper Charles Wendell, steelworker
John Noey.[3]

Murphy's hosts were astonished and pleased by his success with
such men and with working-class and Irish audiences generally. Before
long, however, they discovered distinct limits to their geniality.
Trustees of the Methodist Church that served as Murphy's headquarters began to complain. Unwashed crowds were doing "obnox-
ious things" to their carpets, windows, and pews. They objected to
large expenditures for "material aid and transportion," especially for
a free lunch kitchen which Murphy set up in the church basement.
Surprised by the flood of pledge-signers, the YMTU stopped ad-
mitting Murphy converts indiscriminately.[4]

Murphy was militantly nonpolitical, and it was this fact which
most clearly revealed the fissure between himself and those "whose
chief hope and dependence is in temperance according to law." He
bluntly rebuffed prohibitionists and local optionists who expected
his support. When pushed, Murphy became indignant: "Some people
say [my movement] will be a political movement after a while.
Never! Never!" He insisted his purpose was not to satisfy or "amuse"
sober, middle-class people but to make men "fall in love with
temperance."[5]

Murphy's lack of self-righteousness and class prejudice no doubt
disarmed workingmen accustomed to being lectured to by temperance
preachers. But his appeal was based on more than charm. Practical
experience in organization had already disposed many union men
and their leaders to temperance. One of their earliest arguments in
favor of worker sobriety was also the most straightforward. In the
union hall, on the job, or on the picket line, drunks do not make
good comrades. Neither the "drunken loafer" nor the purveyor of
drink can be counted on in a crisis. Saloons and doggeries are
breeding grounds for strikebreakers.[6]

From their inception Pittsburgh's leading craft unions tried to
legislate against the disruptive consequences of drink. In its constitution the Amalgamated Association of Iron and Steel Workers
stipulated fines against any member who entered a lodge under the
influence of liquor and a series of penalties, including expulsion
from the union, for any member "known to go to his work drunk."[7]
No union occupied itself more strenuously in trying to instill temperate habits in its members than the Window Glass Workers As-

sociation (Local Assembly 300). At its 1883 convention, L.A. 300 resolved to forbid the introduction of liquor into any plant at any time. A year later no fewer than nine motions were offered on the subject of temperance. One resolution specifically condemned men whose intemperance resulted in "brothers losing work." It is clear from the debates that temperance was an issue of serious contention not just at the convention but "in our different Preceptories." In 1886 the union took a hard line, endorsing the right of management to fire any worker who brought liquor into the works. And in 1889 James Campbell, who was publicly committed to the state prohibition amendment, devoted a large part of his presidential address to a blistering attack on glassworker intemperance, insisting that the drunkard "be expelled from the organization, and debarred from work until he proves by his actions that he is worthy to be a member of L.A. 300."[8]

It is true that labor spokesmen occasionally invoked temperance in order to promote their movement's claim to respectability and middle-class support. Sometimes they simply and unselfconsciously shared in the conventions of bourgeois discourse, as, for example, when the *Labor Tribune* included in its list of arguments for sobriety the charge that drunken idleness "prevents the accumulation of capital." Similarly, temperance tales and homilies published in the labor press sentimentalized the horrors of drunkenness and the joys and profits of sobriety in a manner indistinguishable from that of the evangelical press or the popular melodrama. References to "gin shops" as "stagnant ponds and unclean sewers" came from the same rhetorical waters fished by Frances Willard, John St. John, and Washington Gladden.[9]

If in using such language labor spokesmen revealed a susceptibility to *embourgeoisement,* they also showed canny political sense. For example, when John Jarrett and William Wiehe, outgoing and incoming presidents of the AAISW, testified before the U.S. Senate Committee on Labor and Education in 1883, they skillfully played the temperance tune. "[W]e have devoted more time and attention to educating our members on the question of temperance than on any other," Jarrett explained, "for we find that intemperance is productive of more evil among workingmen than any other thing." Having warmed to the theme and developed its variations, Jarrett moved swiftly to his coda: The "better educated" the workingmen, the "less intemperance among them"; education requires money and leisure; therefore, the gentlemen of the Senate could best promote temperance by passing an eight-hour law![10]

The leaders of the AAISW were skilled rhetoricians, but their performances was not merely cynical. If few labor leaders agreed with such prohibitionists as Campbell of the glassworkers that intemperance was a prime cause rather than a symptom of poverty, even fewer believed it did not injure the labor movement. And if most believed that widespread temperance would eventually issue from the triumph of the labor movement, few thought that the matter could be left to the future. Especially at times when clear-headed and aggressive action seemed most vital to the success of organization—at the start of new organizing drives or during strikes, for example—the ideal of "the sober workman" impressed itself most firmly upon the practical reformer.

Thus, John M. Davis promoted temperance during his years of pioneer organizing for the Knights of Labor in western Pennsylvania. Similarly, Andrew Roy, in his early efforts to build communal solidarity among the miners of western Pennsylvania, advocated temperance less as an individual benefit than as a way to "do justice to the sober miners around you." Temperance men were sometimes the most militant organizers and allies of labor. Among persons convicted of conspiracy in the Washington County coal miners' strike of 1885–1886 was "a Methodist local preacher, a devoted Christian and ardent temperance advocate." The leadership of the Catholic Total Abstinence Union in Pittsburgh came not primarily from middle-class or clerical sources but from workingmen such as E.H. McAninch, Hugh McMillan, and Michael Sullivan, all of whom were activists in the Knights of Labor or the Amalgamated Association of Iron and Steel Workers. They were also Greenbackers and Irish nationalists and were among the strongest supporters of Francis Murphy's ecumenical revival in Pittsburgh. They demonstrated the same constellation of values which made *The Irish World and American Industrial Liberator* of New York a national organ of labor, Greenback, Land League, and temperance causes.[11]

When the *Labor Tribune* in 1877 urged workingmen to "Fall into Rank" behind Murphy, therefore, it did so with an eye toward the need for disciplined soldiers in the army of labor. However, it also revealed concerns that were both deeper and broader than those of the shop floor or the union hall. They were deeper in that they pertained to the very process of character formation among labor's foot soldiers, and broader in that they alerted workingmen to the duties of citizenship, to involvement in the larger issues of community, culture, and polity.

The cult of "manliness" occupied an important place in the moral environment of nineteenth-century workingmen.[12] In a sense, it operated as a counterpoint to demands for more thoroughgoing organization by reassuring workingmen that sober, cooperative behavior need not imply emasculation. It is therefore not surprising that labor spokesmen in Pittsburgh responded instinctively to Murphy's appeal to "manhood." The slogan "Be men!" so well complemented their call to worker self-discipline that the *Labor Tribune* could barely contain its impulse to proclaim it over and over again:

Signing the pledge is a good, open, public, courageous step. By it a man proclaims himself to be a man.[13]

The cult of manliness also tapped a strain of moralism that had always run with almost equal vigor alongside the hearty exuberance of plebeian culture. Rooted in the Protestant work ethic and the ethos of the autonomous craftsman, and conditioned by generations of self-righteousness apostrophes to the moral superiority of "nature's noblemen," this plebeian moralism conditioned workingmen to see in "dependency" the chief source of personal and public vice. Images of enslavement and emasculation cluttered the rhetoric of most of the popular movements to which nineteenth-century workingmen gave their support.[14] They were staples of plebeian melodrama and of the stories published in the *National Labor Tribune* and other popular publications.[15] They had also been staples of Republican Party rhetoric since the 1850s, when nativists and early trades unionists, although they disagreed as to whether "monopolists" or "papists" were the chief emasculators, flocked together under the banner of free labor, free soil, and free men. After the Civil War, labor spokesmen easily assimilated the struggles against wage-slavery and against "soul-enslaving appetites" to that recently concluded against chattel slavery.[16]

The central value which, in each of these crusades, had most devoutly to be preserved from degradation was "manly independence." As a spokesman for the Knights of Labor put it, "the man is the happiest who goes to himself for all that he desires, who is independent of outside circumstances." Intemperance was an especially insiduous threat because it installed the "monster" of dependency within the individual himself. It unfitted him for battle before the colors had been raised. For the *Labor Tribune* in 1881, the threat was serious enough to require a stark inquiry into the interior of every working man:

The important question for each individual is, who shall preside over my appetites and propensities?[17]

This preoccupation with the inner life of working men might be thought of as a plebeian version of the search for a "bourgeois interior."[18] Though working people lived in cramped quarters and indulged in the essentially public leisure of the plebeian city, they were not immune to the appeals of domesticity. Especially among better-paid craftsmen, a stable home represented the "independence and respectability" that the constitution of the Amalgamated Association insisted were chief goals of craft organization. Pittsburgh's *Peoples Monthly,* published briefly in the early 1870s and aimed squarely at the craftsmen audience, ran a stream of articles on the need for more home building. "We hold," the editors opined, "that no man occupies a truly independent position, nor can he or his family enjoy life until he owns his own home . . . ." Similarly, the *Labor Tribune* editorialized in 1886 about the centrality of "OUR HOMES" to the lives of workingmen.[19]

What is the greatest prize of the American citizen? . . . It is the home . . . where hours of leisure and repose are spent . . . . Without the home of the American, liberty itself would become impossible . . . . Homes make men, make citizens, make heroes . . . . The man without a home is a barbarian.

Along with the acquisition of property, home ownership also implied expanded domestic consumption. Thus, in the years between the late 1870s and mid-1880s, when business boomed and incomes rose in Pittsburgh, retailers began to appeal more directly to families rather than just to men. The *Tribune* responded to the new emphasis on domestic consumption by inaugurating in 1879 a column called "Household Hints," aimed at wives and featuring recipes and advice about wise consumption. Advertisements for furniture, rugs, musical instruments, jewelry, and other consumer goods, as well as for family excursions packaged by travel agents and railroads, grew to outnumber those for groceries and work clothes. In the *Tribune* and elsewhere, brewers began advertising bottled beer as a family beverage to be consumed at home or on picnics, not in the saloon.[20]

Yet, as Linda Schneider has argued, home was not just a symbol of consumption; it was also "a symbol of autonomy" for workingmen. Although stories and poems published in the *Labor Tribune* indeed showed wife, children, and hearth "civilizing" the intemperate workingman and turning him into a stable burgher, they also showed

*57*

him becoming a self-respecting union man and citizen. By weaning him from self-destructive habits and giving him a powerful motive to plan for the future, home and family worked in harmony with the labor movement to create that very manly self-discipline required to storm "the Vicksburgs of Labor's enemies." Although the cult of domesticity appeared to challenge the masculine world of workplace and union lodge, it might also complement them.[21]

In this respect, union balls and outings, designed specifically as family affairs, harnessed the potentially privatistic family to the engine of labor organization. The union lodge had always been more than a place for doing union business and nurturing male camaraderie. As a site for weddings, wakes, fund-raisers, and balls it welcomed families and friends, thereby associating the union more firmly with the daily lives of workers. In the late 1870s, unions increasingly sponsored temperate versions of such family gatherings, anticipating by several decades the search for "substitutes for the saloon," which so occupied middle-class reformers at the turn of the century.[22] Thus, an Amalgamated ball might be advertised with the warning, "No intoxicated or disorderly person will be allowed to remain in the hall." The Knights could be counted on for a dry Fourth of July picnic or a New Year's "grand temperance supper and ball." For several years the Amalgamated annual reunion was held on a strictly dry basis. At many holiday celebrations, explicit temperance appeals accompanied patriotic and pro-labor speeches as a regular part of platform ceremonies. Although such expedients represented an effort to indoctrinate participants and to modify traditional recreational practices, the bulk of those practices remained perfectly familiar. The holiday picnic retained a "carnival atmosphere," with its ball games, foot-races, dances, and band concerts. At balls, "comic and sentimental songs were sung, suitable to all nationalities," and proceedings resembled those held under other auspices in fire halls and saloons.[23]

Labor leaders believed that sober workmen made better union comrades, but they also had a larger agenda in which temperance played an important part. Within the labor movement, especially the Knights of Labor, the republican vision of citizenship lived on for a quarter-century after the Civil War. It associated the labor movement with the widest currents of reform and social progress. It included the belief that only sober workmen could fully claim their right to participate in community, polity, and civilization. In an 1877 editorial in the *National Labor Tribune,* Thomas A. Armstrong located labor in the forefront of a cultural revolution, "a great change to be wrought" upon the entire fabric of social life:

> It comprehends a sounder, deeper and higher education of the people. It means temperance, not a total abstinence, but a far higher degree of temperance in drink than now prevails. It means a higher type of practical Christianity than prevails in our gilded and painted churches.[24]

Such a view required that the labor movement educate as well as represent the working class. In the abstract, labor spokesmen affirmed the "natural right" of citizenship for all, but they also suggested that workingmen needed to "qualify [themselves] to play their part in the world's drama." The labor movement played a decisive, although not unique part in that education. In addition to schools, specifically political entities such as the Greenback-Labor Party and reform groups such as the Gospel Temperance society might also be understood as "grand instrumentalities" of working-class education. The Knights of Labor looked to education, in this broad sense, "to develop [workers'] intellectual, moral and social faculties . . . , to enable them to share in the gains and honors of advancing civilization."[25]

That some working people shared these views is indicated by the appearance in Pittsburgh of several organizations dedicated to worker self-improvement. Among these were the South Side Mechanics Institute, founded by a glass presser and a laborer for the purpose of building a library and sponsoring lectures, and several lodges of the Sovereigns of Industry, a national organization whose aims included the promotion of both education and sociability among working men and women.[26]

The promotion of working-class education became the life-task of Andrew Burtt, the glassblower turned schoolteacher and organizer for the Knights and the Greenback-Labor Party. Something of a local hero in Pittsburgh, Burtt taught children by day and adults by night, the latter frequently in union halls. Similarly, the *Labor Tribune* sponsored book-buying clubs and urged workers to read books and discuss them with their fellows in the lodge. Disturbed that too many workers saw the lodge as a place for meetings in which officers "go through the order of business in a cold machine-like fashion," the *Tribune* thought it imperative that the lodge become an American "imitation" of the English workingmen's club, where "instructive readings" and discussions combined with sociability. "Why," it asked, "have we got a whole network of influences and agencies at work to educate and strengthen our faculties and capabilities for higher activity?" The *Tribune's* answer to that question is revealing: "Too many men look upon a dollar as able to buy them just so much tobacco or whiskey."[27]

The *Tribune* here revealed a growing suspicion among labor leaders that the saloons and other centers of plebeian sociability, which had done so much to nurture the labor movement, were thwarting its progress. It also reveals something about the importance of the Knights of Labor, even for the *Tribune* and other spokesmen for trade unionism who, in the late 1880s, increasingly criticized the Order's organizing tactics and vague reformist rhetoric. Convinced that trade unions better represented the economic interests of their members than did the Knights, the *Tribune* nonetheless wanted to salvage the Knights as a crucial educational wing of the labor movement:

> The unionist looks to his union for his rights as to terms and wages; he attends the meetings of his local assembly and fraternizes with persons of other trades, joined together in Knighthood for the advantages of those educational objects that will prove elevating to labor.

Having itself insisted that unions adopt "business methods" and operate with "efficiency," the *Tribune* feared that business unions would utterly abandon their responsibility to promote solidarity and educate workers for citizenship.[28]

The ambition to unify economic, political, and social spheres of working-class life lay at the heart of the Knight's vision of the labor movement. To a surprising degree, moreover, it corresponded to social realities in plebeian Pittsburgh. Sprung from the craftsmen's empire and nurtured by plebeian culture, the movement had, in a sense, simply reproduced in somewhat altered form an older set of communal relations that bound workers to one another and to many of their neighbors. Yet, that alteration, based on temperance and "education" in the broader sense, injected a critical distance between the movement and the milieu. The citizen-worker idealized by Knights and labor reformers was not simply a local pleb set in motion, any more than the trade unionist was simply an autonomous craftsman with a union card. He was a new man, sober and cosmopolitan, rooted in the plebeian milieu yet intent upon remaking it.

By the 1880s, however, that milieu had begun to change in ways not anticipated by labor reformers. As trade unions such as the Amalgamated and L.A. 300 moved increasingly toward interest-group tactics and bureaucratic management, plebeian politics was becoming more professionalized and less responsive to initiatives from the bottom up. Although the Knights tried to translate plebeian community into a new form of citizen-solidarity, they were no match for the professionals. Particularly noteworthy was the fact that, in their role as centers of working-class political organization, the union lodge and assembly hall were being bypassed. All the old centers of plebeian politics, including the firehouse, the veterans lodge, the sports club, the grocery, the tobacco shop, and the saloon, appeared destined to be coöpted and harnessed by new political forces. Just as labor seemed at the peak of its political power in the late 1870s, those political forces showed that they had a life of their own.

# CHAPTER 5

# Politicians and Professionals

For workingmen in Pittsburgh, the 1877 upheaval had been a spur
to organization and a demonstration of labor's power in the local
community. While leaders such as Humphreys, Armstrong, Davis,
and Burtt strongly condemned the arson and random violence that
accompanied the strike, they saw such activities as regrettable excesses, the cure for which was further organization. Most respectable
citizens held a similar view or remained silent. Among a growing
minority, however, the specter of the Paris commune evinced a more
militant response. The upheaval convinced them that neither the
labor leadership nor the local police (especially when commanded
by a mayor like William C. McCarthy) could be counted on to
restrain the plebeian population. At the same time, however, local
government was becoming more insulated from citizen initiatives of
any kind. Advocates of law and order therefore sought both to
outflank and to reform local government.

Shortly after the 1877 upheaval, Pittsburgh businessmen joined
their peers in other industrial cities in a successful movement to
transform the weak state militia into a strong National Guard. The
focus of their efforts was the state legislature. There, rural legislators
hardly needed to be convinced of the need for a strong constabulary;
and other legislators found public revulsion against violence—and
sizeable contribution from business lobbyists—sufficiently persuasive.
The Guard they created proved itself for the next half-century a
reliable ally of corporations, a predictable enemy of labor. Financed

largely by coal, steel, and railroad money, and led by elite officers, the Guard subjected recruits to careful screening and rigorous training. Military discipline insured that this force of law and order would be unrestrained by local or class sympathies for its likely targets. Thus, the Guardsmen sent to Homestead in 1892 little resembled the militiamen of 1877. Few openly sympathized with the strikers or the townspeople, and those who did could expect to be treated as mutineers. When one young Guardsman bivouacked at Homestead cheered the news that Henry C. Frick had been shot, his colonel swiftly ordered him "strung up by his thumbs," then shaved his head and drummed him out of service.[1]

On the local level, the recently formed Chamber of Commerce became a leading advocate of law and order. The Chamber claimed some credit for defeating Miles Humphreys in his bid to succeed McCarthy as mayor. It had already begun to take up in its own way the issues upon which McCarthy had run successfully in the past— tax reform for small property owners and an end to the corruption of city officials by railroad money. While smaller shopkeepers represented by the Retail Grocers Association maintained close links with labor, the merchants and manufactures represented by the Chamber possessed large investments in downtown property, homes in the suburbs, and a view of the city which took little notice of life in the plebeian wards. The Chamber's campaign to reorganize the city police won a following among such men. After a decade spent pushing for larger and better-financed police forces, the Chamber succeeded in shaping the new 1887 city charter according to its law and order specifications. The Department of Safety created by that charter was to be controlled by a council-appointed board, not by the mayor; it imposed standards of military discipline and professional efficiency on the expanded police force. Not coincidentally, the first chief of the new department was J. O. Brown, a lawyer and long-time leader of the anti-McCarthy wing of the local Republican party.[2]

Until the 1890s, however, the Chamber's political efforts were halting and sporadic. They certainly never penetrated to the ward and precinct level in a way that seriously challenged the masters of plebeian politics. However, another contender did precisely that.

The rapid rise of the Magee-Flinn machine represented the major fact of political life in Pittsburgh in the 1880s. Dismaying to middle-class reformers, it was even more so to labor reformers. At first, the latter attacked the growing ranks of professional politicians in familiar, moralistic terms. The politicians were alien, part of a network of "cliques, rings, parties, monopolies, knotted together in money interest," a "gentry" seeking to impose itself upon the citizenry. Sometimes they were seen as foolish and effete, "a lot of clowns . . . loafing around City Hall." More often they were taken seriously and merged with the other external enemies of labor:

> Strike against these bankers and money lenders . . . . Strike against political ringmasters who sell you every time . . . .[3]

The very fear of being "sold," however, points to a second and increasingly prominent motif in the labor critique of politics. Labor detested the Magee ring not only because it was the ally of "monopolists" or because its corruption ultimately impoverished the plebeian citizenry, but especially because it threatened to displace the labor movement as the principal organizer and educator of the working class.

Christopher Magee learned to coordinate the administrative powers of the expanding city government after four short years of service as city treasurer in the 1870s. By carefully controlling utility and transportation franchises, the deposit of city funds, and the granting of construction contracts, he quickly developed a devoted following among the city's construction, banking, and traction magnates. His alliance with William Flinn, one of those magnates, sealed the control that Magee exercised over the city council, into which the Pennsylvania Railroad had funnelled large sums of money for years. By 1880, Magee had become the regulator of all such transfers. The key to his success, however, was his control of patronage and his masterful maintenance of a network of ward-level organizations. Magee made allies, and sometimes public employees, of the habitues of those very centers of plebeian sociability that William C. McCarthy had first mobilized in the 1860s. In union halls, boat clubs, and saloons, "festive ward bummers" and "workingmen politicians" advanced the cause of the machine as familiar comrades in labor and leisure, not as agents of an alien interest.[4]

Old Vulcans such as Humphreys and Nate Brokaw and old Knights such as L.J. Booker became party stalwarts, professionals whose job was more often to sell the cause of the Republican Party to labor than vice versa. Big men in labor became prime candidates for appointment to state and even national office. When the rumor that Carroll Wright might resign as head of the United States Bureau of Labor Statistics reached Pittsburgh, both James Campbell of the glassworkers and William Martin of the Amalgamated hotly pursued the opening. Earnestly, though in vain, they advertised themselves to prominent Republicans as good, "conservative" replacements and loyal party men. If the biggest plums eluded Pittsburgh labor leaders, some more modest, though still juicy, ones did not. For example, Humphreys served the state of Pennsylvania as head of the Bureau of Industrial Statistics and Campbell as factory inspector.[5]

Similarly, on the local level, neighborhood retailers and men prominent in union halls and Grand Army of the Republic veterans' posts became party stalwarts and municipal employees on the strength of their plebeian connections.[6] The expansion of city services and employment gave Magee the power to capture not only individuals but institutions that had previously functioned independent of government. For example, within a few years of its transformation into a professional city service, the fire department had become a prime vehicle of patronage. Most of the volunteers who chose to become professionals were kept on, thereby insuring continuity between the old neighborhood firehouse and the new institution. Ensconced on the Board of Fire Commissioners, Magee and his cronies gradually added new firemen to the veteran stock and turned all of them into political retainers.[7] The success of this strategy in neutralizing political insurgency is suggested by the fact that Miles Humphreys ended his long career as Pittsburgh's fire chief, and that, after his last term as mayor, William C. McCarthy was almost never without an appointed job in city government. As the "lure of office"[8] turned union leaders and other plebeian notables into candidates and appointees, scores of smaller figures also found the congenial and profitable world of local politics and municipal employment too hard to resist.

Having spent years promoting the "elevation of workingmen to office," labor reformers began in the 1880s to question their very success. Politics no longer seemed an open channel through which the republican citizenry might impress its interests and values upon the state. It had become an obstacle course or, worse, a destination in itself. In short, politics had become a profession. Against this professionalization some labor spokesmen protested. The *Labor Tribune* urgently pleaded with workingmen to support the Greenback-Labor Party or the independent faction of the Republican Party. However, it found that "prominent workingmen, who are supposed to have much influence in controlling the labor vote, are secretly paid to talk and sing along." Having grown to political maturity in an era when party organization was loose and party loyalties shifting, labor reformers now found themselves in an age of "tickets" pushed by working-class professionals.[9]

Such professionals still responded to well-organized pressure from labor, but they also served a clientele of businessmen and middle-class interest groups whose money and influence might outclass that of labor. Most important, they served themselves and their machinery of power. If labor chose to act politically, therefore, it would have to take on the managers of the machinery or forward its own candidates for the ranks of junior management. As McCarthy, Humphreys, and many others took the latter course, the great labor campaigns of the 1860s and 1870s became a thing of the past.

These local trends were abetted by a nationwide intensification of major party rivalry. The resurgence of the Democratic Party in the late 1870s sparked a Republican campaign to restore and consolidate working-class loyalty to the Grand Old Party. If waving the bloody shirt revived wartime passions, appeals based on Republican policies of tariff protection and economic stimulation counted even more. The Amalgamated, for example, was unwaveringly hostile to any suggestion of lower tariffs. Its first annual reunion had actually been organized in 1880 as a "Tariff Demonstration." It held aloof from the infant American Federation of Labor for four years, until in 1887 the Federation gave assurances that its stand on tariffs would be sufficiently protectionist. Convinced that support for high tariffs was the *sine qua non* of labor politics, the Amalgamated increasingly united with industry to lobby and campaign for tariff Republicanism.[10] While opinion in the Knights of Labor was less singleminded,[11] nothing ever seriously disturbed Pittsburgh labor solidarity on the tariff or motivated the *National Labor Tribune* to question its banner proclamation: "Devoted to the Interests of Labor and Protection of Home Industries."

Local Democrats also intensified their efforts to mobilize citizens. Aiming their rhetoric at corporate corruption of local and state Republicans, they sometimes won the support of the Chamber of Commerce and other reform-minded middle-class groups. More important, they consolidated ward organization among the city's Irish and German Catholics. They also built upon the personal organizations of charismatic figures. One of these was Robert Liddell, officer in a Strip district brewery, patron of James Hamill and other leading oarsmen, and one of several Pittsburgh Protestants active in the Irish nationalist cause. Liddell defeated Humphreys for mayor in 1877 by putting together a coalition of Catholics, the "sporting crowd," and genteel citizens outraged by poor-relief scandals (which happened to involve striking ironworkers, men closely identified with Humphreys).[12] In 1893, Bernard McKenna became Pittsburgh's first

Irish Catholic mayor on the strength of his remarkably wide set of associations. A four-term alderman in the solidly Irish Fourth Ward, McKenna had as a young man "dominated the gangs of the Third and Fourth Wards." He was also a founder of the molders' union, a volunteer fireman, a police magistrate, and a commander in the GAR. In addition, he appealed to former mayor Henry Gourley and other "Independent Republicans" whom Magee had recently purged from the party.[13]

By the mid-1880s, both parties had settled on a common political type to mobilize city-wide electoral support. A "hale fellow, well met," the Pittsburgh politician needed a strong personal organization based on lodge and club memberships and a background in skilled labor or the retail trades. He also needed some experience cooperating with the Magee-Flinn organization. This was as true for Democrats as for Republicans. For, despite their ability to take the mayor's office from time to time, the former could never hope to break Magee's hold on the city council or Flinn's hold on county offices. Since all city departments were staffed by the council and not by the mayor, Magee effectively controlled patronage, franchises, contracts, and funds. Both bosses kept a stable minority of Democrats on the public payroll. Even in the county, which was far more Republican than the city, Flinn staffed 25 percent of his vacancies with Democrats.[14]

Thus, while appeals to the bloody shirt and to the tariff kept Republicans in line during elections to state and national office, the bosses' command of ward-level organization and of patronage kept members of either party from launching third party or intra-party insurgencies. The Greenback-Labor Party was an early casualty of this phenomenon. Having built upon the labor reform campaigns of the post-war years, the GLP enjoyed the ardent support of the *Labor Tribune,* the Amalgamated, L.A. 300, and the Knights' District Assembly. It won especially strong support from Irish unionists and Land Leaguers and from miners in Allegheny County. Although it had little success among German workers, many of whom remained loyal to the socialist Workingmen's Party, the Greenback-Labor Party integrated Welsh, Irish, and British workers in a remarkably thoroughgoing way. Nevertheless, its electoral success was limited, first, by the accessibility of the local major parties to labor influence and, second, by the drive to intensify national party identification around issues like the tariff. Consequently, the GLP was excluded from the local political arena, where it might have succeeded, and confined to the state and national arena, where it was doomed.[15]

Thomas Armstrong's 1882 gubernatorial campaign on the GLP ticket revealed the hopeless tangle of conflicting loyalties within which the third party was snared. Terence Powderly declined to run as Armstrong's ticket-mate, partly because of his Democratic sympathies and partly because he had grown generally wary of labor involvement in partisan politics.[16] Three years earlier, the Knights had gone on record in favor of independent political action "in some form." At the same time, however, the Order ruled that political discussion within local and district assemblies would be allowed only after a three-fourths vote of the membership and only after the close of business meetings. Displaying a similar ambivalence, the *Labor Tribune* in 1880 warned against the disruptive consequences of injecting politics into union meetings while at the same time urging workers to follow the political lead of the labor press.[17]

During the 1882 campaign, Armstrong found himself in the middle of a sticky imbroglio when the son of his old comrade, Andrew Burtt, returned to Pittsburgh to campaign for him. Unfortunately, Joseph H. Burtt proceeded to blast Miles Humphreys as a "sucker" who had been caught by the Republicans and turned against his former labor reform allies. Humphreys was indeed a mainstay of the Republican Party in Pennsylvania and offered no support to the Greenback-Labor effort, yet Armstrong felt compelled to defend him in the highest terms. "If there is one man whom the workingmen of Pennsylvania should support," he declared, "that man is Miles S. Humphreys. He never betrayed them and always did his best for their interests."[18]

Finally, ethnic sectarianism reemerged and pulled former Irish supporters of the ticket back into allegiance to the Democrats. Fearing that the Greenback-Labor cause had become a stalking-horse for Republicans bent on keeping Irish Democrats from office, key Fenians such as Michael Wood, an official of the ironworkers union in Woods Run, followed Powderly's lead and successfully denied the third party all but a smattering of Irish votes.[19]

The 1882 campaign was a disaster for the Greenback-Labor Party. Despite a respectable showing in western Pennsylvania, Armstrong managed to outpoll only the Prohibitionists, falling behind even the Independent Republican vote. The combined small-party vote helped elect a Democratic governor for the first time since before the Civil War, a fact which Republicans were thereafter not slow to impress upon their constitutents.[20]

The year 1882 signalled the end of serious labor initiatives in local or state politics. Union leaders abandoned once and for all the notion of launching a separate labor party. Intent on avoiding the ethnic minefield which the Greenbackers had tried to defuse, but which had exploded beneath them in 1882, unions advocated instead the endorsement of pro-labor candidates regardless of party affiliation. The nature of the new political mood was apparent four years later in the Pittsburgh mayoralty campaign. As calls for a "businessman's candidate," a "newspaperman's candidate," and a "reformers' candidate" surfaced in the city press, labor found itself unable to mount its own challenge to the Magee-Flinn regime. The *Commercial Gazette* suggested that "if Tom Armstrong had moved to Pittsburgh [from his residence across the river in Allegheny City] three years ago when he was asked . . . , he would be your next Mayor. The workingmen and the GAR boys would pull off their coats to a man for him."[21] This may have been an exaggeration, although it reflected Armstrong's unique reputation within and without the labor movement. But it was symptomatic of a problem more troubling than Armstrong's address. Politics had become a series of reactions to and anticipations of the professionals' plans. While names such as Jarrett, Campbell, Martin, and Cline were mentioned as credible labor candidates, none chose to jeopardize his own relationship to the Republican Party or to waste his reputation contending with two such immensely popular and impeccable examples of the new political type as Republican William C. McCallin and Democrat Bernard McKenna.[22]

By the mid-1880s, the confident labor republicanism of the previous decade and a half had given way to an increasingly skeptical, quasi-libertarian view of politics and the state. Already in 1879, the *Labor Tribune* had decided that "the greatest enemy the Republic has [is] centralization." In support of this contention, it reminded workers that the government had sent its "shoulder strapped gentry" to defend the Pennsylvania Railroad against strikers in 1877. The Chamber's campaign to strengthen local and state police powers could only have reinforced the observation. A few years later, the *Labor Tribune* suggested that "the whiskey ring" be purged from politics by eliminating the tax on liquor: " . . . any tax on liquor, thereby giving it a legal existence, is a crime." It similarly opposed federal aid to public schools as a first step toward wresting control over education from families and local communities. Though it continued to advocate the creation of a Federal Bureau of Labor Statistics, it had already grown wary of the Pennsylvania Bureau. The latter had become a haven for "dead-beats" and "political shysters," its reports mere compilations of data, "calculated to give one a headache." Had its funds been "devoted to legitimate work" rather than to "padding and payrolls", the Bureau might well have done something useful. Yet is failed to do so even under the direction of Miles Humphreys. The disappointing results of child labor and maximum-hour legislation only contributed to the growing anti-political mood. Increasingly it seemed that a distant and bureaucratic state would never fulfill the republican expectations of labor reform.[23]

In addressing their frustrations concerning politics in the 1880s, Pittsburgh's labor spokesmen turned to lamentation. "What do you think of such voters as citizens of a republic," they cried, when professional politicians boasted of carrying "the labor vote in their pockets" and were never proven wrong? The *Labor Tribune* continued to rail against corruption and high taxes. It continued to argue that the "producing classes" had only to do their duty and the polity would be healed. "If the mill men of Pittsburgh are desirous to renovate councils and secure measures to their interests," it bravely announced in 1884, "all they have to do is to organize the industrial interests and nominate good tickets." Similarly, the huge Labor Day parade of 1887 led it to imagine that united labor, like an "anaconda" coiled about the city, had "the strength, if properly directed, to carry the municipal elections outright."[24]

But it was obvious that labor was not properly directed. Indeed, in 1887 the labor movement in Pittsburgh was more divided than it had been at any time in the last quarter-century. On several fronts, a battle raged between trade unionists and advocates of broader political and labor organization. Reflecting and intensifying the growing national dispute between the AFL and the Knights of Labor,[25] the local battle pitted the biggest trade union in Pittsburgh, the Amalgamated Association of Iron and Steel Workers, against the Knights' District Assembly 3. Jurisdictional rivalry between the Amalgamated and new steelworker assemblies organized by the Knights erupted into open warfare after 1886. Though the city labor council tried to moderate that warfare, it became itself a battlefield. The Amalgamated tried to wrest control of the council from D.A. 3, while the latter used the council's new *Trades Journal* to blast the Amalgamated and the *National Labor Tribune,* which, particularly after the retirement and death of Armstrong, was becoming an organ of the Amalgamated and a proponent of pure-and-simple trade unionism.[26]

Conflict arose within the Knights of Labor, as well as between it and the Amalgamated. In the glass industry, Local Assembly 300 encouraged skilled workers outside the window-glass trades to follow its lead in creating trade unions affiliated with the Knights but independent of the mixed assemblies that integrated workers of differing skills and trades in one organization. It also disdained to cooperate with glass-house laborers organized by D.A. 3. Although theoretically affiliated with the District Assembly, L.A. 300 acted like a conservative trade union, disinclined to exert itself on behalf of the polyglot constituency of D.A. 3. Moreover, L.A. 300's great financial resources made it a power in the Knights' national organization and gave it great leverage over fellow Knights in Pittsburgh. Thus, L.A. 300 not only went its own way, but moved against its critics. By 1890, President Campbell of L.A. 300 succeeded in getting several of those critics expelled from the Knights and in winning control of the *Commoner,* which had been the journal of D.A. 3. Renamed the *Glassworker,* that journal became, even more than the *National Labor Tribune,* an organ of conservative trade unionism.[27]

This intensification of intra-labor conflict occurred just as labor political solidarity was being tested for the last time by D.A. 3. In 1886–1887 a Citizens League campaigned against the Republican machine and against high taxes, utility monopolies, and poor city services. It ran a Citizens-Democratic fusion ticket in the February 1888 council race. The *Commoner* fully endorsed the new movement. Editor Kelly and two officers of the Knights' telegraphers' assembly served on the League's executive committee, and at least one of the ticket's candidates was a former Knight. Support for the coalition also came from small businessmen and residents of the south side. The latter were especially aroused by the inadequacy of their water supply and by the unfair burden of taxation they still bore as a result of annexation to the city in 1872. Since the south side was a solidly industrial, working-class section and the home of a large portion of the city's Irish population, the Citizen-Democrats had a good chance of winning there. In fact the League won most of the south side council seats. But it had little success elsewhere. In the suburban east end it attracted some of the support that the Chamber of Commerce had begun to tap among middle-class professionals and businessmen. However, in the heartland of the old plebeian politics—the downtown wards, the nearby residential periphery, and the Strip district—the League made not a dent in Magee's organization.[28]

The Citizens campaign also suffered from a rekindling of those sectarian passions that had already helped sink the Greenback-Labor Party. In the fall of 1887, the Irish-dominated school committee of one south side ward appointed a Catholic priest as principal of its public school. When Father McTighe proceeded to import eleven Sisters of Charity to fill the instructional staff, the storm broke. The nuns were "jeered and hooted at on the streets," the Loyal Orange Lodge threatened even stronger retaliation against the "un-American" threat to education, and McTighe called on young Catholics who were neither "lukewarm" nor "liberal-minded" to stand up for their school and their church. After a month of controversy, McTighe withdrew, but the event so colored local feeling that no one could have expected Catholic Democrats and Protestant Republicans to cooperate politically. In this context, the very success of the Citizens with the former guaranteed failure with the latter.[29]

For the *Commoner,* the bitterest part of the campaign involved the failure of the *Labor Tribune,* the Amalgamated Association, and L.A. 300 to support the ticket. Despite the decidedly local character of the issues, the Citizens were tarred with the brush of "free trade Democracy." The new fusionists were trying to build precisely the kind of nonpartisan local coalition which labor spokesmen had once advocated. But times had changed. Displaying a new cynicism toward local politics, the *Labor Tribune* now accepted Magee's "ownership of the town," his considerable managerial skill, and even his superiority to "a fresh man who has not yet made a fortune." Although it had ardently condemned the spending provisions of the new, Magee-drafted city charter, the *Labor Tribune* declined to join the city labor council or the Citizens League in fighting against it. Instead it joined with L.A. 300 and the Amalgamated in gearing up for the 1888 presidential election. Throughout the winter of 1887–1888, therefore, the trade union leadership simply ignored the local campaign (as it had the fall state campaign) and talked tariff instead.[30]

The political legacy of labor reform did not survive the 1880s. The common discourse which had served to unite different groups of workers with one another and with reform-minded groups in the city had shattered. And yet neither the symbols of solidarity nor the patterns and habits of cooperation vanished over night. Events of the year 1887 demonstrate the tension between these conflicting tendencies.

On October 1, 1887, Thomas A. Armstrong died in Pittsburgh. Editor of the *National Labor Tribune,* champion of trade unionism and of the Knights of Labor, spokesman for Greenback and temperance causes, Armstrong had for twenty years embodied labor reform in Pittsburgh. The response to his death amount to a symbolic reaffirmation of old solidarities.[31] Funeral ceremonies were planned and carried out by representatives of the full range of labor organizations in the city: from the Amalgamated, William Martin and William Wiehe; from the Knights, Kelly of the *Commoner,* John Campell and Peter Shields of the telegraphers (all three of whom held leadership positions in the Citizens League), and John F. Doyle of D.A. 3. The typographers' union, which Armstrong had helped found, sent two representatives of whom one was former mayor McCarthy. Representatives of the molders, green-glass bottle blowers, flint glass workers, miners, and carpenters filled out the labor contingent.

Labor was joined by delegates from the GAR, who also commemorated Armstrong at GAR Day on October 4, and from the Union Veteran League. The latter must have felt special regret over Armstrong's passing, for it was at their dedication of a soldiers' monument three weeks earlier that their old comrade had collapsed "while carrying the colors." In the months to come, veterans proved themselves second only to labor in promoting the Armstrong monument fund. In addition to labor and veterans' groups, the local press, the barbers' association, and the Retail Grocers Association participated in memorial ceremonies. Both of the RGA representatives were sons of Armstrong's long-time friend, Thomas Grundy. A Greenbacker, Land Leaguer, temperance man, and Knight, Grundy had been a favorite speaker and entertainer at Labor Reform socials in the 1870s (reportedly capable of singing "'The Runaway's Return,' in a manner which filled many eyes with tears"). Employed at various times in his life as a grocery clerk, carpet weaver, and real estate agent, in the 1880s he helped organize local grocers to resist middlemen and monopolies in the food industry. He also sought to unite clerks, salesmen, and grocers into a single organization closely identified with the labor movement. Thus, when Knights of Labor bakers went on strike in 1887, one of their first actions was to call on the RGA for fraternal support. And in 1892 the RGA would be one of the first organizations outside the labor movement to condemn the Carnegie Steel Corporation and endorse the Amalgamated strike at Homestead.[32]

Armstrong's death evoked eulogies from Presbyterian and Methodist churchmen. Moreover, when the news of his death reached a Murphy temperance meeting on the night of October 2, the hushed audience rose to its feet and an ironworker from Braddock stepped forward to speak of his "comrade."

Young men of Pittsburgh, you for whom the best years of his life were spent, you for whose interests he worked so hard, think of the doctrine he taught through all his life by precept and example. A temperance man as he was, in the name of the dead Tom Armstrong, I ask you to come up and sign the pledge.[33]

The outpouring of feeling at Armstrong's death testified to the persistence of those bonds of plebeian solidarity which he had always sought to strengthen and perfect. Those bonds retained a measure of vitality even in the midst of new conflicts. For example, a contemporaneous Knights of Labor strike at the Black Diamond steel works elicited strong support from the rival Amalgamated and from local allies such as Pittsburgh's theater managers, who vied with one another to sponsor strike benefit performances.[34]

Earlier in the year, a manager of J.H. Gusky's clothing store, which catered to a working-class clientele, had been awarded a gold-headed cane by the Knights of nearby Elizabeth in appreciation of the "patriotic assistance" he rendered to families of jailed miners. As if in return, Gusky donated nearly 4,000 walking canes to Labor Day marchers in Pittsburgh. For Gusky, this was nothing new. Five years earlier he had been the ironworkers' "friend in need," supporting their strike against Carnegie Steel and bailing their president, John Jarrett, out of jail. Five years later, his wife would be listed as one of the "most liberal contributors" to the Homestead strikers' relief fund.[35]

The Knights of Labor tried assiduously to maintain these ties of interdependence by urging and sometimes compelling workers to make good on debts run up during strikes and layoffs and by enrolling "the professional man, the clerk, and the shopkeeper" in the army of labor. While they did not fail to recognize that conflicts of interest often arose between wage-earners and retailers, they refused to attribute such conflict to "class distinctions."

From this logic of plebeian solidarity the trade unions had begun to separate themselves. Two months after Armstrong's funeral, in the midst of a bitter dispute with a Knights' steelworker assembly, the Amalgamated belittled its rival's pretensions:

> It is to be expected that men in business who get their money from those who are entitled to an advance in wages will oppose anything that savors of stopping the mill a week or two. The steadier the mill runs, no matter at what wages to the men, the more the butchers, bakers, etc., expect to realize.

Against such criticism, the Knights argued that all plebeian elements could be brought "into harmonious relation and active sympathy"

*74*

with labor. And they warned that the labor movement could ignore only at its own peril "the relations existing between man and man, members of the same body politic."[36]

The breakdown of labor solidarity thus reflected more than sharpened inter-skill and jurisdictional conflicts. It also reflected the reorganization of public life in Pittsburgh. Whatever reservations labor may in the past have harbored in regard to politics, years of success had buttressed arguments in favor of plebeian alliances and broad reform campaigns. But with the rise of professional political organizations and the intensification of ethnic and party loyalties, labor found itself handicapped by its very successes. Having identified the cause of labor with the progress of republican institutions, having cheered the victories of labor's champions in local politics, having witnessed the value of inter-class solidarities in defending and promoting labor's interests, the heirs of labor reform were not prepared for the bitter choices of the late 1880s. Between the Knights' continued espousal of the grandest of anti-monopoly coalitions and the trade unionists' retreat to limited interest-group tactics, there had opened a chasm too great to bridge.

An even greater chasm opened within the temperance movement. Organized into Law and Order Leagues, a new, harder-edged breed of temperance agitator abandoned any hope of reforming the inner life of workingmen, preferring instead to impose explicit external controls upon them. Springing up in the city's old residential wards, the Leagues mobilized middle-class Protestants troubled by the Magee-Flinn machine, the growing power of Catholic Democrats, and the beginnings of a new wave of immigration in the late 1880s. They sought a direct and immediate way to control the alien tide and to preserve the residential character of their neighborhoods: fierce enforcement of license and Sabbath laws. In the process, by equating sobriety with subordination, the new agitators ended forever the labor reform hope of consecrating temperance on the altar of "manliness." They drove workingmen into the arms of the "festive ward bummers" who promised to forestall, or at least to moderate, the new tide of repression.

Law and Order had the advantage of drawing at once upon the traditional Sabbatarianism of Pittsburgh's Presbyterian elite and upon the growing respect for organization and efficiency within the "new middle class." Well funded by city churches, the Leagues asserted "the absolute necessity of regularly employed and reliable agents." The tactics of the first League set the pattern. In May of 1885 a group of church people in the eleventh ward hired a lawyer to prosecute the proprietor of a new roller coaster which had begun operating on Sunday. Winning a quick conviction, they proceeded to bring suits, most of them successful, against thirty-two saloon-keepers and vendors who defied the Sunday closing laws.[37]

Leagues soon appeared in the fifth, eight, and seventeenth wards, which were, like the eleventh, mixed residential wards on the fringes of the central business district. On May 10, 1887, three days after the state legislature passed a strict saloon licensing law, the Pittsburgh Law and Order League was founded to coordinate the activities of a growing number of ward organizations. Within six months it had overseen 325 convictions. Moreover, in July it began a campaign against prostitution based on the same principles that had made its earlier efforts so effective. The League "never proposed to reform anyone, but solely to *enforce the law* and leave the reformation of the inmates to those societies whose particular province it may be." It mocked the sentimental notion that prostitutes were just poor girls gone wrong and in need of loving care. Drawn from "the very lowest dregs of society," they "entered upon their life of shame simply to escape from honest work, and . . . they laugh deep and long at the sentimental gush that is periodically indulged in at their expense."[38]

The Republican Party gave no encouragement to the movement. Harsh enforcement of the blue laws could only redound to the benefit of the Democrats, who never tired of embracing the cause of "liberty" and of reminding plebeian Protestants that their customary amusements would fall under the same axe that threatened Catholic immigrants. Thus the Magee-Flinn machine stoutly resisted efforts to make it an engine of purification. Police Chief J.O. Brown announced he would not interfere with unlicensed liquor sellers "unless they keep disorderly houses or sell on Sunday," and even in those cases would only respond to direct complaints. His successor, Nate Brokaw (formerly an officer in the Amalgamated Association), wrote a letter urging an alderman to "fix" cases brought by the Law and Order League against ten bawdy houses in his ward. The letter was discovered and published, but Mayor McCallin ignored the incident.[39]

Similarly, although the state Republican Party had to pay attention to more dry-minded rural constituents, it responded to well-organized temperance and church groups with much rhetoric and little reform. "Doing the Straddle Act With the Parsons and the Publicans," as the Democratic *Post* caricatured the strategy, became a Republican specialty in the late 1880s and the 1890s. Thus, in 1887, a year after the party ran a stalwart temperance man, Gen. James A. Beaver, for governor, it approved a referendum on the prohibition amendment sponsored by its militant dry faction. Although party regulars and voters had strongly supported Beaver, they were far less enthusiastic about the amendment. In the big cities, in mining counties, and in the "Dutch" regions of eastern Pennsylvania, local Republicans let the amendment sink. State Senator James Rutan of Allegheny County was one of several Republican legislators who openly campaigned against it.[40]

Even many long-time temperance advocates saw legal prohibition as a will-of-the-wisp, incapable of realization and expensive of time and energy. When some prominent followers of Francis Murphy joined the prohibition campaign, they provoked a storm of local controversy. Murphy's son, Edward, denounced the prohibitionists and called for the "re-establishment of the Murphy Gospel Temperance Union on the old lines." Most Murphyites concurred, reaffirming the "non-sectarian and non-political" character of the organization by holding a special election in which all the prohibitionist officers were defeated.[41] As the referendum approached in 1889, it became clear that, outside the Presbyterian and Methodist Churches and the WCTU, prohibition had won little organized support.

The crushing defeat of the prohibition referendum confirmed the Law and Order League in its strategy. Unlike prohibitionists, Law and Order Leaguers entertained no grand hopes of political reform. Having passed the licensing law in 1887, the state had done all it could for them. The rest was their responsibility. Even the obstructionism of local officials did not deter them. Instead, they relied on the ability of their own investigators to win cases before the county courts. Except for supporting the licensing bill, the League ventured actively into politics only to elect tough county judges. By transferring the power to grant liquor licenses to county judges and out of the hands of the Flinn-controlled county commission, the new licensing law minimized the problem of obstructionism. Anti-urban voters in the out-county could be relied on to elect judges who dealt harshly with violators and responded favorably to the Leagues' well-prepared briefs against applicants for new and renewed licenses. Thus, J.W.F. White won the strong support of such voters and of the city-based League in his race for a judgeship by vowing a "terrific cleaning out" of saloons in Allegheny County, especially in the vicinity of steel mills. True to his word, Judge White deferred to the League's judgment in most license hearings, reducing in two years the number of licensed establishments in the county from 3,500 to 389 and in the city from 1,500 to 223.[42]

If the campaign for state prohibition had not already alienated most workingmen from the cause of temperance, the activities of the Law and Order League certainly did. What infuriated most people was the League's petty cruelty. Its agents swooped down upon crippled cigar vendors and seventy-year-old candy sellers with a cool self-righteousness that working people accurately attributed to class and ethnic bias.[43] The courts reinforced that impression. In 1888 and 1889, the state Supreme Court upheld the convictions of two Allegheny County men—one a milk dealer, the other a baker—for selling on Sunday. At about the same time, however, it reversed the convictions of two Pennsylvania Railroad employees, ruling their Sunday labor a "necessity." These were landmark cases which overturned the precedent set in 1853 in Johnston Versus the Commonwealth of Pennsylvania. In that case the court had ruled that neither competition nor public convenience was sufficient grounds for permitting a bus driver to work on the Sabbath. Twenty-five years later it was clear that what was merely convenience for the plebs had become necessity for the Pennsylvania Railroad.[44]

Given free rein, the new enforcers levelled their sights at the operators of pool halls and other amusements and at the purveyors of milk, groceries, ice-cream, tobacco, and liquor. Between 1887 and 1890, they precipitated a kind of guerrilla warfare which pitted middle-class Protestants against working-class Catholics. At trials and license hearings, League lawyers humiliated witnesses and provoked nasty exchanges between neighbors called upon to testify against one another. Against this "star chamber business" popular reaction was strong. In September of 1887, William A. Herron, distinguished figurehead president of the Pittsburgh Law and Order League, resigned from the organization in protest. The League tried to ascribe Herron's departure to ill-health, but the old man had confided his real reasons to former labor leader John Jarrett, who promptly made them public: "He is opposed to this stystem of Persecutions, and told me that he would not be a party to it."[45]

The *Labor Tribune* kept up a drum beat of criticism of the League. It asked why the organization's chief agent "does not turn his attention to industrial establishments that run their works on Sunday." It quoted the reliable Francis Murphy as saying, "If there were 10,000 saloons in Pittsburgh, instead of less than a hundred, there would not be any more drunkenness than there is to-day." The Murphyites joined high-church Protestants in denouncing the League's hard-hearted pietism. The Personal Liberty League, organized by retail liquor dealers to fight the Law and Order crusade, was blessed by Lutheran pastors who rose to defend "the German Sunday" from attack. Democrats took full advantage of these events, cultivating the anti-pietist backlash and nearly electing to the Common Pleas Court John Bailey, whom critics labelled "the candidate of the Liquor League." Although he narrowly lost the election, Bailey carried the city of Pittsburgh by 1,500 votes. Moreover, his victorious opponent, J.F. Slagle, was no temperance man but rather a stalwart machine Republican, unfriendly to the Law and Order cause.[46]

Thus, although the Law and Order movement disrupted hundreds of lives, it accomplished few of its long-term aims. By the early 1890s it had lost its bite. Law enforcement remained weak and the popular desire to evade the law strong.[47] The League seemed in the end nothing more than a rear guard covering the retreat of the very people most interested in disciplining the chaotic city: middle-class Pittsburghers who were succumbing to the lure of the streetcar suburb. In retreat the bourgeoisie seemed to have conceded to professional politicians the right to control the industrial city.

In fact, however, the concession was temporary. For the League, along with the more sophisticated and less evangelical Chamber of Commerce, reflected a growing organizational activism among the business and professional classes in Pittsburgh. Like the professional politicians, the new activists recognized that the craftsmen's empire and the plebeian moment were at an end. And, as the balance of social forces that had undergirded the Iron City was subverted by vast demographic and economic changes, only the best financed and organized actors could contend for a part in shaping the emerging Metropolis of Steel.

# CHAPTER 6

# Steel City

Approaching Pittsburgh around 1910 after a long absence, a visitor could be forgiven only momentarily for imagining that little had changed in the past thirty years. From a distance, perhaps, Pittsburgh was what it had always been—a place dedicated to nothing more than the making of metal and smoke, seemingly in equal proportion. Yet, the impression of changelessness could not have survived the trip toward town; well before he reached Pennsylvania Station, the visitor would have noticed, beneath the blanket of "everlasting smoke," a new city—indeed a new metropolitan area—risen on the site of the old.[1]

His first clue to the character of these changes would have been the smoke that came out to greet him much sooner than expected. As his railroad car descended into the Allegheny Valley, he might easily have confused the fires of New Kensington or Etna or Sharpsburg for those of Pittsburgh itself. The industrial city had expanded its borders, filled them, and finally spilled over into its hinterland. By 1910 the metropolitan district contained over a million people, twice as many as it had in 1890 and nearly three times as many as in 1880. This growth outpaced the old city's not inconsiderable rate of 127 percent between 1880 and 1910 (Table 4).

Population had followed industry. By the end of the century, growth in the iron and steel industry was occurring almost entirely outside the city, in nearby suburbs, farther along the river valleys, and well beyond these in Ohio, Illinois, and other western sites. Steelmasters moved nearer markets and nearer the great Mesabi ore fields in Minnesota. Superior rail systems and Great Lake shipping

Table 4. Population of Pittsburgh, 1880–1920 (to the Nearest 500)

| | City* | Metropolitan District** | City as % of District |
|---|---|---|---|
| 1880 | 235,000 | 356,000 | 66 |
| 1890 | 344,000 | 552,000 | 62.3 |
| 1900 | 451,500 | 775,000 | 58.5 |
| 1910 | 534,000 | 1,018,500 | 52.4 |
| 1920 | 588,500 | 1,186,000 | 49.6 |

SOURCE: U.S. Census 1920, vol. 1, pp. 85, 586–587.
* Combined figure for Pittsburgh and Allegheny City until their consolidation in 1906.
** Through 1900, this figure represents Allegheny County; thereafter, it represents the standard census metropolitan district.

also drew them westward. But even in the environs of Pittsburgh, investments and jobs moved away from the old city. Intent on building new, technologically advanced steel plants, manufacturers looked beyond the crowded urban core for large tracts of cheaper real estate. Natural gas, increasingly available as a fuel for manufacturing, made locational choice more flexible, while the opportunity to withdraw from centers of unionization and plebeian politics made suburban and rural sites attractive.[2]

Along the Monongahela in particular, a proliferation of steel mills transformed the environment. Upriver from the Point, Jones and Laughlin had greatly expanded its huge complex of rolling mills, blast furnaces, wharves, train yards, and residential rows on both sides of the river. Because J&L had exploited the last of the large tracts of river property in the city, other steelmasters built mill towns virtually out of pastures—across the city line in Braddock and Homestead, and farther upstream in Duquesne, Monogahela, McKeesport, and a dozen other places. Westward in the Ohio Valley, such villages as McKees Rocks and Mansfield (soon to be renamed Carnegie) turned into dense industrial suburbs, outside the city yet tied to its economy.

The approaches to the city were marked by residential as well as industrial development. The east end filled up with homes for the upper and middle classes, and in East Liberty a new hub of commerce began to draw business from downtown. Just east of the city line, Swissvale grew from a mere backwoods into an elite suburb of nearly 7,500 people in 1910. "The Hills"—North, East, and especially South Hills—suddenly sprouted houses in the 1890s. New bridges spanned the rivers. Across the Monongahela, tunnels directed traffic through the precipices which for half a century had marked the southern boundary of settlement. North of the Allegheny River, the city of Allegheny expanded its boundaries and population and consolidated with Pittsburgh in 1906.

Although it had long been true that "nearly all whose means or occupation permit reside at the east end . . . or in some railway suburb,"[3] transportation technology limited the extent of suburbanization until around 1890. Commuter railroads were too few, horse cars too slow, and both too expensive to draw any but the wealthiest out of the city. It was the inauguration of cable car service in 1888, followed in a few years by electric service, that effected the suburbanization of most of Pittsburgh's non-wage-earning population. The new cars were more powerful and thus able to negotiate the hilly terrain at high speeds. As lines multiplied and expanded their service, fares dropped, allowing most white-collar workers and some of the best-paid skilled wage-earners to leave the dense central wards. The latter filled such sections of the older residential periphery as Herron Hill, Lawrenceville, and Bloomfield. They also moved into neighborhoods in East Liberty and Oakland, where residential, commercial, and industrial development proceeded apace. However, to the least dense sections of the east end—Shadyside, Squirrel Hill, Point Breeze, Highland Park, Homewood—and to the exurban communities of Edgewood, Swissvale, and the distant Hills, few workers commuted.[4]

Suburbanization was accompanied by the functional and spatial reorganization of the old city. In the 1890s, Pittsburgh developed a recognizable central business district, and skyscrapers began to change its skyline. As the middle class moved to the east end, and as workers crowded into formerly mixed or bourgeois neighborhoods in the near periphery, the four wards at the juncture of the three rivers together lost 35 percent of their population and 26 percent of their dwelling units in one decade. New corporate and government offices took their place. Great capitalists bought large tracts of downtown property not only to build corporate headquarters but to profit from the boom in real estate values. Thus, as Diamond and Virgin Alleys lost their names to Mellon and Oliver, respectively, the honored gentlemen acquired immortality and profit at a single stroke. More important, the rise of the central business district, combined with suburbanization, confirmed a new social geography for Pittsburgh, which sharply segregated work from leisure and one social class from another.[5]

The transformation of Pittsburgh into an industrial metropolis was thus not a matter of simple growth. Nor did it consist merely of the greater functional differentiation of space into commercial center, residential periphery, and so forth. The most powerful changes involved the shattering of those bonds of class and community which had undergirded the social balance of power in the Iron City. The consequences of that shattering were amply documented in the Pittsburgh Survey of 1907.[6]

The Survey described a city in thrall to an industry. The center of the most "progressive" industrial establishment on earth, Pittsburgh lacked the political and cultural wherewithal to constitute itself a community. Some inhabitants found relief in trade unions and ethnic societies and in the favors of the political machine, but, by and large, they were forced to accommodate to the mastery of steel. In the view of the Survey team, the city's only hope rested with an aroused professional-technical class and a few businessmen who were disgusted with corrupt politics and civic ugliness and who possessed the ability to organize collectively.

The Survey's picture of Pittsburgh at the turn of the century merits qualification,[7] yet its basic outlines endure. The bitter experience of labor struggle after 1890, culminating in the 1919 Great Steel Strike, confirmed the fact that Pittsburgh had become a big company town. The plebeian city which in 1877 had risen against the alien railroad monopoly no longer existed. In its place the Steel City arose on a foundation of intimidation. After the crippling of the Amalgamated Association at Homestead in 1892, little stood in the way of the steelmasters and their allies. Freed finally from the limits placed upon them by the craftsmen's empire and the plebeian community, they could remake the workplace and the metropolis into clearer expressions of their interests and aspirations.

The capitalists' triumph had been made easier by the ideological and jurisdictional conflicts that internally weakened the labor movement in the 1880s. But even had labor's solidarity remained intact, workers would have been hard pressed to meet the external challenge. It was the enormity and pace of economic and social change that swamped the working class in Pittsburgh. Technological revolution, work reorganization, massive immigration, and the restructuring of urban space all occurred simultaneously with the anti-union drive and transformed the character of everyday experience at work, at home, and in the streets of the city.

In 1887, the *National Labor Tribune* condemned the growing prevalence in the mills of a kind of work which made the worker "a mere machine tender." "Such a life is not life," it insisted. "One respects a man for hating such work."[8] Skill degradation was one

*83*

consequence of the new mechanization that especially troubled autonomous craftsmen. Nothing in their values or experiences disposed them to rebel against bigness or technology per se. What repelled them about the open hearth steel mills, however, was the extent to which new machines and regimens subordinated free men to external disciplines. As iron gave way to steel, therefore, their concerns increased.[9]

Conversely, managers saw as steel's greatest virtue the fact that it required little craft skill to produce. Before the late 1880s, ironmakers saw no way to increase productivity and profit other than through machinery designed to maximize the efficient employment of skill: better heating furnaces, faster and stronger rolls, etc. And they tried to improve the quality of ores and coke in order to guarantee a product smoothly worked from molten form to finished bar or sheet. That is, they tried to make individual craftsmen more productive.[10]

Skilled iron craftsmen took some part in suggesting and implementing new techniques. They, like craftsmen in the Window Glass Workers Association, expected each increase in productivity to increase their return according to the negotiated scale. In window glass, nothing threatened this expectation for some time. While the capacity of glass pots increased and methods of cooling glass steadily improved, it was not until the early twentieth century that glass-makers perfected a way of drawing glass that could compete successfully with the traditional methods of gatherer, blower, and flattener. Moreover, there was no alternative to glass itself, nothing that could stand in relation to glass as steel stood to iron.[11] Thus, the proletarianization of work in Pittsburgh is synonymous with the progress of steel.

Steel was superior to iron for a number of industrial and structural purposes, especially for rails. But it was not superior in all cases—not for metal plate, sheet, or pipe. Nonetheless, steel rapidly replaced iron for almost all uses beginning in the late 1880s. In 1892, steel production surpassed that of iron for the first time.

The key to steel's success was that it did not have to be puddled. Manufacturers could vastly increase its production to meet new demands without doling out a considerable share of the profit to craftsmen and, most important, without meeting craftsmen's selective resistance to mechanical improvement. Costs could be cut ruthlessly because the open-hearth process circumvented that technological bottleneck which had enabled an organized and self-confident body of skilled employees to limit production.[12]

*84*

By the mid-1890s, most major iron producers in Pittsburgh and elsewhere had shifted to steel. Moving rapidly into expanding domestic and international markets, Carnegie and his competitors thus found a way to outflank the craftsmen's empire and to shift dramatically and suddenly the terms of battle between the Amalgamated and the industry. Carnegie and Frick could demand unconditional surrender at Homestead in 1892 precisely because the Amalgamated dominated what had become distinctly secondary sectors of the industry: iron and tin plate finishing and iron sheet and tube manufacture. The union could be permitted to hold these islands of skill while being expelled completely from steel.

For a decade before the *coup de grâce* at Homestead, the masters of iron and steel had been testing their strength against the powerful Amalgamated Association. By working together against the puddlers' strike of 1882, they managed to administer to the union its first serious defeat. They also learned to exploit the tension between puddlers and the more secure finishers, on the one hand, and between craftsmen and less-skilled workers, on the other. In particular, managers cultivated rollers and other finishers, who had a future in steel. These craftsmen had by the late 1880s gained the balance of power in the national union at the expense of the iron puddlers, who were more militant because more beleaguered by technological change. By 1890, when the national union voted down their demand for a scale increase, the iron puddlers were talking seriously about withdrawing from the Amalgamated and resurrecting the old Sons of Vulcan.[13]

However, the intensely competitive iron and steel barons were not yet capable of uniting against their common enemy below. In 1888, employers prematurely tested the strength of their infant trade association with an industry-wide lockout of the Amalgamated. Its failure made the employers look weak and the union look stronger than ever. In fact, however, employer solidarity was young and growing stronger, while the Amalgamated had only barely held together. *Iron Age,* the industry journal, noted gravely and prophetically that, although workers were "considerably elated over their recent victory," employers still intended some day "to treat with employees directly and personally, . . . without dictation from committees of labor associations."[14]

The 1888 struggle impressed employers once again with the advantages of steel over iron. During the lockout, it had been the steel producers who held out longest against the Amalgamated scale; they had lost only because they were bound to iron producers who depended so completely on skilled workers. Indeed, the only reason the Amalgamated (or the Knights of Labor) had any hope of organizing the steel industry was because the iron producers continued to certify organized labor in the industry as a whole.[15] In 1888, therefore, all the signs pointed in the same direction. The steel men had determined to master the increasingly competitive market by lowering prices; to lower prices by cutting costs; to cut costs in a number of ways including controlling raw material supplies and transportation, but especially by cutting wages; and to cut wages by breaking the union. The road to Homestead was clearly marked out by a single-minded intention to usher in the age of steel by burying once and for all the champions of the age of iron.

In plebeian Pittsburgh this strategy seemed most imperative. Between 1887 and 1894 Pittsburgh ranked behind only New York and Chicago in the incidence of labor disturbances, as management and labor engaged in an intense struggle for control of the mills. Pittsburgh ranked first in number of lockouts and first in amount of formal assistance from labor organizations against lockouts. It also ranked first in wage loss due to lockouts and second in wage loss due to strikes.[16] Although the industry's center of gravity was shifting westward to Ohio and Illinois, Pittsburgh remained the seat of union power. Entrenched in Pittsburgh, the Amalgamated followed the drift westward, making the new mills among the best organized in the country. By 1890, however, management no longer needed the union's cooperation in getting the new mills into successful operation. Moreover, once the mid-decade slump had lifted, employers more than ever resented having to share with workers the augmented surplus that the new mechanization generated.[17]

In Pittsburgh steelmasters were already cutting loose from the old subcontracting relationship with organized craftsmen. The renovated J. Edgar Thompson works in Braddock, just outside the city line, served as the prototype of the coming industrial order: integrated, continuous, mechanized steel production on a vast scale, twelve-hour shifts, and no union. After replacing with machines five out of every six skilled men in the furnace and rail mill departments, the Thompson management might have dispensed with a formal open-shop declaration—the Amalgamated lodges were silently disbanding for lack of members. But the declaration was indispensable because the steelmasters intended to foreclose the possibility that the old union, based in the iron crafts, might sponsor or inspire organization of the steel mills.[18] In a sense, steelmasters recognized what social historians have only recently rediscovered: that, despite tension between skilled and unskilled workers, industrial unionism proceeds more rapidly and thoroughly when its link to the craftsmen's empire remains unbroken.[19]

Carnegie's victory at Homestead in 1892 dealt the deathblow to labor organization in the mills for at least a generation. Having called in the military to accomplish that end, he gave the lie to his past professions of sympathy for labor and flew in the face of a solidly pro-labor plebeian community in Homestead.[20] But the power of local communities was everywhere on the wane; and Carnegie could count on his reputation as philanthropist and self-made man to shield him from potential middle-class criticism (he probably knew that the public would shift much of the blame for the company's tactics at Homestead to his draconic lieutenant, Henry Clay Frick). In any case, neither he nor his colleagues in steel ever doubted that the effort had been worth it. Freed to reorganize work in the mills, the steelmasters moved to subordinate skilled men and to differentiate supervision more sharply from labor. Within the next two decades, as the wages of unskilled labor rose, those of skilled workers in steel declined precipitously, in some cases by as much as 70 percent. It was only by increasing their pace and their hours that the tonnage men managed to keep losses in daily earnings from exceeding 30 percent.

Moreover, the steel mill little resembled the congeries of workshops that had been the old iron mill. Whereas authority had once been dispersed among a large number of semi-autonomous craftsmen, the lines of command in the new mill were clear and hierarchical. A more homogeneous force of semi-skilled workers dwarfed the declining ranks of the skilled.[21]

Brutalizing though such machine-tending appeared to craftsmen, it represented a step up for unskilled common laborers. Higher pay and greater responsibility more than compensated for whatever regimentation the new machines and procedures imposed. Men who had never had power, who had probably been excluded from the helper system and hence from the chance of advancement in the iron trade, could not be expected to condemn the proletarianization of labor with the craftsman's poignant sense of lost status and independence. Nor could they be expected to lament the passing of a union that neglected them and had only grudgingly agreed to admit some of them to membership. Nor, finally, could they be expected to resent as bitterly the swarm of clerks and supervisors that Andrew Carnegie loosed upon the floor of the modern steel mill.

Between 1890 and 1910, the salaried force increased from 5.6 percent to 13.9 percent of the total manufacturing work force in

Allegheny County, growing faster than the wage-earning force and earning an increasingly larger share of total labor charges. Convinced that "nothing was more profitable than clerks to check up on each transfer of material from one department to another," Carnegie wanted to know precisely "who saved material, who wasted it, and who produced the best results." He instructed his clerks to find out "what each of the many men working at the furnaces was doing," and to "compare one with another." In the age of steel, craftsmen no longer directed the work team or trained newcomers in the skills required for production. Instead, clerks, engineers, and technicians devised and transmitted work instructions to machine-tenders who lacked the customary expertise of the craftsman.[22]

The steelmasters successfully reduced the need for skilled labor and mechanized much of the hauling and loading work that used to occupy common laborers. At the same time they created numerous and minute gradations among the seemingly undifferentiated semi-skilled work force. These gradations operated against the tendency toward homogenization of the working class. Indeed, piece rates, premium plans, and elaborate pay schemes tended to fragment the work force and to encourage workers to see the labor system as a ladder constructed of regular and individuated steps. Moreover, as David Brody has shown, many of those workers did rise slowly through the ranks of semi-skilled and even skilled labor.[23]

Most important, the new semi-skilled work was taken over by a polyglot army of immigrants from southeastern Europe. Called "Hunkies" by their English-speaking hosts, the new immigrants were in fact incredibly heterogeneous. Croats, Serbs, Slovenes, Slovaks, Lithuanians, Hungarians, Ruthenians, Bohemians, Romanians, Poles, Ukrainians, Russians, and others, speaking a dozen languages and practicing as many religious rites, joined Italians and southern blacks in the mills and neighborhoods of Pittsburgh. By 1910, they and their offspring accounted for three and a half times as many residents of metropolitan Pittsburgh as did the offspring of native whites. They largely replaced the Irish, German, Welsh, and English immigrants who had formerly filled the expanding ranks of labor in the iron industry and who had, by the 1880s, become fairly well integrated into the life of the city, its work force, labor unions, retail trades, political parties, and cultural institutions. By 1910, most of these old-stock employees were on the privileged side of that line which divided "Hunkies" in the ranks from "Americans" in the skilled and white-collar strata. They accounted for only two of every ten semi-skilled operatives in the blast furnaces and rolling mills and for only one in every fifteen common laborers.[24]

For men like John Jarrett of the Amalgamated Association, himself an English immigrant, the newcomers were very much "foreigners— Hungarians, Poles, Italians, Bohemians, men that really don't know the difference . . . between light work and heavy work, or between good wages and bad wages . . . . In investigating these matters," he went on, "I have been disgusted to find that those people can live where I think decent men would die." Another craftsman complained to a Survey investigator: "These fellows have no pride . . . ; they are not ruled by custom. When the foreman demands it they will throw down the saw and hammer and take the wheelbarrow."[25]

The vast expansion of the steel industry and the new social relations that it engendered led to changes in the shape and organization of the city and to multiple fragmentations within the working class and the community at large. In the first place, Pittsburgh became a city of more rigidly segregated ethnic enclaves. Topography greatly contributed to that segregation, for hills, ravines, and bluffs sharply marked off neighborhoods from one another. Natural demarcations were accentuated by mills and railroads which controlled large swaths of territory along the flatlands and thereby forced residences up hillsides and down into hollows.[26]

More important, the industry's labor policies encouraged the "Balkanization" of the population. Employers and foremen purposefully recruited different ethnic groups for different departments within the mills. The effects of such policies may be clearly observed in the Strip and Lawrenceville sections. This area of Allegheny River flatland had long been the site of intensive industrial development, including Carnegie's Clark Mill and Lucy Furnace, the Black Diamond Steel mill, the Pennsylvania Railroad yards, and the Iron City Brewery. American, English, Irish, and German workers made their homes within the narrow band of territory between river and railroad. Beyond the tracks, steep bluffs sharply marked off the zone of settlement.[27]

The area had always been a collection of identifiable ethnic quarters: Three exclusively Irish parishes surrounded without touching, a German Catholic island in the Arsenal neighborhood. Until 1880, however, there were few blacks in the Strip and 95 percent of all foreign-born there (as in the city) were from Germany and the British Isles. Then, beginning in the late 1870s, the masters of Black Diamond and Clark began recruiting southern blacks to break Amalgamated strikes. At the same time, German Poles, possibly attracted by the

German Catholic community in Lawrenceville, began finding work in the train yards and at Heppenstall's iron mill. As the flow of blacks increased and that of Poles turned to a flood in the late 1880s, the newcomers displaced their predecessors, especially the Irish, in the lower ranks of steel mill labor.[28]

While blacks were less concentrated in any plant, the Poles and other Slavs took root. For English-speaking supervisors, these new immigrants answered many needs. As one Survey investigator put it, "employers of labor give the Slavs and Italians preference over English-speaking applicants because of their docility, their habit of silent submission, their amenability to discipline, and their willingness to work long hours and overtime without a murmur."[29] Unlike most other Slavic immigrants to Pittsburgh, however, Poles usually arrived as families, seeking to settle into stable homes and neighborhoods. In the Strip (as on the south side) they moved steadily up through the ranks of semi-skilled and skilled labor in the mills and bought homes in the neighborhoods surrounding them. In both sections they bought less desirable single-family or attached houses, fixed them, and stayed in them for years. They paid for their investments with the labor of children, and, in return, the children expected to become a part of the same community of work and residence their parents had built.[30] To an extent, employers complied with those expectations. They virtually guaranteed specific jobs to the representatives of ethnic communities in return for a steady supply of labor. Eventually they promoted Poles and other Slavs to low-level supervisory positions, thus delegating recruitment and hiring responsibilities to the immigrant communities themselves.[31]

Such accommodations could be mutually rewarding. The employer who advertised, "To Work In Open Shops. Syrians, Poles and Romainians [sic] Preferred; Steady Employment And Good Wages to Men Willing to WORK,"[32] knew he could forestall unionization and acquire cheap labor at the same time by giving immigrants a modicum of job security. Having thus been acquired, the workers won for themselves a foothold in a desperately unstable industrial milieu. For the Poles of Pittsburgh's sixth ward, it meant jobs for men and their sons, and homes for their families and relatives. It meant a place to build a church, later a major basilica, a Polish Falcons organization, and a network of retail establishments catering to their needs and tastes. It meant the chance to build a community. Perched above the mills and trainyards of the Allegheny River flatland, it remains to this day "Polish Hill."[33]

Not all newcomers fared as well as those on Polish Hill. Blacks fared worst, although in the Strip they won promotions and other favors in return for strikebreaking services for the managers of Clark Mill. A few moved into skilled and supervisory posts, but blacks were never patronized as a community. Most filled the pool of casual, unskilled labor in the mills. "As a rule," noted the Survey, "Negro boys do not remain in the mills long, nor work up in them." Unable to guarantee their childen jobs or stable homes, black parents socialized them for individual survival in the industrial city. Blacks dominated transport and several other services and succeeded as barbers and retailers for a black clientele. Most of them had to live in places like Skunk Hollow, the Survey description of which rivals in horror that of any other slum in the industrial world.[34]

For most immigrants, as for blacks, the needs of expanding capital seldom meshed benignly with individual or group aspirations. Although managers sometimes gave newcomers a stake in the factory, more often they relied on the simple logic of labor surplus to keep workers in line. As David Brody has demonstrated, steelmasters stabilized their industry by combining real, if limited, benefits for English-speaking skilled workers and discrete groups of immigrants, with ruthless exploitation of the proletarian surplus. Moreover, even among more stable workers, the management policy of playing ethnic groups against one another silenced complaints and discouraged organization. Immigrant workers who tried to build cross-ethnic or class solidarity faced formidable odds.

Margaret Byington noted in the Survey that in Homestead, "There are no labor unions . . . to give a common interest to Pole, Slav and native born, and pave the way for mutual understanding and citizenship." Differences in language and religion, and long-standing national hostilities, often kept immigrants from cooperating outside the mill. "The Slavic lodges are usually limited to the members of one nationality, Slovak, Hungarian, Polish," noted Byington, "and so far as they tend to perpetuate racial and religious feuds, miss their opportunity to amalgamate the immigrant colony." Most ethnic churches and lodges were too busy meeting their countrymen's basic needs for worship, sociability, accident and death benefits, and liaison with American institutions to enage extensively in pan-Slavic, labor, or other inclusive forms of organization. Some efforts were made to broaden the jurisdiction of particular ethnic organizations. In 1898, for example, P. V. Rovnianek, editor of the *Slavonic Gazette,* tried to rally Bohemians, Poles, and his regular Slovak readers behind a campaign against the anti-immigrant Republican candidate for Governor. But homeland nationalist causes often divided the immigrant population, turning Pole against Lithuanian, Bohemian against Slovak, Croat against Serb.[35]

Most immigrant workers bravely hung on between layoffs and speed-ups, building their lodges, churches, and neighborhoods under the bitterest of circumstances. All had to struggle for shelter in one of the worst housing markets in America. Competition for real estate in the downtown periphery, along the Strip, and on the south side abetted the dissolution of the old plebeian wards. A doubly archaic school and land tax system lifted most of the tax burden from both the commercial Point and the suburban east end and laid it squarely upon the small property holders of the old residential wards. Onerous taxes discouraged new building and turned small property owners into slumlords. The bulk of Pittsburgh's working-class population moved from one subdivided house to another. Most probably hoped not to fall to the level of those three hundred squatters who inhabited twenty-nine shanty boats docked at the south bank of the Monongahela, at the foot of the Jones and Laughlin mill.[36]

In the face of such fragmentation and instability, the labor struggles of Pittsburgh workers in the early twentieth century were both heroic and doomed. A weak and defensive Amalgamated Association neither welcomed nor sought out the unskilled "Hunkies." Fumbling for a footing after the defeat at Homestead in 1892, the Amalgamated veered erratically between supine accommodation and hysterical bluff in its relations with the steel companies. An ill-timed and bungled strike in 1901 not only sapped the union's remaining strength, but also discredited unionism, even in the eyes of many critics of the new U.S. Steel trust.[37]

Although in Pittsburgh and in small mill towns shopkeepers and other middle-class citizens sometimes supported strikers, on the whole workers had lost their allies. As the income, power, confidence, and sheer numbers of skilled craftsmen declined, they no longer performed the crucial role of mediating relations between working class and middle class. Machine politicians and elements of the press could still be counted on to oppose prohibitionists and other cultural chauvinists, but it was clear that the city whose labor movement had once boasted, "our press generally . . . give out to the public what we want them to give out," had been mastered by Big Steel. One Survey investigator captured the character of the regime under which the working class labored:

. . . the Pittsburgh employers' point of view, more than that of any other city of the country, is like that of England in the early days of the factory system,—holding employees guilty of a sort of impiety, and acting with sudden and sure execution, if they undertake to enforce their claims in such a way as to embarrass the momentum of great business administration.[38]

And yet, labor not only dared such impieties, it sometimes won battles. In 1897 every labor organization in western Pennsylvania threw its weight behind the United Mine Workers' fight against the New York and Cleveland Gas Coal Company. Run by William DeArmit, Carnegie's man in the bituminous fields, NY&C refused to submit to the established system of yearly conferences between the coal operators association and the UMW. Labor used all its influence upon Senator Matthew Quay and other Republican leaders to commission a state investigation into DeArmit's practices. State factory inspector James Campbell (formerly head of the Window Glass Workers) convinced the governor not to send militia to aid the company. In western Pennsylvania labor mobilized every friendly newsman, businessman, and clergyman it could find and sent them to Harrisburg to testify. A delegation from Pittsburgh's United Labor League, headed by the venerable Thomas Grundy, convinced the common council to rescind the city's contract with NY&C and to label the company an "irresponsible bidder."[39]

One year later, local labor again mobilized its energies to good effect, denying a county judgeship to John S. Robb, one of the most vehemently anti-labor prosecutors at the Homestead trials of 1892–1893.[40] Such victories reflected the continuing worth of old political ties, but they may also have falsely magnified their value. In each case peculiar circumstances contributed to the victorious outcome. In the case of the coal strike, DeArmit had been cast in the role of outlaw within an increasingly oligopolistic industry. Politicians and the press joined businessmen in praising the yearly conference as a "progressive" mechanism for ensuring industrial peace. As for Robb, his extraordinarily anti-labor rhetoric at the Homestead trials lived on in the memory of all workingmen. The name "Homestead" remained a tocsin capable of rousing organized labor to denounce the erection of a Carnegie library in Pittsburgh or the scheduling of a Welsh Eisteddfod (singing festival) at Carnegie Hall in Homestead. Moreover, Robb's unreformed rhetoric permitted all critics of "unrestricted capital" to portray him, like De Armit, as an atavistic obstacle to the "search for order."[41]

While existing organizations and political relationships, however vestigial, proved useful to workers, another source of power was of far greater importance for the future. As the first decade of the twentieth century drew to a close, new militance and new forms of solidarity emerged from the bottom up. Driven to the limit by the depression of 1907–1909, having given up on the Amalgamated as an ally, and having increasingly sunk roots in the industrial city, immigrant steelworkers organized themselves. At the Pressed Steel Car Works in McKees Rocks in 1909, a polyglot immigrant work force stunned the unions, the public, and the bosses by overcoming ethnic divisions and launching a tenacious, although ultimately unsuccessful, strike. Even before they won outside support from the IWW (International Workers of the World) and others, the workers at McKees Rocks had proved that "Hunkies" were not unorganizeable transients.

Together with the equally impressive strike at Bethlehem Steel a few years later, McKees Rocks also inspired proponents of the "new unionism." In Pittsburgh, those members of the nearly moribund Amalgamated Association who advocated industry-wide organization across skill lines took heart from the new militance below, as well as from that of machinists, electrical workers, and others outside Big Steel. Moreover, McKees Rocks and Bethlehem supplied ample ammunition for those muckrakers and politicians who, fortified by the revelations of the Pittsburgh Survey and the Stanley Committee hearings in the U.S. Senate, increasingly identified the steel industry as an appropriate object of their progressive outrage.[42]

Despite continuing effort and occasional success, however, Pittsburgh's working class would have to wait for the 1930s to mobilize a successful challenge to their masters. Until then, neither militance from below nor progressive allies from above seriously disturbed the logic of labor surplus and repression. It is true that, in response to strikes and mounting public criticism in the second decade of the century, U.S. Steel inaugurated a successful safety program and a wide range of welfare benefits for white-collar and skilled workers. Even old-line, cost-cutting steel men like Charles Schwab came to accept the gospel of cooperation preached by U.S. Steel chairman Elbert Gary and other financier-organizers of corporate consolidation. But in steel, and therefore in Pittsburgh, the new gospel never went very far. It certainly never inspired modification of the open-shop line. Given the absence of a strong craft union, and the still widespread antagonisms between natives and immigrants, Big Steel paid attention to muckrakers and progressive critics only when doing so made economic or public-relations sense.[43]

Turning from the workplace they had mastered, Pittsburgh capitalists contributed in a similarly conservative way to efforts aimed at reforming the working-class city. Indeed, in the 1890s, some of them began to develop that sense of civic duty that James Parton had found lacking in their predecessors. Though many lesser reformers advocated higher taxes and criticized the steel companies' labor policies, big businessmen had no trouble linking their company welfare programs and their investments in suburban and downtown redevelopment with the movement to beautify the city and bring "efficiency" and "business methods" to its government. Especially for those invested in real estate and retail trade, civic improvement was just good business. Around the turn of the century, the Chamber of Commerce and other industry spokesmen took sharp aim at the problem of smoke pollution and "civic ugliness." Concerned that businessmen and professionals would leave or refuse to come to Pittsburgh because of its squalor and lack of cultural amenities, the boosters knew that "Pittsburgh the Powerful" was being grievously weakened by the failure of its industrial elite to tidy up.[44]

Far from rebelling against such charges of civic irresponsibility, many capitalists were glad of the opportunity to renounce the cruel, competitive past and to set out upon the high road of philanthropy and civic leadership. Nevertheless, although great capitalists contributed to the movement for reform, it was to smaller businessmen and to the new middle class of professionals and white-collar workers that leadership fell. In striving to "civilize" the industrial city, these middle-class reformers shared many of the values of the welfare capitalists. And yet, notwithstanding the distance that had grown between their suburban world and the life of the proletarian wards, some of the reformers came to recognize—often grudgingly—that the same steel barons who had mastered the working class had mastered them.

# CHAPTER 7

# Leisure Class, Ruling Class

At the end of the nineteenth century the Pittsburgh social elite, which had hitherto been neither a leisure class nor a ruling class, strove to become both. Although not always complementary, these ambitions marked a sharp break with the past, one dramatized by the withdrawal of the bourgeoisie from the old city. Among the greatest capitalists, withdrawal was nearly total: Mellon retreated to his Laurel Highlands duchy, Frick to his New York City palazzo, and Carnegie to his Scottish castle. Most of Pittsburgh's business and professional families, however, neither imitated nor approved (although they may have envied) such absenteeism. Seeking after elegant interiors and pastoral landscapes, they remained bound nonetheless to the old wards and the alien and disorderly masses who inhabited them. Their lives were thus characterized by a continual tension between escape and involvement, between an urge to achieve the pastoral ideal and a determination to master the urban, industrial environment.

In the pastures of the east end, middle-class Pittsburghers found escape not only from the vicious, but also from the confinement of their own narrow virtue. By 1890 they had begun to cultivate finer tastes and more cosmopolitan ideals. The change first registered within the walls of the new suburban homes. The provincial and intensely Protestant elite seemed suddenly to have heard and absorbed "The Gospel of Relaxation." As early as 1881, the *Christian Advocate* had begun to disparage "the goddess *WORK*" and to encourage the cultivation of domestic leisure. "Neighborhood sociables, where music, mental entertainment and innocent fun form the program, are to be recommended . . . . "[1] Within the next two decades, a virtual revolution in private recreation took place among middle-class Pittsburghers. Except for the prejudice against drinking, almost every leisure taboo lost its grip. Within Elizabeth Moorhead's east end circle, the "worse mid-Victorian taste," along with "the whole Presbyterian repression," gave way before the appeals of fine music, cuisine, art, and other entertainments.[2]

The Moorhead villa in the east end little resembled General J.K. Moorehead's old house on Herron Hill. As his granddaughter remembered it, the main room in the General's house had proudly displayed "two big oil paintings of the upper reaches of the Monongahela ordered by my grandfather from a local artist and framed heavily in gilt, for the General firmly believed in encouraging home industries, and the river was dear to him; it was almost his own property. He never knew how bad the pictures were, nor would he have cared had he known." His descendants did care and had their home professionally decorated. Moreover, they and their neighbors in the east end installed Pittsburgh's first generation of such modern conveniences as indoor plumbing, gas furnaces, electrical appliances, and telephones. They also owned most of the automobiles purchased in the city before World War I.[3]

At about the same time, the suburban elite began giving gracious parties catered by such new establishments as Hubley's and Schlosser's and offering entertainment by professional society musicians. Sometimes they entertained themselves with "Merry Twelve Socials," "Tuesday Musical Clubs," "Euchre Parties," and the like. Elizabeth Moorhead traces the evolution of one form of domestic entertainment, the amateur theatrical, from the "strictly censored" Shakespeare Reading Club to the "more frivolous" Crusaders and, finally around 1890, to the Tuesday Night Club, which was "more elaborate than the Crusaders, for Pittsburgh society was progessing in sophistication and made greater demands." It was in response to such demands that "New York" theaters were built in the 1890s and the early twentieth century.[4]

Moorhead's reminiscence reveals two additional features of the new elite culture. Besides being more expressive, it was also more highly organized and more cosmopolitan. The clubs that sponsored domestic entertainments often evolved into formal societies with permanent quarters and more sophisticated programs.[5] This trend was especially apparent in the field of music, where, until the late 1880s, only the German community had sustained serious activity. By 1890, many new choirs and chamber groups offered ambitious programs to the middle-class public at large. A virtual explosion of musical programming within a hitherto severely Low Church community served as the crucial mediator of the musical development of the city as a whole. Such elite churches as Calvary Episcopal, Shadyside Presbyterian, and East Liberty Presbyterian retained professional organists, directors, and soloists. Often imported from New York, these professionals provided the moving force for such groups as the Mendelssohn Quintet Club, the Orpheus Singing Society, and the Mozart Club. They also encourged the men and, especially, the women of the east end to take up, resume, or perfect their musical training. Finally, they cultivated the audiences for whom the professional Carnegie Music Hall series and the Pittsburgh Symphony Orchestra were established in the 1890s.[6]

Similar developments marked the local art scene. New galleries and art shops and an Art Society cultivated a more sophisticated public for professional art among the growing ranks of the educated middle class. Reflecting such cultivation, French Impressionism finally penetrated Pittsburgh's militantly provincial art scene in the 1890s. For example, it helped work an autumnal transformation in the style of George Hetzel, one of the best of the old "Scalp Level" school of regional landscapists. The erection of Carnegie's museum and the inauguration of the quadrennial Pittsburgh International completed the remaking of the city's art scene. Some of the old portraitists continued to prosper by duplicating successful portraits of thirty years earlier at the request of their subjects' descendants, but most prominent Pittsburghers looked to such famous east coast portraitists as Chartran and Zorn. Increasingly, they turned their attention to the walls of the new museum and, through them, to New York, Paris, and the international art world.[7]

By the turn of the century, the "Classic East End" contained not only beautiful homes but a whole range of exclusive services, including fine retail establishments, a market, a theater, a dancing school, the city's only auto club, and two preparatory schools. In 1907 it witnessed the erection of the city's first luxury high-rise, the Bellefield Dwellings, advertised as the last word in comfort, privacy, and security ("Each dwelling has a forged steel wall safe, while watchmen patrol the building day and night"). In 1897 the east end spawned Pittsburgh's first "society" journal, the *Index,* a paper that mirrored "the spirit of the socially elite, in society, in literature, in the fine arts and in politics." Providing its readers with "social news" that was "always accurate, always exclusive," it also tutored them in the new attitudes and postures appropriate to a civilized and progressive ruling class.[8]

By the turn of the century, therefore, the suburban life style had bred a suburban point of view. Before all else, that point of view was exclusive. The new elite inhabited a "magic circle . . . where life is worth living and nature smiles sweetly, undefiled by smoke and grime." To Samuel J. Fisher, author of *Our Suburb,* the village of Swissvale and suburban life in general provided the basis of a new, anti-urban ideology. Against those who "found a continuous pleasure and inspiration in the city," Fisher asserted that "some [urban] evolution is discouraging." Thus, to retreat from the over-developed city to a garden, wherein the highest culture and morality might flourish, seemed the wisest course. Indeed, as transfigured by Fisher, the commuting process itself attained almost mythic pro-portions. It became an "eternal return" from the profane and tur-bulent city back to that balanced milieu within which learning, religion, and the refined arts might coexist with salubrious nature. It is not surprising that from such an Edenic perspective "the apparent majority seems devilish."[9]

Though Fisher's ideology of suburban retreat no doubt struck sympathetic chords within the middle class, it had to compete with strong counter-currents. Principal among these was the movement toward self-conscious cosmopolitanism, already noted in regard to local theater, music, and art. Cosmopolitanism took a great stride forward in 1895 with the erection of that complex of structures— music hall, library, museum, and art institute—that bore the name Carnegie. For Elizabeth Moorhead and her generation, the phrase, "before the founding of the Carnegie Institute," signified a past sunk in provinciality and repression.[10] Immense and imperial, the *belle-époque* Carnegie complex offered suburbanites the grand entertain-ments hitherto lacking in Pittsburgh and confirmed their right to think of themselves as members of a leisure class with cosmopolitan tastes and connections.

In the realm of sociability, too, the suburban elite showed that its interests extended beyond the rural garden. The Duquesne and Pitts-burgh Clubs, both founded in the 1870s and devoted to small gatherings of closely allied steel and financial magnates, blossomed in the late 1880s and 1890s into crucial organizers of official elite culture. Both were quartered downtown and drew to their balls and cotillions the first families of the entire metropolis, from Allegheny City to the South Hills, from Sewickley to the east end. These clubs also began to link the local elite with the society of the East Coast.

Thus, an important feature of any cotillion at the Pittsburgh Club was the opportunity to meet "prominent visitors from New York."[11]

Similarly, shopping at Horne's or Kauffman's, the city's new department stores, brought suburban women together for an afternoon downtown. At the same time, it linked them to a network of fashion and consumption based in the East. One interesting consequence of the new pattern of elite consumption was a change in the way Christmas was celebrated in the Steel City. For the old iron elite, Christmas had been a pious and private holiday, centered around home and family. By the turn of the century, however, it had become a signal opportunity for public display. Christmas gift buying became "the bright particular custom of the day." Along with the department stores and other exclusive shops, the Women's Exchange attracted women downtown for tea and showing of luxury gift items, some of them imported, others produced by talented women among the "deserving poor." For the display of these and other commodities, a round of Christmas *fêtes* became "recognized social requirements." The season now also meant lavish musical, theatrical, and art shows. It was a time for seeing and being seen, for assuring oneself and one's peers that all was right—if not with the whole world then at least with that segment of it to which one was crucially connected.[12]

Greater cosmopolitanism also expressed itself in education and marriage. By the 1890s, the children and grandchildren of the iron barons were joining their eastern counterparts in prestigious pre-partory schools, St. Paul's in New Hampshire being a particular favorite. A majority of them now went to post-secondary schools, most leaving the region to attend Yale, Princeton, and other socially prominent colleges. Moreover, the rate at which children of upper-class families chose mates from outside the region rose steadily.[13]

Among the more visible and enduring institutional espressions of the new cosmopolitanism was the theatre-building wave of the 1890s. Convinced that "the theatre should be commensurate with the importance of Pittsburgh as he saw it," Henry W. Oliver mobilized the finances and bought the land on which the Nixon Theater rose. With department store magnate Joseph Horne, Oliver also helped erect two other downtown theaters that gave Pittsburgh's aspiring middle class what it wanted: "New York theatre," i.e., syndicated shows and great stars such as Maggie Mitchell, Laurence Barrett, Thomas Keene, and Sarah Bernhardt. The halls in which they performed had "Moorish" and "rococo" designs and no galleries. Unlike the inclusive plebeian theater, which mixed touring shows and local productions and which tried to serve a varied audience, the new theaters consciously served an exclusive audience intent on the conspicuous consumption of "culture."[14]

The Exposition Society was another popular institution reformed in the spirit of cosmopolitanism.[15] Although financed by businessmen and intended as a great advertisement of the city's industrial and mercantile advantages, the Exposition had, for a few years after its founding in 1875, remained a decidedly plebeian affair. Billed as a "Tradesmen's Industrial Institute," it operated for five weeks under canvas on its own grounds in Allegheny City. Manager William C. Smythe was a local reporter, a former manager of one of Ellsler's theaters, and singer with the Stephen C. Foster Serenaders—just the man to make the Exposition a popular attraction of the first rank. Indeed, during his tenure, crowds flocked to Horticultural Hall, Machinery Hall, and the local art display; they patronized the horde of candy and soda vendors that cluttered the grounds.

In the early 1880s, however, Smythe's successors began slowly to make the Exposition more respectable. For a time "People's Day" was set aside for such amusements as horse races, fireworks, and band concerts, and management allowed illegal gambling wheels and card games to run without interference. But changes were occurring under the main shed. Management increasingly pitched displays and lectures to a cosmopolitan business audience. As early as 1881, the *National Labor Tribune* protested that "the Pittsburgh Exposition management this year propose[s] to have a show based on snobocratic principles, and workingmen will not, of course, be invited." The Exposition, it continued, threatened to become an "annual show of emptiness," the increased fee for which "might be put to a better purpose and the time expended devoted to something like genuine recreation." In the early 1890s the Exposition was running for eight weeks in a large new building and devoting itself, on the one hand, to the work of the Chamber of Commerce and, on the other, to "high culture." In the early twentieth century the Exposition Society set out to make Pittsburgh "a Convention City," a task requiring large subsidies from the city council. Although the *Labor Tribune* had long ceased to care about what went on at Exposition Park, it rebelled against the use of tax monies to subsidize "a cooperative advertising scheme backed by the merchants of this city."

With the exception of band concerts and pony rides for children, the Exposition all but abandoned its popular entertainment function. For a time in the 1890s, however, before the Carnegie complex became the focus of elite attention, the Exposition provided sophisticated amusement for the city's middle and upper classes. "Mrs.

Morgan's—*the* Catering Establishment of the city" replaced the petty vendors on the grounds, and Exposition Hall became the place to hear Walter Damrosch conduct Wagner and Liszt—the place, that is, for the aspiring bourgeois spirit to receive an infusion "from that Land of Culture, the East."

Along with this spread of cosmopolitanism, a new emphasis on energetic and assertive living arrived to correct tendencies toward suburban retreat. Indeed, Pittsburgh's middle and upper classes responded to the impulse to "the strenuous life" that John Higham has identified as one of the ruling passions of the age.[16] An international phenomenon, the cult of strenuosity can first be observed in America in the midcentury "Muscular Christianity" movement. Inspired by the English public school ethos, the movement won the adherence of New England preachers and moralists. By the 1880s, *mens sana in corpore sano* had become the ideal of a growing number of middle-class Americans. To those who worried that the promotion of physical play might weaken the compulsion to work, promoters argued that exercise strengthened individual character and restored a zest for work. Moreover, they warned, an enlightened Christian nation could take no heart from the sight of an army of slack, pasty-faced young men, chained to desks and incapable of vigorous assertion. Clearly, under such circumstances, "Physical culture has become a plain moral duty."[17]

Among men such as Rudyard Kipling and Theodore Roosevelt, glorification of the strenuous life might be closely associated with the martial spirit and with nationalism and imperialism. Yet, however much the cult of strenuosity found an outlet in chauvinism, it sprang from a revolt against bourgeois gentility and Protestant repression. While the gospel of relaxation worked cautiously to dissolve the latter, the cult of strenuosity moved confidently to shatter the decrepit sanctum of "the nice." Thus, while borrowing partly from aristocratic traditions of leisure, the cult leaned heavily on distinctly plebeian attitudes towards deportment and physical exertion. It encouraged boys and, significantly, girls, to unbutton their collars and let down their hair. In its romantic affirmation of naturalness, the cult also offered an antidote to the increasing regimentation and organization of life in the industrial city. On the other hand, with its emphasis on hygiene and right-living, it suggested an image of nature devoid of the primitive, anarchic, and pessimistic implications which European contemporaries were exploring. It was, in brief, optimistic and stoutly progressive.[18]

*102*

Among suburban Pittsburghers the new mood spawned a "delight-ful epidemic" of tennis, golf, and archery. Clubs devoted to those sports, as well as to cricket, riding, and shooting, sprouted in the east end and other suburbs. In the more exclusive sport and country clubs the urge toward vigorous physical assertion blended happily with conventional notions of respectability and elegance. Among the younger and more energetic, gymnastics, swimming, camping, tennis, and especially bicycling were the rage.[19] The "great cycle craze" enlisted in "the democracy of the wheel" young men and women from the broadest reaches of the middle class. Pittsburgh's earliest bike club was formed by three young east enders, a student, a harness-maker, and a mechanical engineer. Although the cycling craze never penetrated deeply into the working class, Pittsburgh's first competitive cycling champions, the Banker brothers, rose from the ranks of labor to become proprietors of the area's most successful cycle dealership. In the 1890s, bicycle advertisements by hardware and sporting goods stores appeared regularly in the city directories and newspapers. As early as 1887, the bicycle meet had become a regular feature of Memorial Day and July Fourth celebrations.[20]

Another feature of those celebrations revealed even more clearly the trend in middle-class sport. The heroes of organized holiday track and field events in the 1890s were all amateurs, either students or alumni of school teams. As they did elsewhere in the 1880s, team sports flourished in Pittsburgh's private academies and at Central High School, the east end public school which fancied itself "one of the best preparatory schools outside new England." By 1889, Central had adopted standardized cheers, colors, mottoes, and in-signia. Clearly "*espirit de corps* . . . , intensified by the discipline of wholesome athletics," had become the *sine qua non* of middle-class student life.[21]

School spirit was even stronger among college students and alumni. On July 4, 1892, twenty thousand spectators saw the college boys dominate holiday track and field events at Schenley Park. Awarding prizes to the winners after the meet, Mayor Henry Gourley found it "gratifying . . . to see so many college boys among the number, and thought it another proof of the necessity of physical as well as mental training." Collegians not only won most of the medals, they also filled the stands and led the crowd in "vehement applause" and "college cries."[22] When Western University sponsored the state's first trans-Allegheny intercollegiate track meet in 1898, "Pittsburg's lead-ing society people . . . subscribed to boxes." Even upper-class Ivy Leaguers, far from their own college grounds, could follow the progress of their teams in the Pittsburgh papers and could simulate college camaraderie and rivalry at such social events as the annual Yale and Princeton Christmas Eve Concert.[23]

College graduates carried "the old-time enthusiasm" into local amateur athletics. Since the 1880s, the Allegheny Athletic Club and the East End Athletic Club (renamed the Pittsburgh Athletic Club in the mid-1890s) organized young clerks, professionals, and businessmen into track, baseball, and football teams. They competed against each other and against clubs and college teams in the area. There is some evidence that the PAC-AAC rivalry reflected a division within the local elite, one that pitted a Princeton–east end new elite against a Yale–Allegheny City old elite. That division generated a rivalry intense enough to cause serious scandals. In the most notorious of these, six members of the Chicago Athletic Club sold their services to PAC in 1886 for a big game against AAC. For a short time, buying sandals also marred the history of local college football. Although they soon stopped buying players, however, the local colleges did not stop trying to buy victory. By increasing its athletic budget and hiring the estimable Glenn S. ("Pop") Warner as head coach in 1907, the University of Pittsburgh succeeded in bringing champion-caliber football to the city for a decade.[24]

Though seemingly unrelated to developments in elite consumption or to the evolution of more cosmopolitan tastes and values, the rise of college team sports contributed to the same growth in class consciousness to which the Women's Exchange and the Duquesne Club gave more obvious testimony. It certainly fortified those who rejected the counsel of retreat in favor of activism and self-assertion, but who nonetheless renounced the austere and obsessive style of the Law and Order League. They could, it seemed, realize the suburban ideal and at the same time venture into the hurly-burly, compete for the attention of the masses, and put their stamp upon the life of the city.

Thus, even in withdrawal to the suburbs, middle-class culture evolved in counterpoint to the changing culture of the working-class city. Pastoralism, cosmopolitanism, and strenuosity represented different modes of a continuing interaction with those variously characterized as dangerous, parochial, and debauched. However earnestly middle-class suburbanites sought not to be of the metropolis, they could not escape that fact that they lived in it. Whether they lived within or beyond the "zone of residence" that had been annexed by the city, suburbanites could not afford the luxury of confusing pastoral fantasies with reality. The east end and the distant hills afforded a secure and eminently satisfying private milieu, but they were neither socially nor politically autonomous.

Even if they had sought to ignore the alien masses, the suburbanites could not have done so merely by avoiding the old city. For the city had already begun to come out to them. The east end was surrounded by industrial zones in the river valleys to the west, north, and south. When the wind was right, even Swissvale suffered from the smoke and smell of steelmaking. In East Liberty, the studied calm of suburban life was already disturbed by pool rooms, taverns, a popular theater, and the city's two amusement parks. Perhaps most telling, the Pittsburgh Free Dispensary found it necessary before the turn of the century to open an east end branch.[25]

Clearly, elite residential communities were themselves enclaves within the great metropolis. In the twentieth century true escape was vouchsafed only to the Mellons, Fricks, Carnegies and their peers. The bulk of Pittsburgh's business and professional families could not doubt that the fate of the few was bound to that of the many. From that growing certainty the Progressive movement drew nourishment.

The erection of the Carnegie complex in 1895 thus announced more than the arrival of a self-conscious leisure class. It also announced the ambition of that class to reform culture in the Steel City. The latter intention could be inferred from the very siting of the complex, which confirmed Oakland's status as the "cultural and civic center" of Pittsburgh.[26] Already the site of the relocated campus of Western University (soon to be renamed the University of Pittsburgh and to be joined by the Carnegie Technical Schools), of the Bellefield and Athletic Clubs, and of the exclusive new Schenley Hotel, Oakland was also the locus of Schenley Park, the jewel of the emerging metropolitan park system. Poised as it was midway between downtown and the east end, Oakland served as the pivot for a middle class trying to balance pastoral vision and social ambition. It was a kind of frontier of east end culture, at once a buffer against encroachment and a staging ground for new efforts to evangelize the plebeian masses.

Unlike private clubs or commercial theaters, the Carnegie complex was a public institution with an explicit social agenda: to define, create, and disseminate "the highest culture" and thereby to civilize the inhabitants of the industrial city. An early expression of this cultural mission was the inauguration in 1896 of free Sunday organ recitals at the music hall. The recitals reportedly attracted "the people for whose benefit they have been established—viz., the wage workers."

*105*

Organist and music director Frederic Archer planned Saturday programs for students and Sunday programs for the general public. About the latter he explained:

> In order to develop the musical instincts of the people *en masse,* the adoption of a *repertoire* of diverse character is absolutely necessary, for by such means alone can universal interest be aroused and catholicity of taste promoted. My Sunday programmes are therefore constructed on this plan, although all music of low or vulgar character is excluded.[27]

It is difficult to determine the identity of those who attended Archer's recitals, and it may be doubted that workers who could barely afford the necessities of life expended precious time and money on a trip to Oakland. Nonetheless, up to his death in 1901, Archer reported an average attendance of one thousand. In its first five years the series drew an astonishing 381,000.[28] The first free public concert series in Pittsburgh, the Carnegie recitals were also the first organized attempt to elevate working-class sensibilities.

Like the erection of the music hall, the development of Schenley Park reflected first the elite's desire for a more gracious and sophisticated way of life and second its search for social harmony. Since before the Civil War, genteel Pittsburghers had regretted that their city possessed "neither public park, fountain, [n]or garden."[29] Their discomfort was relieved somewhat in 1867 when the state legislature authorized and the city of Allegheny laid out a public common of a hundred acres. Around it quickly rose the district's most exclusive residential precinct. Two years later, however, Pittsburgh voters declined to underwrite a more ambitious venture, rejecting a bond issue intended to finance the purchase of the huge Schenley estate in Oakland. The plebeian electorate (and many tax-conscious businessmen) saw no reason to finance suburban development and doubted the need for such a "public pleasure ground."[30]

Despite growth in industrial and residential demand for urban real estate, for at least a decade after the Civil War citizens took advantage of numerous and relatively undisturbed natural sites in and around the city for swimming, sledding, picnicking, riding, fishing, pigeon-trapping, and other kinds of informal play.[31] Well into the 1880s, therefore, the debate over public parks proceeded in familiar terms. Those Pittsburghers with sufficiently expanded sensibilities and purses offered Romantic apostrophes to nature, advocated publicly financed preservation of land, and were for the most part ignored by the plebeian majority. Increasingly, however, park promoters joined utilitarian to aesthetic arguments. As natural beauty gratified the height-ened sensibilities of the already-civilized, so, they argued, it restrained the baser instincts of the yet-to-be-civilized. Parks might uplift base temperaments or at least provide a safety valve to vent the frustra-tions of urban, industrial life.[32] Whether park promoters believed it or merely employed it to convince reluctant burghers, the idea that a Schenley Park could serve as substitute for saloons and rowdy pastimes and thereby create civic harmony weighed heavily in sub-sequent debates.[33]

The massive industrial and demographic changes of the late 1880s made utilitarian arguments more and more convincing. In 1889 Edward Bigelow, the city's aggressive new chief of public works, won from heiress Mary Schenley a gift of three hundred acres and an option to buy one hundred more for $125,000. In promoting his program, Bigelow appealed both to the rapidly suburbanizing middle class, which sought a pastoral preserve, and to the immigrant masses from whom the suburbanites were escaping. In appealing to the latter, Bigelow recognized that popular opposition to park devel-opment was disappearing along with old neighborhoods and informal recreational sites. Moreover, with increasing persuasiveness, the scarred and vanishing natural landscape made it own case.

Almost simultaneously with the Schenley deal, Bigelow announced plans to develop the Highland Reservoir site, in the more distant reaches of the east end. Long-time residents of the area were dis-concerted by the news. The prospect of hordes of undesirables violating their hills and glades aroused them to militant opposition. They saw in Bigelow's proposal not simply a plan to preserve beautiful landscapes—they had already accomplished that privately—but a direct threat to their golf course, their country club, and their exclusive way of life. No less than the poor southsiders who fought the creation of McKinley Park in 1898—and no more successfully—the highlanders couched their resistance to planned development as a defense of nature and of received patterns of leisure. By the 1890s, however, the argument for "democratic planning" had won the day.

Despite that victory, Bigelow's park plans remained relatively modest, examples less of social engineering than of grand rhetoric. Like the nearby Carnegie complex, Schenley Park extended to the urban masses in whose name it was built a welcome that was at best tacit. Thus, in the early years of park development, the city made only a few improvements on nature, most designed to facilitate elite leisure—driving and bridal paths and, at Schenley, a golf course run by a private club. Like Highland, which one progressive critic complained "does some social work although far from the desired amount," Schenley was "typically . . . the East End's park, adapted fairly well to its neighborhood, but not at all serving the democratic needs of Greater Pittsburgh."[34]

Neither the Carnegie center nor Schenley Park was fitted to perform social work. Organ recitals, picture galleries, and stacks of books were, like park lawns and trees, simply made available to the public. For middle-class Pittsburghers concerned to ameliorate social disorder and decay, mere availability was not enough. Because they doubted that the distant cathedrals of Nature and Culture could do the necessary missionary work, reformers turned to more direct and active methods of influencing working-class leisure. These included expanding the functions of parks, building neighborhood playgrounds, and launching a library extension service.

Bigelow's most obvious attempt to do social work involved redesigning the celebration of the Fourth of July. By 1890 the plebeian Fourth was a thing of the past, a victim both of demographic change and of elite pressure for a reformed celebration. The latter took the form of calls for a more reverent and somber observance to replace the kind of celebration which the great park planner, Frederick Law Olmsted, referred to as "grotesque performances by montebanks [sic] with fireworks and music."[35] Appalled by such displays and by the drunken fights and fire company brawls that frequently marred such celebrations, pietists tried for a decade following the Civil War to promote Memorial Day as a sober substitute for the plebeian Fourth. By the 1880s, however, they admitted failure. "There is much puerility in our observance of our nation's anniversary," lamented Pittsburgh's *Christian Advocate,* "and yet better this than nothing." In the turbulence of the 1880s, moreover, pietists rediscovered the virtues of the "old-time Fourth of July," finding it preferable to Memorial Day because the latter recalled rebellion and civil war at a time when people needed a message of unity.

A generation has grown up in almost entire ignorance of the "old Fourth." Many of them have never heard the Declaration of Independence read to a public assembly. . . . Other thousands have come in among us . . . who are equally ignorant of these things, and of those for which they stand. The old celebration is a good way to impress them with these great lessons, . . . in all the varied and changing phases of life and labor among us. . . .[36]

Ironically, the anti-labor *Advocate* found itself echoing the *National Labor Tribune* when it asserted, "It lies with labor organizations to revive old-time celebration of the Fourth of July . . . , the one particular holiday of the year which wage-workers should mark with patriotic ardor."[37] What pietist and unionist had in common was a desire to focus the celebration, to impose serious, thematic content upon a holiday that had always been more carnival than somber ceremony. Their concern increased in the 1880s as the loose integrity of the plebeian Fourth gave way to scattered observances and private pleasures. On July Fourth, ethnic, labor, fraternal, religious, and elite groups increasingly went their different ways—to commercial amusements, sporting events, and private parties. Picnics and excursions drew more people to more distant sites as railroads, boat companies, and agents devised excursion packages with special holiday rates.[38]

Thus, in 1887, after Terence Powderly called on workingmen to turn the Fourth into an expression of labor unity and patriotism, local Knights began organizing modified versions of the plebeian Fourth of July. While they filled the day with the usual games and events, they also made temperance the order of the day and strove explicitly to associate the cause of labor with the republican heritage. Though the effort to put labor at the head of a movement to revive the old Fourth succeeded in many smaller towns in western Pennsylvania, it made little impact in Pittsburgh. There, as powerful groups competed for control of patriotic symbols, the Knights were in no position to dominate the holiday. Only a year later they complained of the expense of organizing a celebration of any kind and doubted their ability to attract much of a crowd.[39]

The year 1887 also witnessed a very different attempt to organize the holiday: Leading politicians and businessmen tried to develop a decentralized celebration in keeping with the more fragmented and dispersed character of life in the Steel City.[40] In at least a dozen sections of the expanded city, prominent men financed and organized fireworks displays and other festivities. Boss Magee spent $500 on downtown pyrotechnics, and other area patrons, such as Henry C. Frick in the east end community of Point Breeze, may have spent as much. On the other hand, the efforts of the butcher and boilermaker who took charge of one of the south side celebrations were doubtless more modest. In any case, this experiment in neo-feudalism was not repeated. For, even as it was being carried out, Edward Bigelow (whose brother Thomas had sponsored the 1887 celebration in the Hill district) was formulating his plans for Pittsburgh's modern park system, one part of which was the mobilization of massive July Fourth festivals in Schenley Park.

Bigelow took the Fourth of July seriously. Unlike pietists, however, he sought not to spurn the plebeian Fourth but to absorb it. To the park he invited vaudeville performers, Punch and Judy shows, ethnic dancers, balloonists, pyrotechnicians, horse and mule racers, and a myriad of other plebeian entertainers. On the other hand, he mounted elaborate ceremonies in which business and political leaders took center stage. And by containing the celebration within Schenley Park, Bigelow centralized the observance and detached it from plebeian associations in the old city. He then reinforced that detachment by allowing only licensed vendors in the park, by banning liquor and peddling, and by deploying large police contingents to maintain order. Moreover, the ceremonies themselves asserted the new cooperative ideal on which the hierarchical social reality of the Steel City was to be based. Extolled in poems and speeches, enacted in dramatic tableaux and chanted in choral anthems, patriotism became a kind of service, a doing one's part for the larger, progressive purpose.[41]

Although ambitious and well financed by business contributions, and well designed to celebrate the status quo, Bigelow's patriotic extravaganzas may not have had their desired effect. Their intended message could be variously interpreted or ignored. Moreover, the official veneer could simply break down, as it did dramatically on July 4, 1892. Then "eloquent old Tom Marshall" cried the one word which no one on the platform wanted to hear: "Homestead." An old Mugwump, founding member of the Republican Party, former local and state official, and labor arbitrator, Marshall was universally respected and had a reputation for fiery oratory. More to the point, perhaps, he was too old to imbibe fashionable progressivism and too cranky to acquiesce in a charade intended to celebrate unity even as, a few miles away, the social tinder of the Steel District was about to explode. His bitter excoriation of monopoly capitalism and his endorsement of labor's crusade to "assert the manhood of man" fell "like a bombshell" on the audience. But it was a fugitive dissent from an otherwise smooth performance, and it was never repeated.[42]

More persistent threats to Bigelow's plans were public indifference and the danger that, in his effort to appeal to the masses, the medium might overwhelm the message. Thus, the *Gazette,* one of the city's more straightlaced newspapers, saw in the 1892 celebration little more than a vulgar "country fair" run for the benefit of the political machine and the "street-railway combine" which Boss Magee owned. Oblivious to any intended preachments about social order—which it would have applauded—the *Gazette* noticed nothing but "moneymaking schemes."

"Everything goes" was the order of the day. . . . Organ grinders, peddlars and fakirs of all classes took hold early . . . , while many merchants and others took advantage of the supposed solemn and patriotic occasion to advertise their respective concerns to the fullest extent.[43]

Indeed, promoters could only be certain that the very attractions they had hoped would draw crowds—picnic grounds, ball games, and the ever-reliable "montebanks with fireworks and music"—had done just that.

The *Gazette*'s obliviousness suggests that Bigelow's success lay not in indoctrination but, as the fate of another holiday suggests, in his ability to define public space. For a time in the 1880s, Labor Day inspired a working-class version of what pietists had hoped for Memorial Day, i.e., the mobilization of huge crowds in a sober and serious affirmation of citizenship. However staid those demonstrations—in 1887 ironworkers marched under the banner of "Unity, Stability, Conservatism"—they were at least implicitly class-conscious expressions of the same social context that was producing an extraordinary number of strikes and other labor disturbances. Even more important, however, they were vestiges of a passing era. The Labor Day parade customarily wound its way through the wards of Allegheny, the south side, and the old city. As it did, neighborhood merchants and other middle-class residents joined in the sort of plebeian festivities that their suburbanized peers had left behind. For workingmen, the celebration of Labor Day demonstrated just that distinction between capitalist enemies and middle-class neighbors which the passing of the plebeian city would soon make anachronistic. Indeed, by Labor Day of 1892 the city had so changed that labor leaders contemplating ways to mark the day could think of no better place to demonstrate than Schenley Park. By the end of the decade they had shifted to a less obviously supervised but still clearly contained space, Kennywood amusement park.[44]

While Bigelow redefined public space, other reformers delved into inner space. Library extension workers, for example, revealed some of the diverse, even contradictory, motives that inspired such efforts. Though partly motivated by benevolence and by professional ambition, extension workers aimed at social control through literacy. Books were an "important socializing factor" through which the librarian was able "indirectly to instill lessons of courtesy, cleanliness, care of public property, respect for the rights of others and many other valuable lessons."[45] In a city of immigrant workers toiling, perhaps seething, under the yoke of a militantly authoritarian in-

*111*

dustrial regime, the library's socializing function could not have seemed unimportant to the suburban businessman or professional.

In effect, then, extension was a publicly sponsored form of welfare capitalism. This is especially apparent in a company town such as Homestead. There the Carnegie Library oversaw a full range of cultural services for town residents, nearly all of whom were employees of Carnegie Steel. Unlike Pittsburgh, where all efforts to influence the behavior of employees had to be mediated through a complex of cultural and political institutions and conventions, where, in brief, history intervened between people and those aspiring to shape or master them, Homestead had only recently and suddenly risen around Carnegie's mill. In such a virgin context, Carnegie discerned a unique opportunity to develop the "three natures in the make-up of every human being," that is, "the mental, moral and physical." As his dedicatory speech of 1898 reveals, he allowed himself to believe that, through wise intervention in the cultural environment, great capitalists might complete the process already begun in the mill. Having reorganized the world of work, they could now turn to the larger world of leisure. "How a man spends his time at work may be taken for granted," he announced (though it is a striking announcement, coming from the man who knew better than any of his colleagues that the craftman's empire had had to be obliterated), "but how he spends his hours of recreation is really the key to his progress in all the virtues."[46]

Homestead's library thus reflected its master's plan. Mill officers dominated the library board and the professional staff seemed to know its duty:

> If it is proper for the library to furnish books for the people, it is right that they should be good books. If the library has the right to control the character of the reading, it has a right to direct the reader to the desired information. . . . [47]

In addition to the desire for social control, extension work reflected the efforts of professionalizing librarians to sell their services. They strove to convince the public that librarians were no longer amateurs, antiquarians, or mere clerks. They were professionals, their products literacy and good habits, their main task, distribution. "To this end," asserted the chief of the Children's Department of the Carnegie Library of Pittsburgh, "the library is organized like a business house into departments under the control of a head librarian." Instead of waiting for the public to come to them, these new professionals strove to define, locate, and serve their market. "To reach the working men, the foreigners and their children in their homes," the Pittsburgh library created seven branches and 177 distribution stations. In one twelve-month period alone, it circulated more than 31,500 foreign-language books. Although 13,000 of these were written in German and thus reached few of the newer immigrants, the rest represented the languages of those recently arrived southern and eastern Europeans.[48]

The library set up extension stations in factories, department stores, churches, YMCA buildings, firehouses, public and private schools, Sunday schools, settlements, bathhouses, vacation schools, playgrounds, and juvenile detention facilities. It even allowed children to establish "home libraries" for the use of friends and neighbors, and it sent librarians to lead weekly "library hours" in readers' homes. Inspired by Jacob Riis's call to fight "the gang" with "its own weapon—the weapon of organization," librarians did special work among boys' gangs.[49] It may be doubted that such outreach activities affected working people precisely as intended, but there can be no doubt about the initial seriousness of the effort.

While extension workers tried to reform behavior by means of literacy and the cultivation of sensibility, playground workers looked instead to the strenuous life and, in particular, to team sports. "Play is a social inheritance," announced Beulah Kennard, the moving force behind Pittsburgh's playground movement. Unlike Romantic park planners, who envisioned the tired worker reviving his spirit in verdant and tranquil solitude, Kennard insisted that play "has almost no existence away from group life."[50]

Less confident than park planners about the curative powers of Nature, playground promoters were also less patient of a cure. Investigating the lives of immigrant children in 1896, Kennard noted with impatience the ignorance of her colleagues in the Pittsburgh Civic Club:

> The members having never lived next to a mill and always having had yards and doorsteps of their own, could not understand that these children did not know how to play. The committee could not believe it. Some of them do not believe it now; they think that the children played when they were not looking.[51]

Playground promoters thus took as one of their first responsibilities the education of the middle class in the sordid realities of the industrial city. When promoters failed to secure from the Homestead school board the funds necessary for continued operation of a vacation school, Margaret Byington regretted the loss, not only to the children but also to "the intelligent women of the town" who had, through the program, "come into personal contact with the problems of their Second Ward neighbors." Appalled by the "indescribable" character of life among immigrant children, stung by their own ignorance, Kennard's middle-class constituency wanted nothing more than to know "what to do next."[52] The playground movement supplied a seemingly practical answer to such demands.

Linked closely to public schools and settlements, the campaign for playgrounds tapped the optimistic and strenuous strain in middle-class culture. With confident blandness, the motto of their national association advertised their intention "To promote normal wholesome play and public recreation." They believed that the disorder of urban life resulted from society's failure to socialize children and that playgrounds would teach isolated and stunted children the satisfaction and creative power of collectivity. Since the "play spirit" was the spirit of civilization itself, only by harnessing the instincts through strenuous team play could social health be restored. Only after "we give free rein to what is caged and leashed in us" might human beings begin cooperatively to cultivate "the Higher Life."[53]

Thus attuned to instinctual demand and convinced of organizational solutions, playground workers promoted the healthy release of energy through a myriad of group activities. To achieve "positive educational results," they created playgrounds and programmed activities in working-class neighborhoods wherever they could find space—school, settlement, and church yards, factory grounds, and empty lots. They also took to politics, sponsoring bond proposals and competing for park development funds, arguing always that "schools of play" were more effective agents of socialization than were schools of Nature. What they wanted for their charges was not "breathing space" but ceaseless, directed activity. Playgrounds had to be close at hand, easy of access, and supervised so that no child would be left with hands or thoughts unengaged. Imagining themselves free of Romantic illusions about natural morality, the new activists were in fact obsessed with "the whole hygienic aspect of life among the working people." Unable to trust their charges to God, to Nature, or to themselves, however, playground workers eventually found their "persistent attention" inadequate to the task of "comprehensive social formation."[54]

In fact, most playground workers probably never realized the neo-puritan expectations raised by their rhetoric. Experience with working-class children and their families taught most playground workers that, beyond the simple provision of service and the spontaneous demonstration of kindness, their ministrations were coolly received. When they became censors or moral instructors, their clients retreated. If they chose to serve the working class, they would have to do so on terms dictated by a clientele which recognized with acute discrimination the difference between service and domination.

Moreover, it may be that playground workers came to pay no more than lip service to their own professional uplift jargon. Despite talk of developing the "physical, social and educational" well-being of the working class and of turning every playground into "the headquarters of a kind of neighborhood guild" wherein would grow an "invaluable village . . . loyalty," playground workers were compelled to settle for more modest, yet real, achievements. They created safe places for children who were crowded into mill neighborhoods; they supplied equipment and some instruction in sports, arts, and crafts. Despite pronouncements about socialization, in practice they endeavored "to keep the activities spontaneous, childlike, and joyous, without strain and without self-consciousness."[55]

Similarly, in their work with children, extension librarians probably communicated less censoriousness and pedantry than sheer earnestness and friendly interest. In claiming that they purveyed only "suitable stories illustrating ethical subjects," librarians may have been broadcasting what trustees and superiors wanted to hear. Even when they did intend to instill values and habits in their charges, the librarians gave as much emphasis to the need "to think independently" as to the wisdom of decorum and submission to authority. Whatever they intended, moreover, librarians often did little more than read stories and fairy tales to children. Like their colleagues in the playgrounds, librarians learned to avoid the hard-sell:

> The methods of the children's librarians are those of informal teaching. The children come and go as they wish, there being no compulsion in their attendance at the library.[56]

To working-class parents, the library was probably just a pleasant place staffed by pleasant people into whose hands children could safely be deposited for a few hours on weekends.

Finally, library staffs were often too busy providing services to keep clearly in mind the utimate aims of profession or institution. This was especially true when, as in Homestead, the staff included recreation workers, music directors, teachers, and other auxiliary workers who were expected to organize and maintain most of the town's athletic and cultural activities, from basketball, gymnastics, and bowling teams to bands, choruses, and instrumental clubs.[57] Thus to whatever extent it intended to "Americanize" its clientele, the library staff could be certain only that it provided welcome diversion, especially for youngsters. However serious its efforts to bend play to ulterior social ends, the staff had eventually to treat play as an end in itself.

Whatever their role in the lives of children, the playground and the library extension mattered little to working-class adults. As playground workers had no luck with "neighborhood guilds," so librarians found extension work among mill men frankly discouraging and gladly turned their attention to children, who welcomed, or at least tolerated, their ministrations. "The library and the lecture course are fine things for business men, women and children," but not for himself, one steelworker told John Fitch. His indifference reflected motives mixed but not unrelated. In addition to competition from bars and pool halls, "Conditions at the mill, overtime work, and the fact that the men are not readers, or distrusted the company's motives" were cited for the failure of extension stations in factories. Similarly, Fitch noted that, while the twelve-hour day made self-improvement of any kind practically impossible, there also existed "a great deal of prejudice against the gift of Mr. Carnegie on account of the several labor conflicts that have occurred in the mills." The conservative glassblowers union scorned Carnegie's alleged magnanimity, finding only irony in the claim that his library was "Free to the People." On the contrary, argued the union,, the taxpayers would forever sustain Carnegie's monument to himself and to the money sweated from the workers at Homestead. His self-glorification, like his use of Pinkertons, was "a challenge to the manhood of free American laborers."[58]

Indeed, working people viewed Carnegie's philanthropies in the way they viewed most forms of welfare capitalism, i.e., as company public relations and as attempts to appease and distract them. Whereas in the 1880s the *Labor Tribune* and other labor spokesmen had been in the habit of praising Carnegie for his enlightened labor policies and philanthropies,[59] after Homestead their attitude cooled considerably. Even earlier, they had begun questioning the wisdom and morality of such gestures. In 1890, for example, workingmen and their representatives in Allegheny raised serious questions about who would control the library that Carnegie had offered the city. Carnegie and other upper-class citizens naturally assumed that a blue-ribbon board of trustees should administer the institution, but the *Labor Tribune* and, as it turned out, a majority of the city council disagreed:

> A committee of [the city council] would represent the people; a special committee of unofficial citizens might be composed of snobs who would make the Library anything but popular.[60]

Though the issues were often very different, questions of power and authority lay behind all working-class criticism of public and private paternalism. It is therefore not surprising that some of the earliest and most comprehensive programs of welfare capitalism were first attempted by companies which, like the famous Lowell mills, hired predominantly female labor forces. Over women, management might exercise a paternalistic authority that would have provoked greater resistance if applied to men.[61]

The best example of such paternalism in Pittsburgh was the so-called "German Welfare System" administered to six hundred women employees by the H.J. Heinz Company.[62] Besides providing scrupulously clean surroundings, uniforms, and equipment, Heinz gave each "girl" a weekly manicure and supplied free treatment from company physicians and dentists. Several times every summer, each employee had the chance to "climb into a horse-drawn wagonette with eight other girls and spend a morning or afternoon, at no loss of pay, being driven through the park and downtown areas." On the Fourth of July she could board the company paddle-wheeler for the slow trip to Beaver County, where the lavish annual picnic took place. She could use the company roof garden, the pool, the washroom, and the lunchroom, where one penny bought coffee, milk, and sugar and where she was serenaded by piano music. Even more impressive was the great auditorium:

> It had a musical director, 1500 opera-type seats, a gallery with two proscenium boxes, 2000 incandescent bulbs, a pipe organ, a Pianola, a Steinway Concert Grand Piano, an Edison Stereo-Projecting Kinetoscope, and a splendid large dome with artistically designed stained glass . . . , on which appeared the motto, "The World Our Field."[63]

The auditorium featured professional shows as well as employees' theatrical, choral, and instrumental productions, an annual dance, and a Christmas party.

Owned and managed by Germans, staffed largely by German and Bohemian workers supervised by Matrons, the Heinz plant may for a time have operated according to its founder's grand paternal design.

*117*

By the turn of the century, however, when Elizabeth Butler investigated the firm for the Pittsburgh Survey, most of the workers were Slavs, and the veneer of paternalistic benevolence had worn thin. Although there was little open rebellion, Butler sensed resentment against that cheerful and sterile regime under which women might, like "girls," be "summoned to the auditorium at noon to hear an address by some visitors or to sing. . . . " She also recognized the brute hardship under which the women labored: "A girl who cuts onions at $.75 a day cares very little for the polished piano in the lunch room, or for the roof garden." To exceptionally noxious and unrewarding work at very high speeds, Heinz's welfare measures added only indignity. "When high wages are paid, even if fewer gifts are given, women employees have the precious opportunity to work out their own lives."[64]

Paternalism evoked in the working class a proletarian version of laissez-faire,[65] an instinctive demand simply to be let alone. That instinct was revealed in the similarly dubious reception that working people gave to nearly all varieties of public and private welfare work. They refused to be patronized, whether by employers or by reformers who were deeply critical of those very employers. They especially resisted the efforts of those who proffered service in return for good behavior, usually defined in middle-class, Protestant terms.

Thus, the Playground Association failed to attract to its Lawrenceville field house the very Polish and black working women of the Strip and lower Hill areas for whom it had been built in 1907. Instead, only German, Irish, and "American" women—nearly all clerks, stenographers, and other white-collar employees—took advantage of the classes, concerts, and athletic facilities. Settlement houses had similar experiences. Although the Kingsley and Columbian settlements in the Hill district attracted some immigrant boys to their basketball courts, they and others made little impact on blacks or on the Slavic majority.[66] Similarly, in Lawrenceville and on the south side, the YWCA failed to attract working women to its lunchrooms or to its evening programs, with their evangelical bias and their emphasis on "Character building." With extreme understatement, John R. Commons noted that the YWCA "has yet to reach the rank and file of girl wage-earners, especially factory employees." Like the Carnegie Library extension, the YWCA put the best face on its failure and anticipated a more fruitful field for service in the "army of clerks [and] stenographers . . . who daily traverse the thoroughfares" downtown.[67] Eventually, however, in order to salvage some credibility in a city of immigrant workers, it had to bend its evangelicalism to the social gospel. Indeed, so earnest was its belated endorsement of collective bargaining, minimum wage laws, and "industrial democracy," that it won in 1921 the outraged opposition of the Pittsburgh Employers Association.[68]

As the behavior of the YWCA shows, some reformers learned that what working people most wanted from them was not uplift or therapy but elementary support in their struggle to survive in the industrial city. However, many reformers missed the lesson or learned it late. From the perspective of the leisure reformers, in particular, the immigrants remained an alien mass, locked in impenetrable ethnic and class enclaves. And, indeed, although public schooling would eventually make a partial contribution toward "Americanizing" immigrant children, middle-class uplift never succeeded in creating loyal and pious citizens. It would be a mistake, however, to attribute that failure entirely to the defensive and inward features of immigrant life. For, although the immigrants sustained durable ethnic subcultures, they also demonstrated at odd moments, a willingness to affirm their own version of Americanism.

A striking example of such a moment came to view when Leroy Scott, an investigator for the Survey, discovered "Little Jim Park," a tiny plot of U.S. Steel property on Pittsburgh's south side. Opened with children's choir, skits, and other flourishes on Decoration Day, 1909, Little Jim was built by neighborhood men—"when any of us was laid off at the mill"—from remnants of the church that had last occupied the site. The park sported brick flower beds, benches, iron gate, arch, canopy, and flagpole topped by the American flag. When asked "Who gave the park?" one man answered, "We took it."[69]

Almost lost within the bulk of the Survey, Scott's brief description casts a withering light on the uplift rhetoric that informed many of the reports surrounding it. At once heroic and pathetic, the building of Little Jim may be taken as emblematic of a wider working-class struggle for cultural space. That struggle took place not only on the limited and tightly-held terrain of the ethnic neighborhood, but beyond it as well. Escaping from regimentation and reform, working-class immigrants found in mass culture a "free-and-easy" version of America quite different from that offered by the promoters of "Progressive Recreation." Mediated by "merchants of leisure"[70] who pursued profit with little regard for bourgeois opinion, new commercial entertainments displaced or transfigured those rooted in the plebeian city and began to create a mass audience.

# CHAPTER 8

# The Triumph of Commerce

No conclusion emerges more clearly from the study of leisure reform in Pittsburgh than that it failed. That failure bears a curious resemblance to the experience, chronicled by Peter Burke in *Popular Culture in Early Modern Europe*,[1] of Christian reformers who sought the "Triumph of Lent" over traditional, semi-pagan culture. Although such efforts partially succeeded, Burke locates the major source of cultural change in the "commercial revolution" that permanently transformed communications, markets, and consumption in "ways which no contemporary could have foreseen." Similarly, at the dawn of the twentieth century in Pittsburgh, commerce overmatched reform and contributed to the remaking of working-class culture. Militant leisure reform only accelerated the rush of working people (and many of their betters) into the arms of merchants of leisure who were fashioning a new mass culture.

By the 1880s, vast demographic and institutional changes had already begun to subvert plebeian culture, which had nurtured local initiatives in politics and labor organization in Pittsburgh for a quarter-century. In addition to the Knights of Labor assembly hall, the volunteer fire company, and the old Exposition, which have been discussed already, major casualties of these changes included the plebeian theater, the workingmen's boat club, and the amateur baseball team. The new entertainments that took their place, however, did not simply fill a vacuum. Rather, they successfully competed for popular attention, reshaped tastes and habits, and created a new mass audience.

*120*

Even before the ascendance of steel and the new immigration in the late 1880s, nationwide changes in the theatrical business had put local houses in jeopardy. In 1879, the last stock company in Pittsburgh disbanded. In a few years, John Ellsler, who had referred to the company as his "acting school," left the city. Critics who had lambasted his effort to provide mixed programs for mixed audiences much preferred the impressive touring shows of the New York and Philadelphia syndicates.[2]

However, genteel critics did not in themselves put the plebeian houses out of business. On the one hand, syndicated shows simply outclassed the locals in spectacle and splendor, and thereby won over a larger audience. On the other hand, by guaranteeing the local theater manager a series of predictably impressive features, the syndicates could package a season at a cost that compared favorably with stock company productions.

If the new arrangement proved profitable to some managers, however, it also created new problems. First, it turned local managers into booking agents for legitimate, vaudeville, and burlesque syndicates. Once incorporated into the system, they lost the ability to control their schedules and to resist syndicate demand for higher prices. Second, in the late 1880s and 1890s, managers found themselves confronting both bourgeois patrons who demanded more exclusive fare, and poor, alien audiences unfamiliar with the conventions of theatrical comedy and melodrama. Some of the old houses tried to straddle the social cleavage pulling their audience apart. But they could no longer rely for patronage on hard-pressed skilled workers nor, after the erection of "New York" theaters in the 1890s, on the bourgeois audience. They also failed to attract the immigrant customers of the "ten-cent houses" which, for the price of a drink, offered a comedy act or a little song and dance.[3]

By the turn of the century, therefore, the theatrical business had become specialized and the audience fragmented. While the fancy theaters offered high-priced productions for an elite, and vaudeville tried to repackage the variety show into a more respectable product for the white-collar lower-middle class, burlesque appealed to less respectable audiences.[4] Anti-elitist and contemptuous of snobs and do-gooders, burlesque made up for the loss of local reference and topical interest with a libertine demeanor and a frenetic pace. Still, in the first decade of the twentieth century, burlesque too began losing its audience—now to nickelodeons and movies.

Produced and distributed by small-time operators, many of them Jewish immigrants, the new medium was undemanding and militantly escapist. It won over the audiences of the burlesques and the ten-cent houses, and it generated new ones. John P. Harris, whose "Museum" had been the most successful ten-cent house in Pittsburgh, quickly sensed the trend and built "the first all-motion picture theater" in America. In 1905, the *Post* began a series explaining to an intensely interested public the process of filmmaking. And by 1915, the *National Labor Tribune* was celebrating Charlie Chaplin as a "national hero, whose funny hat, walk, cane, and mustache are now better known than the prayer book."[5]

Regarding the nickelodeon in Homestead, Margaret Byington of the Pittsburgh Survey exclaimed: "The part these shows play in the life of the community is really surprising." That children were "always begging for five cents to go to the nickelodeon" she found less noteworthy than that men on their way from work, women out shopping, and, on Saturday nights, whole families regularly sought "a glimpse of the other side of life." Similarly, Elizabeth Butler noted the working girls lined up outside downtown picture shows on Saturday evening, "hot and tired and irritable, but willing to wait" and "determined to be amused."[6] Out of such determination was created the audience for Chaplin's "The Tramp," "The Immigrant," etc. With their fugitive assertions of freedom and their images of unconquerable dignity amid the wreckage of urban industrial society, such films demonstrated that the new medium could offer more than mere escape. On the other hand, almost any kind of one-reeler could draw an audience from a population so desperately in need of consolation and escape.

Although they could not rival the popularity of the movies, Pittsburgh's three amusement parks, all of which were built in the first decade of the twentieth century, drew large working-class crowds. Dream City, the larger of the two east end parks, opened on Memorial Day, 1906, to a crowd of 37,000. Operated by a national amusement corporation, it offered "pavilions, theatres, 'shoot the chutes,' . . . pony tracks, miniature railroad, and similar attractions." It also featured dance halls and skating rinks, two varieties of entertainment that were especially popular with young people because they permitted physical contact between the sexes. The amusement parks also offered hundreds of acres of wooded grounds and picnic sites, thus competing successfully with the public parks for the holiday crowds (including union workers celebrating Labor Day).[7] Amusement parks appealed to the wide cross-section of urban citizenry in search of excitement that was relatively inexpensive, always exciting, and unreformed.

At the same time, similar changes were occurring in the realm of sports. The last boat race on the Allegheny River took place in 1887, and the clubs soon passed out of existence. Their disappearance was the result both of growing demand on river property by industry and of the departure of skilled craftsmen from the old city. For several years thereafter professional oarsmen from Pittsburgh continued to race in national competitions, but they were increasingly plagued by scandals involving gambling and race-fixing. Meanwhile, at the same time that new immigrant spectators were being won to other spectacles, collegiate amateurs rewrote the rule book along British lines and won for boating the attention of new enthusiasts. By 1890 rowing had joined track and football as a sport of the college-educated middle class.[8]

Boxing emerged as a favorite workingman's spectacle. Although illegal and thoroughly condemned by neo-puritans, boxing attracted larger purses and wider publicity as the century drew to a close. While numerous local challenge matches continued to be run by small operators, attention increasingly turned to nationally reported fights between such symbols of ethnic identity as John L. Sullivan, Harry Greb, and Jack Johnson. Moreover, newspapers and athletic clubs became the sport's leading sponsors, and their influence made boxing respectable, despite persistent opposition from churches and reform groups. Indeed, the consolidation of athletic-club sponsorship of boxing represents the first example of elite patrons successfully dominating lower-class sport in Pittsburgh. In the twentieth century, the typical prize fight featured immigrant-stock fighters in the ring and a combination of immigrant workers and "prominent businessmen" in the seats.[9] Although Queensbury rules and club oversight made the game marginally more respectable, the significance of the new arrangement had little to do with what went on in the ring. More important, each fight became, in a sense, an enactment of a new set of social relations. Working men might enjoy their leisure, but they were now dependent on elite patrons who supplied a professionalized, nationally distributed product for mass consumption.

No spectator sport won a following as large or as devout as that of baseball. The game, however, was markedly different from that brought home by Civil War veterans. After shedding the gamblers and sharpers who made notorious the old "Beer and Whiskey League," the National League gained respectability and a broader financial base in the 1890s. It professionalized, tightened its organization, codified its rules, and raised its ticket prices. It also weathered the defection of many of its stars to the Baseball Brotherhood and turned back a loosely organized campaign to lower ticket prices (both of which won the support of Pittsburgh's Knights of Labor).[10]

But the game never became too respectable. Instead, it quickened its pace and began successfully to exploit its natural market, the urban working class. Although higher ticket prices and weekday games limited working-class spectatorship, when the factories in Pittsburgh let out on Saturday afternoon, hundreds of workers streamed to the ball park. Pittsburgh's team president, William C. Temple, exemplified the new breed of market-oriented baseball man. Originally an ironworker with a zest for sports, Temple became an enthusiastic inventor of baseball promotions, the most enduring of which was the National League All-Star game. Most important, he and his successors hired first-rate managers and players whose success on the field brought success at the box office.[11]

Thus, far more than did boxing, baseball gained respectability as a result of popular success and not vice versa. Important people took respectful note of it because they wanted customers or votes, and the change in attitude was striking. In 1887 Judge J. W. F. White (of Law and Order fame) administered to the defendant in a larceny case a severe lecture about the dangers of baseball:

> You should never go to a ball game. A majority of the persons connected with base ball bet on the result of the games, and all betting is gambling. Base ball is one of the evils of the day.[12]

Such a lecture would have been inconceivable in 1910, when the stolid William H. Taft became the first President to throw out the pitch that opened the baseball season. In that same year, John K. Tener, who would shortly accept the presidency of the National League, sat in the Governor's chair in Harrisburg. Earlier in his career, before rising from bank clerk to bank officer, Tener had been a professional baseball player. Indeed, in 1887, only a few days after Judge White's admonition and only a few miles from the court house, Tener had pitched an exhibition game in Pittsburgh.[13]

Thus, after Barney Dreyfuss's Pirates won their first World Series in 1909, the city's elite toasted the manager at a fancy reception in the Fort Pitt Hotel. After the party, Mayor William A. Magee, accompanied by National Guard units and political clubs, led a parade of thousands to Forbes Field, the new arena in Oakland. There Congressman J. F. Burke introduced each player to the crowd. And there is in fact an ironic sense in which the players needed introduction. Pirate heroes (with the exception of the great Honus Wagner, who came from nearby Mansfield) were nationally recruited professionals, not locals. Although amateur teams continued to flourish in Pittsburgh, they did so under the new dispensation in which the line between amateur and professional was sharply drawn. Thus, while neighborhood and factory teams continued to offer exercise and sociability, little remained of their audience or their public function. The heroes of the diamond now played in Forbes Field.[14]

By the onset of World War I, the outlines of a new popular culture had taken shape in Pittsburgh as elsewhere in America. Some features of that new pattern emerge clearly: the failure of leisure reform and the triumph of commercial amusements in shaping popular tastes; the beginnings of a shift from elite condemnation to elite toleration, even sponsorship, of popular amusements; and, despite continuing subcultural commitments, the integration of local, ethnic, and class fragments into mass audiences.

In regard to the last especially, mass culture, like partisan politics, may have constituted a "safety valve"[15] of popular discontents, giving release to suppressed urges for liberation and channelling them into relatively harmless paths. Such a mass culture was at once more alluring and more distant from everyday life than had been the culture of the plebeian city. In this sense, the inhabitants of the Steel City were part of the first generation of truly contemporary people. As sociologist Joseph Gusfield has argued, such people live in a world "immersed in and surrounded by a culture of dramatic excitement," one which gives compelling shape to everyday experience and replaces or subsumes more limited and pragmatically-rooted interpretations.[16] As working people were integrated into that culture, therefore, the commitment they made to defending it sometimes competed with that devoted to class struggle. It is not surprising, for example, that until the 1930s, organized labor in Pennsylvania fought as long and as hard for Sunday baseball and against Prohibition as it did for almost any other cause.[17]

As the latter indicates, however, the defense of mass culture could create opportunities for working-class mobilization. In this sense, both mass culture and ethnic subculture became symbolic grounds for the development of working-class consciousness in twentieth-century America, the latter reinforcing parochial resistance to "Americanization," the former incorporating all such separate efforts into an affirmation of wider commonality. One recent student of British working-class culture has noted that "twentieth-century cultural forms expressed and helped to forge a greater cultural homogeneity within the working class, or at least helped to erode older forms of divisions."[18] In Pittsburgh they did both, but the resultant homogeneity—implied, if not fully realized—comprehended more than just the working class. Well before sophisticated "captains of consciousness" turned their attention to shaping consumers' values and habits, working people had already constituted themselves into what Asa Briggs has called "a vast new audience," the boundaries of which lay well beyond those of the industrial working class.[19] Becoming part of that mass may have weakened immigrant workers' sense of themselves as a class, but it also offered them the opportunity to become American without having to identify with their enemies.

To whatever extent it empowered or coopted the working class, however, mass culture remained unconsolidated until after World War I. For at least another decade, working people in Pittsburgh escaped their round of brute labor and social isolation be alternately retreating into ethnic enclaves and foraying into the still marginal world of the free-and-easy. Unlike their plebeian predecessors, they could not count on the power of a local culture to integrate the scattered fragments of their lives. And unlike their successors in the 1930s, they could acknowledge only dimly a wider culture that affirmed a pluralistic version of American nationality. It was thus between two cultures that in 1919 they faced the massed power of corporate capital, public authority, and "public opinion."

# CHAPTER 9

# Epilogue: 1919 and Beyond

> For why this war? For why we buy Liberty Bonds? For mills? No, for freedom and America—for everybody.
> —a Polish steelworker, 1919

Given the nearly unrestrained repression inflicted upon immigrant workers in the 1919 steel strike, it may seem far-fetched to argue that those workers had begun to Americanize themselves in the early twentieth century.[1] In breaking the back of industrial unionism, Big Steel not only wielded its corporate power with immense daring and brutality, but also successfully enlisted the aid of local police, sheriffs, state troopers, and hundreds of vigilantes from among the "American" population. Choosing to interpret the strike as a "bolshevik" insurgency, the latter population clearly demonstrated its intention to defeat not only the strikers' economic demands but their efforts to achieve basic civil rights.

However, it is precisely because immigrant workers had for a decade prior to the strike demonstrated their intention to become American that their adversaries in 1919 strove to interpret them as un-American. In repudiating the "Hunkies'" claim to a place in America, the respectable classes of western Pennsylvania signalled in fact the extent to which that claim had been winning greater legitimacy in the second decade of the twentieth century. Thus, the steelworkers of western Pennsylvania earned the counterattack of 1919 not because they had failed to Americanize, but because they had, with increasing assertiveness, begun to succeed, and because their success was only part of a wider national reassessment of the meaning of "freedom and America."

Since the McKees Rocks strike of 1909, immigrant workers in Pittsburgh and beyond had shown that they were capable of overcoming ethnic differences and mobilizing tenacious labor struggles. They had also demonstrated a capacity to attract attention and support from liberal and radical elements in the middle class—from muckrakers, social surveyors, and politicians. As progressive insurgents in both major political parties increasingly lent at least rhetorical support to organized labor and to the idea of a regulatory and welfare state, they were prodded from below by an immigrant working class that had begun to sink roots[2] and to contend for power in places like Pittsburgh.

By the second decade of the twentieth century, the minority of immigrant workers eligible to vote was increasing, and that fact began to reshape politics in the Steel District. Although slow to respond to the new mood, established politicians in Pittsburgh—Republicans and Democrats, stalwarts and reformers—found themselves forced to search for new voters.

After the death of Christopher Magee in 1901, the Republican machine nearly disintegrated in the face of intense factionalism and a wave of scandals that exposed it as a pack of corrupt insiders, even more buccaneering than most critics had imagined.[3] Struggling to stabilize the machine, both the Flinn faction and the Bigelow faction sought support from different elements of the state Republican Party, and at the same time actively recruited new voters.

East end reformers, in alliance with the Democratic Party, likewise sought out the new vote. In the absence of detailed voting analysis, the success of such efforts cannot be gauged, but it is safe to suggest that the victory of the Democratic "progressives" in 1906 cannot simply be ascribed to their ability to mobilize elite cosmopolitans.[4] George Guthrie, elected mayor in 1906, was a patrician, but he was also a Debs elector in 1908 and a proponent of a modest version of municipal socialism.[5] Although he eventually alienated lower-class citizens with his saloon closings and other leisure reforms, he also equalized taxes, increased public employment in the 1908 recession, and funnelled a larger share of public money into schools and municipal services in poorer precincts, especially on the south side. Perhaps most important, he delivered on the promise that had probably been most responsible for drawing in 1906 the largest total vote in the history of municipal elections in Pittsburgh: He pushed to completion a municipal water treatment plant. After a decade of

Republican wrangling over contracts and other spoils, Guthrie's action removed from Pittsburgh its most dubious distinction, that of being the typhoid capital of the western world.[6] Since the scourge of typhoid fever had fallen disproportionately on residents of the poorest precincts, Guthrie's treatment plant was tangible evidence of the way in which intelligent voting could significantly improve the lives of working-class Pittsburghers.

Given Guthrie's reformist biases, working-class voters doubtless took note of other evidence in assessing his short-lived administration. More important, beyond major party politics, there is clear evidence that they had begun to endorse new alternatives. After the strike wave of 1908–1909, a surge of Socialist voting elected a mayor in Newcastle, Pennsylvania, and several sheriffs and councilmen in Pittsburgh and other steel towns in the district. In 1912, Eugene Debs won forty percent of the presidential vote in the most heavily immigrant mill precincts of Pittsburgh and western Pennsylvania.[7]

Socialist voting was clearly associated with increased labor militance, but it represented less a rejection of America than an effort to fulfill its promise. As Socialists in the United States competed with Wilsonian Democrats, Bull Moose Progressives, and stalwart Republicans for the new vote, politics demonstrated on a broader canvass what it had already shown on the state and local level: that despite corruption and organizational rigidity, the political process could deliver benefits to working-class voters. Something could be gained by voting for water treatment or against saloon closings, for factory inspection or against conspiracy laws, for workmen's compensation or against immigration restriction.

Thus, if politics constituted a "safety-valve" for working-class discontent, as Alan Dawley has argued,[8] it also served as a vehicle for real, if limited, achievement. As working-class voters used the vote, they also helped to reorient the political process, prodding "progressives" and "urban liberals" to abandon narrower conceptions of "freedom and America" and to generate broader ones, which new citizens could more readily embrace.

The experience of war mobilization in 1917 indicated the extent to which immigrant workers were ready to incorporate their lives into a broadened version of the American way. With an enthusiasm that surprised their betters, "Hunkies" and other workers affirmed a commitment to the nation that fought to make the world safe for democracy and to reform its domestic social order.[9] In parades, bond drives, and recruitment campaigns, immigrant Americans responded to the new invitation—from bosses, politicians, and patriots of all kinds—to join "our country." Because that campaign accompanied improved wartime wages and working conditions and an unprecedented legitimation of organized labor by the Wilson administration's mobilization apparatus—because, as William Z. Foster put it, "The gods were indeed fighting on the side of Labor"[10]—the invitation was all the more convincing. Indeed, as workers responded, steelmasters and other "Americans" feared that the invitation might have been misinterpreted. Those suspicions proved well-founded when, in 1919, steelworkers sought to secure and extend the gains made possible by the exigencies of war.

In crushing the strike, steeltown America seemed to succeed in putting the genie back into the bottle. "Hunkies" were readily separated from their native allies in the labor movement and from their erstwhile patrons in the Wilson Administration. The status quo that had prevailed before 1917—perhaps, before 1909—was reimposed. But the victory, if massive, was not total. The Red Scare and the anti-labor offensive never succeeded entirely in wresting from the immigrant working class the banner it had snatched in the years of mobilization. Even in the midst of repression in 1919, workers assailed their enemies' "war upon organized labor" as "un-American." In the town of Clairton, for example, when state troopers (called "Cossacks") rode down upon the uniformed and flag-bearing veterans who marched along with their laboring brethren, workers fought back "in defense of our flag."[11] Far more than any act of renunciation, such working-class determination to contend for control of patriotic symbols provoked those who preferred the "Hunkies" to be either subservient or invisible.

Defeat no doubt disillusioned and embittered many working-class patriots. Had the wartime experience been unprecedented, not just in degree but in kind, that disillusionment might have been total. In fact, however, the war merely realized in a dramatic and concentrated way what had been emergent in the politics and culture of the pre-war years. It showed that, given the hope of achieving some measure of security and freedom, immigrant working people would choose to build a future in industrial America.

Too radical for those who mastered events in 1919, the demands of immigrant workers were modest enough for those who, in the 1930s, redefined in more inclusive and perhaps more clever terms the meaning of American citizenship. In a city so dominated by Big Steel, where organized labor and the Democratic Party remained unusually weak until the Great Depression, the path to that future was narrower and less certain than in many other places. The repression of radicals after 1919 further narrowed the range of possibilities for a new generation. Yet, even in Pittsburgh, the way had already been pointed, if not paved, by the workers who had ventured beyond the ethnic retreat to forge new links of class and national solidarity. It had also been pointed by those progressive reformers who came to recognize the parochial character of their own values, and who insisted that building a decent social order required addressing workers' fundamental demands for security and dignity. And it had been pointed by politicians and merchants of leisure—such as Edward Bigelow, the park builder, John Harris, the movie king, and William Magee, patron of the baseball crowd—who learned to tolerate, sometimes to celebrate, and often to profit from new audiences and constituencies. Along that compromised way, despite lockouts, Red Scares, and Prohibition crusades, another America could nearly always be discerned, one that legitimized ethnic roots, ridiculed pious self-righteousness, and opened the door to a society as apparently democratic as those audiences at the movies, the amusement park, and the baseball field.

# Notes

---

## Abbreviations

*Manuscript Collections:*

AIS: Archives of Industrial Society, University of Pittsburgh
CLP: Carnegie Library of Pittsburgh
HSWP: Historical Society of Western Pennsylvania

*Government Publications:*

U.S. Census reports will be cited in simplified form, e.g., U.S. Census 1880, vol. 2, pp. 107–108. Reports of the Pennsylvania Bureau of Industrial Statistics will be cited similarly, e.g., Pa. Statistics 1887, p. 125.

*Organizations:*

AAISW: Amalgamated Association of Iron and Steel Workers
LA 300: Knights of Labor, Local Assembly 300, Window Glass Workers Association
DA 3: Knights of Labor, District Assembly 3

*Newspapers:*

*NLT: National Labor Tribune*

*Journals:*

*WPHM: Western Pennsylvania Historical Magazine*

*Pittsburgh City Directories:*

Identified simply by date; full citation in bibliography.

## Notes to Introduction

1. James Parton, "Pittsburg," *Atlantic Monthly,* January 1868, p. 17. It should be noted that the modern spelling of Pittsburgh—with the final *h*— was not standardized until the early twentieth century. When it appears otherwise in quoted material, the reader should assume that the variant spelling is in the original.

## Notes to Chapter 1

1. On the 1877 upheaval, see Robert V. Bruce, *1877: Year of Violence* (Indianapolis 1959), pp. 115–183; Clarence E. Macartney, *Right Here in Pittsburgh* (Pittsburgh 1937), pp. 110–116; James Caye, Jr., "Violence in the Nineteenth Century Community: The Roundhouse Riot, Pittsburgh, 1877" (Unpub. manuscript); Henry Mann, *Our Police: A History of the Pittsburgh Police Force* (Pittsburgh 1889), pp. 101–114; Pennsylvania General Assembly, *Report of the Committee Appointed to Investigate the Railroad Riots in July, 1877* (Harrisburg, Pa. 1878); Edward C. Martin, *History of the Great Riots* (Philadelphia 1877); *NLT,* 7 January 1882; Pittsburgh Chamber of Commerce, *The Insurrection among the Railway Employees . . .* (Pittsburgh 1877). See also Herbert G. Gutman, "Trouble on the Railroads in 1873–1874: Prelude to the 1877 Crisis?" *Labor History* 2 (1961), pp. 215–235, reprinted in the author's *Work, Culture, and Society in Industrializing America* (New York 1977).

2. On McCarthy and local politics, see Allen H. Kerr, "The Mayors and Recorders of Pittsburgh, 1816–1951 (Unpub. manuscript, HSWP), pp. 127–175.

3. Entry for 24 July 1877, B.F. Jones Diary, Jones and Laughlin Corporation Papers, AIS.

4. Ibid.; see also Bruce, *1877,* p. 120; Macartney, *Right Here in Pittsburgh,* p. 111.

5. *NLT,* 7 January 1882; Mann, *Our Police,* pp. 111–114; Kerr, "Mayors of Pittsburgh," pp. 175–176, 180; John W. Bennett, "Iron Workers in Woods Run and Johnstown: The Union Era 1865–1895" (Ph.D. dissertation, University of Pittsburgh 1977), p. 105; Shelton Stromquist, "Working Class Organization and Industrial Change in Pittsburgh, 1860–1890" (Unpub. manuscript), p. 19.

6. Caye, "Violence," p. 54.

## Notes to Chapter 2

1. U.S. Census 1870, vol. 1, p. 776; U.S. Census 1880, vol. 18, p. 862; U.S. Census 1890, vol. 7, pp. 403–405; Peter Temin, *Iron and Steel in Nineteenth-Century America* (Cambridge, Mass. 1964), ch. 3; James Kitson, "Iron and Steel Industries of America," *Contemporary Review,* May 1891, p. 630; Kenneth Warren, *The American Steel Industry, 1850–1970* (London 1973), pp. 35–38.

2. U.S Census 1880, vol. 2, pp. 11–12, 15; vol. 18, p. 857; Warren C. Scoville, *Revolution in Glassmaking: Entrepreneurship and Technological*

*Change in the American Industry, 1880–1920* (Cambridge, Mass. 1948), ch. 1; Pearce Davis, *The Development of the American Glass Industry* (Cambridge, Mass. 1949), ch. 5 and pp. 118–120.

3. The following two paragraphs are based on U.S. Census 1860, vol. 2, pp. 338–339, 493–495; U.S Census 1870, vol. 3, pp. 562, 721; U.S. Census 1890, vol. 7, pp. 348–352; Temin, *Iron and Steel,* pt. 1; Warren, *American Steel,* ch. 2.

4. Temin, *Iron and Steel,* chs. 4, 5, 7, 8; Harold C. Livesay, *Andrew Carnegie and the Rise of Big Business* (Boston 1975), p. 105; Robert Hessen, *Steel Titan: The Life of Charles M. Schwab* (New York 1975), pp. 61–63.

5. Temin, *Iron and Steel,* p. 95.

6. Ibid., pp. 87, 109–111; Livesay, *Carnegie,* pp. 83–84.

7. U.S. Census 1870, vol. 3, pp. 562, 721; U.S. Census 1880, vol. 2, pp. 338–339; U.S. Census 1890, vol. 6, pt. 2, pp. 450–459.

8. David Montgomery, "Workers' Control of Machine Production in the Nineteenth Century," *Labor History* 17 (1976), pp. 489. See also Daniel Nelson, *Managers and Workers: Origins of the New Factory System in the United States 1880–1920* (Madison, Wisc. 1975), ch. 3; Benson Soffer, "A Theory of Trade Union Development: The Role of the 'Autonomous Workman'," *Labor History* 1 (1960), pp. 141–163; Bennett, "Iron Workers," pp. 40–74.

9. Ralph Keeler and Harry Fenn, "The Taking of Pittsburgh, Part III," *Every Saturday,* 18 March 1871, p. 262; for other contemporary accounts, see John H. Bridge, *The Inside History of the Carnegie Steel Company: A Romance of Millions* (New York 1903), p. 142–143; James J. Davis, *The Iron Puddler: My Life in the Rolling Mills and What Came of it* (Indianapolis 1922), pp. 85–111; see also Bennett, "Iron Workers," pp. 10–25. N.B. The terms "boiler" and "puddler" were interchangeable, though local preference usually made one or the other standard in a given community.

10. Keeler and Fenn, "The Taking of Pittsburgh, Part III," p. 263; for a detailed description of glassblowing in nineteenth-century France see Joan W. Scott, *The Glassworkers of Carmaux* (Cambridge, Mass. 1974), ch. 2.

11. J. Davis, *Iron Puddler,* pp. 110–111; U.S. Senate Committee on Education and Labor, *Report upon the Relations between Labor and Capital* (Washington, D.C. 1885), vol. 1, p. 1149; "The City of Pittsburgh," *Harper's New Monthly Magazine,* December 1880, pp. 63–64; Scoville, *Revolution in Glassmaking,* p. 13.

12. "The City of Pittsburgh," p. 63; Bennett, "Iron Workers," pp. 10–39; Scoville, *Revolution in Glassmaking,* pp. 13, 27–29; P. Davis, *American Glass Industry,* pp. 120–123; see also Mary E. Bakewell, "Pittsburgh Fifty Years Ago as I Recall It," *WPHM* 30 (1947), pp. 1–8.

13. U.S. Senate, *Labor and Capital,* vol. 1, pp. 1145–1146.

14. Ibid., vol. 1, p. 27; vol. 2, pp. 7, 14; Jesse S. Robinson, *The Amalgamated Association of Iron, Steel and Tin Workers* (Baltimore 1912), p. 105–109.

15. John Fritz, *Autobiography* (New York 1912), p. 53.

16. LA 300, *Report of Fourth National Convention* (Pittsburgh 1886), pp. 23, 27; U.S. Senate, *Labor and Capital,* vol. 1, p. 21; Robinson, *Amalgamated Association,* pp. 112–113; John A. Fitch, *The Steel Workers* (New York 1910), p. 177.

17. Pa. Statistics 1872–1873, p. C.6; LA 300, *Report of Third National Convention* (Pittsburgh 1884), p. 15; P. Davis, *American Glass Industry,* pp. 128–129; Montgomery, "Worker's Control," p. 493; U.S. Senate, *Labor and Capital,* vol. 1, p. 30; Keeler and Fenn, "The Taking of Pittsburgh, Part II," *Every Saturday,* 11 March 1871, p. 238. Flint and Green Glass workers usually took one month off: Pa. Statistics 1876–1877, pp. 536–539.

18. Parton, "Pittsburg," p. 33; see also Kitson, "Iron and Steel," pp. 629–630; "The City of Pittsburgh," p. 64; U.S. Senate, *Labor and Capital,* vol. 1, pp. 1138–1139.

19. See also U.S. Senate, *Labor and Capital,* vol. 1, p. 21; vol. 2, pp. 25–27; U.S. Census 1880, vol. 2, p. 50; P. Davis, *American Glass Industry,* pp. 119–120.

20. U.S. Senate, *Labor and Capital,* vol. 1, pp. 20–21.

21. Clarence D. Long, *Wages and Earnings in the United States 1860–1890* (Princeton 1960), pp. 89, 98, 105, 109–118. While earnings in the U.S. rose by 60 percent between 1870 and 1890, those in glass rose 73 percent, in iron, 72 percent.

22. Warren, *American Steel,* p. 49.

23. Pa. Statistics 1887, p. C.28.

24. Pa. Statistics 1876–1877, pp. 686–687; also *Post,* 30 April 1863.

25. Pa. Statistics 1876–1877, pp. 686–687; also U.S. Senate, *Labor and Capital,* vol. 2, p. 22.

26. Nelson, *Managers and Workers,* p. 20; see Montgomery, "Workers' Control," pp. 489–491, on the translation into an industrial setting of pre-industrial work values; see also Brian D. Palmer, *A Culture of Conflict: Skilled Workers and Industrial Capitalism in Hamilton, Ontario, 1860–1914* (Montreal 1979); Daniel T. Rodgers, "Tradition, Modernity, and the American Industrial Worker: Reflections and Critique," *Journal of Interdisciplinary History* 7 (1977), pp. 655–681.

27. Nelson, *Managers and Workers,* pp. 35–40; Montgomery, "Workers' Control," p. 487.

28. John H. Ashworth, *The Helper and American Trade Unions* (Baltimore 1915), p. 30–31, 49, 75–76; Nelson, *Managers and Workers,* p. 20; P. Davis, *American Glass Industry,* p. 129.

29. Pa. Statistics 1887, p. C.22–25.

30. Ibid., pp. C.12–28; Pa. Statistics 1879–1880, p. 208n; Ashworth, *The Helper,* pp. 73–74, 125–126; U.S. Senate, *Labor and Capital,* vol. 1, p. 21; and see Table 1.

31. Stromquist, "Working Class Organization," pp. 3–5, 105–107, 235–236, 384.

32. Montgomery, "Workers' Control," pp. 489–494; the remainder of the paragraph draws on Charles G. Foster, "The Amalgamated Association of Iron and Steel Workers," in Pa. Statistics 1887, p. G.1, and Fitch, *Steel Workers,* pp. 76–77.

33. J. Davis, *Iron Puddler,* pp. 1114–115.

34. Ibid., pp. 85, 96; Soffer, "Autonomous Workman," p. 151; U.S. Senate, *Labor and Capital,* vol. 1, p. 26; vol. 2, p. 21; P. Davis, *American Glass Industry,* p. 129.

35. U.S. Senate, *Labor and Capital,* vol. 2, p. 15; J. Davis, *Iron Puddler,* pp. 62, 110–111.

36. Keeler and Fenn, "The Taking of Pittsburgh, Part III," pp. 262–263; U.S. Senate, *Labor and Capital*, vo. 1, p. 30; compare health hazards in the French industry in Scott, *Glassworkers of Carmaux*, pp. 42–43.

37. Kitson, "Iron and Steel," pp. 629–630; U.S. Senate, *Labor and Capital*, vol. 1, pp. 1138–1139; vol. 2, p. 8; Parton, "Pittsburg," p. 33; "The City of Pittsburgh," p. 64.

38. Robinson, *Amalgamated Association*, pp. 51–53, 126–127; Stromquist, "Working Class Organization," pp. 10–11; Temin, *Iron and Steel*, p. 227; James M. Swank, *History of the Manufacture of Iron . . .* (Philadelphia 1892), pp. 448–451; *Iron Age*, 13 September 1888; *Journal of United Labor*, 11 July 1889; J. Fetter to T. Powderly, 7 March 1880, *Terence V. Powderly Papers*, microfilm reel 2, University of Pittsburgh Library (original in Catholic University of America).

39. Swank, *History*, p. 393; David Brody, *Steelworkers in America: The Nonunion Era* (Cambridge, Mass. 1960), ch. 1.

40. Livesay, *Carnegie*, chs. 6–7; Hessen, *Steel Titan*, pp. 25–26; Temin, *Iron and Steel*, ch. 8.

41. Foster, "Amalgamated Association," pp. G.25–26; Bennett, "Iron Workers," ch. 2; see also Daniel J. Walkowitz, *Worker City, Company Town: Iron- and Cotton-Worker Protest in Troy and Cohoes, New York, 1855–1884* (Urbana, Ill. 1978), chs. 3, 6, 7. In "Strikes in Nineteenth-Century America," *Social Science History* 4 (1980), p. 82, David Montgomery argues that the incidence of strikes did not simply vary in response to economic cycles; however, my concern here is not with strikes alone, but more generally with labor organization, the pace of which does seem to have varied in response to cycles.

42. Nelson, *Managers and Workers*, p. 40.

43. *Post*, 22 and 23 April, 15 May 1863; Foster, "Amalgamated Association," p. G.1; Fitch, *Steel Workers*, pp. 76–77.

44. Stromquist, "Working Class Organization," pp. 5–7; Robinson, *Amalgamated Association*, pp. 138–141.

45. Montgomery, "Workers' Control," pp. 492–493.

46. David Montgomery, *Beyond Equality: Labor and the Radical Republicans 1862–1872* (New York 1967), pp. 390–392; George E. McNeill, ed., *The Labor Movement: The Problem of Today* (New York, 1887), pp. 273–274; Stromquist, "Working Class Organization," pp. 18–19. On Armstrong, see Montgomery, *Beyond Equality*, pp. 177, 208, 462–463; *NLT*, 8 and 15 October 1887; *Commercial Gazette*, 3 October 1887.

47. *NLT*, 9 July, 6 August 1881; *Post*, 8 July 1867; Montgomery, *Beyond Equality*, pp. 211, 389–392; James A. Beck, "The Old Fifth Ward of Pittsburgh," *WPHM* 28 (1945), p. 117; Kerr, "Mayors of Pittsburgh," pp. 143–145.

48. John R. Commons et al., *History of Labour in the United States*, 4 vols. (New York 1918–1935), vol. 2, pp. 201–202.

49. AAISW, *Constitution* (Columbus 1876), pp. 6–7; Robinson, *Amalgamated Association*, p. 140.

50. AAISW, *Proceedings of Fourth Convention* (Pittsburgh 1879), p. 224.

51. Robinson, *Amalgamated Association*, p. 21; James Holt, "Trade Unionism in the British and U.S. Steel Industries, 1880–1914: A Comparative Study," *Labor History* 18 (1977), pp. 9–10.

52. P. Davis, *American Glass Industry*, pp. 127–131; "The Passing of the National Window Glass Workers," *Monthly Labor Review* 29 (1929), p. 1, 6–7; Norman Ware, *The Labor Movement in the United States 1860–1895* (New York 1929), pp. 196–199; Leon Watillon, *The Knights of Labor in Belgium*, trans. Frederic Meyers (Los Angeles 1959); LA 300, *Third Convention*, p. 6, and *Report of Fifth National Convention* (Pittsburgh 1889), pp. 14ff; Terence V. Powderly, *Thirty Years of Labor 1859–1889* (Columbus 1889), pp. 342–345.

53. McNeill, *Labor Movement*, p. 251; Ware, *Labor Movement*, pp. 32–45; Stromquist, "Working Class Organization," p. 8.

54. *NLT*, 31 October 1874.

55. *Ibid.*, 19 December 1874, 6 February 1875, 22 and 29 July 1876, 20 August 1879, 7 January 1882; McNeill, *Labor Movement*, p. 606. On Callow, see *Gazette*, 13 April, 22 and 24 May 1867; *Peoples Monthly*, June 1871, p. 1; Montgomery, *Beyond Equality*, p. 463.

56. *NLT*, 21 June 1874, 4 December 1875, 1 July 1876, 17 February 1877, 3 January 1880, 22 January 1881.

57. *NLT*, 15 January, 22 and 29 July, 15 and 30 August 1877.

58. *NLT*, 13 March 1875.

59. On this issue, Montgomery, *Beyond Equality*, and Alan Dawley, *Class and Community: The Industrial Revolution in Lynn* (Cambridge, Mass. 1976) are illuminating. See also essays by Sean Wilentz and Leon Fink in Michael H. Frisch and Daniel J. Walkowitz, eds., *Working-Class America* (Urbana, Ill. 1983).


### Notes to Chapter 3

1. Keeler and Fenn, "The Taking of Pittsburgh, Part IV," *Every Saturday*, 25 March 1871, p. 274.

2. In "Beyond Class: The Decline of Industrial Labor and Leisure," *Telos* 28 (1976), pp. 55–80, John Alt overstates the autonomy of craft-related culture within the industrial city, in an otherwise enlightening discussion. For a broader conception of the cultural context within which craftsmen and other nineteenth-centuiry urbanites lived, see Neil Harris, "Four Stages of Cultural Growth: The American City," *Indiana Historical Society Lectures: History and the Role of the City in American Life* (Indianapolis 1972); Harris's "second stage" corresponds closely to this description of plebeian culture in Pittsburgh. In "Patrician Society, Plebeian Culture," *Journal of Social History* 7 (1974), pp. 382–405, E. P. Thompson uses the term "plebeian" to refer to a culture that proceeds clearly neither from the top down nor the bottom up, although it does include a "horizontal solidarity" whose center of gravity is among the lower classes. While I borrow the term, I need to qualify its usage here. Like the eighteenth-century English variety, plebeian culture in nineteenth-century Pittsburgh included commercial as well as customary pastimes (although the latter were relatively more important in England); it nurtured oppositional movements, but it was not "proto-revolutionary;" it implicated workers in a web of relationships and meanings that were not fully under their control, but it was not "deferential." Unlike the culture Thompson describes, however, plebeian culture in Pitts-

burgh was not "the other side of the medal" of hegemonic elite culture. Indeed it was toward hegemony that the steel elite moved later in the century, but until that time there was nothing resembling a patriciate in Pittsburgh.

3. U.S. Census 1880, vol. 1, pp. 536–538, 895; see also Susan J. Kleinberg, "Technology's Stepdaughters: The Impact of Industrialization upon Working Class Women, Pittsburgh 1865–1890" (Ph.D. dissertation, University of Pittsburgh, 1973), ch. 2.

4. Parton, "Pittsburg," p. 17; also Keeler and Fenn, "The Taking of Pittsburgh, Part II," p. 238.

5. See sources for Table 3, and U.S. Census 1880, vol. 2, pp. 381, 426; also see Joel A. Tarr, *Transportation Innovation and Changing Spatial Patterns: Pittsburgh, 1850–1910* (Pittsburgh 1972), pp. 2–3, and Bernard J. Sauers, "A Political Process of Urban Growth: Consolidation of the South Side with the City of Pittsburgh, 1872," *Pennsylvania History* 41 (1974), pp. 265–269.

6. Tarr, *Transportation,* pp. 11–13; U.S. Census 1880, vol. 18, p. 863; *Commercial Gazette,* 8 December 1886; *Evening Telegraph,* 23 October 1873; on the rural character of Pittsburgh's immediate hinterland, see William G. Johnston, *Life and Reminiscences from Birth to Manhood* (New York 1901), pp. 106–108, 119–120, 282–285; Keeler and Fenn, "The Taking of Pittsburgh, Part IV," p. 274; *A Visit to the States . . .* (London 1887), pp. 342, 348.

7. Sam Bass Warner, *Streetcar Suburbs: The Process of Growth in Boston 1870–1900* (Cambridge, Mass. 1962), ch. 3.

8. Tarr, *Transportation,* pp. 13–17.

9. Samuel P. Hays, "The Development of Pittsburgh as a Social Order," *WPHM* 57 (1974), pp. 444–445.

10. *Atlas of the Cities of Pittsburgh and Allegheny* (Philadelphia 1882); Kleinberg, "Technology's Stepdaughters," ch. 2; Victor Walsh, "'A Fanatic Heart': The Cause of Irish-American Nationalism in Pittsburgh during the Gilded Age," *Journal of Social History* 15 (1981), pp. 189–195.

11. Hays, "Development of Pittsburgh," pp. 443–444; Bennett, "Iron Workers," pp. 121–123, 126; Beck, "Old Fifth Ward," p. 118; P. W. Siebert, "Old Bayardstown," *WPHM* 9 (1926), p. 94, 179; *NLT,* 19 December 1874, 22 and 29 January, 8 April 1876, 29 January, 29 July 1887.

12. Parton, "Pittsburg," pp. 19, 31–32; see also George H. Thurston, *Pittsburgh as It Is* (Pittsburgh 1857), p. 37; Keeler and Fenn, "The Taking of Pittsburgh, Part IV," p. 274.

13. John N. Ingham, "The American Urban Upper Class: Cosmopolitans or Locals?" *Journal of Urban History* 2 (1975), pp. 70–75, and "Rags to Riches Revisited: The Effect of City Size and Related Factors on the Recruitment of Business Leaders," *Journal of American History* 63 (1976), pp. 618–621, 624–627, 634; see also Elizabeth Moorhead, *Whirling Spindle: The Story of a Pittsburgh Family* (Pittsburgh 1942), p. 208, and Parton, "Pittsburg," p. 32.

14. Pittsburgh Central High School, *Class Book of 1880* (Pittsburgh 1906), pp. 77–80.

15. Moorhead, *Whirling Spindle,* pp. 262–269; Shakespeare Reading Club Programs, HSWP.

16. Johnston, *Life*, pp. 114, 162, 166–171.
17. Moorhead, *Whirling Spindle*, pp. 251–256; for local Methodist objections to theater, see Pittsburgh's *Christian Advocate*, 12 July 1877 and 10 November 1887; Macartney, *Right Here in Pittsburgh*, pp. 32–33.
18. The unassertiveness of Pittsburgh's social elite contrasts with the large public role played by elites in eastern cities. In Boston at midcentury, for example, "no serious disagreement as to the utility of culture for business families" hindered the shaping of "a durable (and worthy) upper class within the capitalist order": Ronald Story, "Class and Culture in Boston: The Atheneum, 1807–1860," *American Quarterly* 27 (1975), pp. 178–199; see also M. J. Heale, "From City Fathers to Social Critics: Humanitarianism and Government in New York, 1790–1860," *Journal of American History* 63 (1976), pp. 21–41; Sam Bass Warner, *The Private City: Philadelphia in Three Periods of Its Growth* (Philadelphia 1968), ch. 5.
19. A review of city directories from 1860 to 1890 reveals very little occupational or residential persistence among musical personnel. For occasional musical entertainments, see *Post,* 30 April 1863, 21 June 1867; *Gazette,* 19 July 1867; *Christian Advocate,* 22 December 1881; *Commercial Gazette,* 16 November, 8 December 1886, 2 July, 1 October 1887; George T. Fleming, *History of Pittsburgh and Environs* (New York and Chicago 1922), vol. 2, p. 624; Edward G. Baynham, "A History of Pittsburgh Music, 1758–1958" (Unpub. manuscript, CLP), vol. 1, passim; records of the Philomathic Club in the Hailman Papers, HSWP; also see Donald M. Goodfellow, "Centenary of a Pittsburgh Library," *WPHM* 31 (1948), pp. 21–25.
20. See receipts for purchases of sporting goods in the Albree Papers, HSWP; Pittsburgh Gymnastic Association, *By-Laws and Constitution* (Pittsburgh 1860) in Adams Papers, HSWP; *Directory of Pittsburgh and Allegheny Cities* (Pittsburgh 1870), p. 22.
21. On McKelvey, information from directories was used to supplement *Post,* 27 April, 6 and 19 May 1863, and *Evening Telegraph,* 25 October 1873.
22. Kankakee Sporting Club, *Constitution and By-Laws* (Pittsburgh 1872); Sportsmen's Association of Western Pennsylvania, *Charter . . . and By-Laws* (Pittsburgh 1882); *Sportsmen's Association of Cheat Mountain* (Pittsburgh 1889); see also certificate of membership in the South Fork Fishing and Hunting Club (1882) in the Semple Papers, HSWP.
23. *Post,* 29 May, 6 and 10 June 1863; *Gazette,* 2 September 1867; see picnic notices and excursion receipts in the Barr, Slease, and Albree Papers, all in HSWP; on the post–Civil War boom in rural excursions, see John Rickard Betts, *America's Sporting Heritage: 1850–1950* (Reading, Mass. 1974), p. 173.
24. Parton, "Pittsburg," p. 35.
25. Keeler and Fenn, "The Taking of Pittsburgh, Part IV," p. 274.
26. Parton, "Pittsburg," pp. 34–35; also *Post,* 27 May 1863. Robert Layton of the Knights of Labor decried the Sunday draping of these windows since they constituted an important part of working-class recreation: U.S. Senate, *Labor and Capital,* vol. 1, p. 31.
27. On Blythe see Bruce W. Chambers, *The World of David Gilmour Blythe* (Washington 1980); Dorothy Miller, *The Life and Works of David Blythe* (Pittsburgh 1950); John O'Connor, Jr.., "David Gilmour Blythe,

Artist," *WPHM* 27 (1944), pp. 29–36; Dorothy Daniel, "The Sanitary Fair," *WPHM* 41 (1958), pp. 154, 159–160; *Gazette*, 14 June 1864.

28. Thurston, *Pittsburgh as It Is*, p. 202; *Post*, 14 June 1863. I am indebted to David G. Wilkins, Professor of Fine Arts and Director of the University Gallery, University of Pittsburgh, for allowing me to peruse an unpublished manuscript and other materials pertaining to the nineteenth-century art scene in Pittsburgh; see the exhibition catalog, *Art in Nineteenth-Century Pittsburgh* (Pittsburgh 1977), to which Prof. Wilkins contributed an introduction.

29. Charles T. Dawson, *Our Firemen: The History of the Pittsburgh Fire Department* (Pittsburgh 1889), p. 120; *Gazette*, 23 February 1850; *Commercial Gazette*, 18 October, 16 November, 1886; *NLT*, 8 and 29 July 1876; *Christian Advocate*, 19 July 1877; Russell B. Nye, *The Unembarrassed Muse: The Popular Arts in America* (New York 1970), pp. 186–188.

30. *Gazette*, 18 July 1867; *Evening Telegraph*, 15 July 1876; *Commercial Gazette*, 13 October 1882, 5 July, 1 October 1887; *Post*, 1 September 1887; Baynham, "Pittsburgh Music," vol. 1, pp. 7–8; picnic notice in the Barr Papers, HSWP; concert program dated 19 November 1865, in Vigilant Fire Company Papers, CLP; Siebert, "Old Bayardstown," p. 98; Nye, *Unembarrassed Muse*, pp. 194–195.

31. On Weiss, information in city directories was used to supplement *Evening Telegraph*, 11 July 1873; *Commercial Gazette*, 24 June, 2 July 1887.

32. On Christy, see directories 1870–1890 and Beck, "Old Fifth Ward," p. 124; on musicians John McMeniman, Jacob Byerly, John N. Forger, and Jerome Staley, see directories 1870–1900, *Gazette*, 19 July 1867, and *Evening Telegraph*, 23 October 1873.

33. *Commercial Gazette*, 13 October 1882.

34. Baynham, "Pittsburgh Music," vol. 1, pp. 143–145; Moorhead, *Whirling Spindle*, pp. 270–271; *Commercial Gazette*, 15 November 1886, 15 October 1887.

35. George Korson, ed., *Pennsylvania Songs and Legends* (Philadelphia 1949), pp. 426–427; Bennett, "Iron Workers," pp. 119–125; *NLT*, 1 April 1876, 10 February 1877; see also Siebert, "Old Bayardstown," p. 92.

36. On American theater in the nineteenth century, see Nye, *Unembarrassed Muse*, pp. 140–168, and David Grimsted, *Melodrama Unveiled: American Theater and Culture, 1800–1850* (Chicago 1968). The following account of theater life in Pittsburgh draws heavily upon James A. Lowrie, "A History of the Pittsburgh Stage, 1861–1891" (Ph.D. dissertation, University of Pittsburgh 1943); another useful source is the file of nineteenth-century theater programs in the Carnegie Library of Pittsburgh; see also regular reviews and comment on the theater in the *NLT, Post, Gazette, Commercial Gazette,* and *Evening Telegraph.*

37. Parton, "Pittsburg," pp. 34–35; Keeler and Fenn, "The Taking of Pittsburgh, Part IV," P. 274.

38. Comments of Harry Ellsler,, treasurer of the Opera House, quoted in Lowrie, "Pittsburgh Stage," p. 178; Johnston, *Life*, pp. 112–114; *Gazette*, 17 August 1866.

39. *Post*, 11 and 12 May 1863; see also Andrew Carnegie, *Autobiography of Andrew Carnegie* (New York 1920), pp. 46–50. On street urchins, see *Peoples Monthly*, February 1872, p. 143.

40. Gareth Stedman Jones, "Working-Class Culture and Working-Class Politics in London, 1870–1900; Notes on the Remaking of a Working Class," *Journal of Social History* 7 (1974), p. 491.

41. Lowrie, "Pittsburgh Stage," pp. 142, 150; *Gazette,* 3 September 1867; *Post,* 22 May 1876.

42. Percy F. Smith, *Memory's Milestones: Reminiscences of Seventy Years of a Busy Life in Pittsburgh* (Pittsburgh 1918), p. 26, 37; for a distinguished visitor's interesting view of the American stage and, in particular, of ethnic characterizations, see Knut Hamsun, *The Cultural Life of Modern America,* trans. B. Morgridge (Cambridge, Mass. 1969), pp. 90–103; on Uncle Tom, see Nye, *Unembarrassed Muse,* pp. 153–155, and *Post,* 15 May 1898.

43. On Henderson's company, see the Palmer Papers, HSWP, and *Post,* 29 April 1863, 24 and 28 June 1867; on the Ellslers, see John A. Ellsler, *The Stage Memories of John A. Ellsler* (Cleveland 1950), pp. 142, 144, 146, 157–158; William G. Rose, *Cleveland: The Making of a City* (Cleveland 1950), pp. 228, 259–260, 368, 382, 404–405, 479.

44. On *The Lower Million,* see Lowrie, "Pittsburgh Stage," pp. 138–139, and reviews in *Post* and *Gazette,* 22 November 1878; on Campbell, see Smith, *Memory's Milestones,* p. 84.

45. Cited in Philip S. Klein and Ari Hoogenboom, *A History of Pennsylvania* (New York 1973), p. 354; see J. Davis, *Iron Puddler,* pp. 68–70, for a description of popular involvement in local theater in Sharon, an iron and steel town north of Pittsburgh.

46. In *Melodrama Unveiled,* p. 248, Grimsted has noted that such plays "took the lives of the common people seriously and paid much respect to their superior purity and wisdom. It elevated them often into the aristocracy, always into a world charged with action, excitement and a sense of wonder."

47. For examples of advertised betting, see *Post,* 27 April, 6 and 19 May, 25 June 1863; *NLT,* 2 December 1876; *Commercial Gazette,* 15, 16, 22, and 30 November 1886, 4 July, 17 October 1887. On traditional pastimes, see Henry Oliver Evans, "Life in Pittsburgh in 1845," *WPHM* 28 (1945), p. 24; Chet Smith, *Pittsburgh and Western Pennsylvania Sports Hall of Fame* (Pittsburgh 1969), p. 12; Beck, "Old Fifth Ward," p. 124.

48. Beck, "Old Fifth Ward," p. 118; Siebert, "Old Bayardstown," p. 94.

49. *Post,* 24 June 1867; *Gazette,* 2 and 7 September 1867; *Evening Telegraph,* 23 October 1873; *NLT,* 1 and 18 July 1876; Frederick G. Leib, *The Pittsburgh Pirates* (New York 1948), pp. 3–40; William E. Benswanger, "Professional Baseball in Pittsburgh," *WPHM* 30 (1947), pp. 9–12; a disapproving description of the post-war baseball "craze" appears in a letter to Joseph A. Albree from his father, 19 September 1865, in the Albree Papers, HSWP; P. Smith, *Memory's Milestones,* p. 23; see also Betts, *America's Sporting Heritage,* pp. 89–98.

50. On fishing clubs, see *NLT,* 28 January 1882; Stefan Lorant, *Pittsburgh: The Story of an American City* (Garden City, N.Y. 1964), pp. 168–169; Kleinberg, "Technology's Stepdaughters," p. 83. On the boating craze in post-war America see John Allen Krout, *Annals of American Sport* (New Haven 1929), p. 79; Samuel Crowther and Arthur Ruhl, *Rowing and Track Athletics* (New York 1905), pp. 147–160; Robert F. Kelley, *American Rowing: Its Background and Traditions* (New York 1932), pp. 25–26; Dale A. Somers,

NOTES

*The Rise of Sports in New Orleans, 1850–1900* (Baton Rouge 1972), pp. 151–153.

51. On the Blackmore campaign, see Kerr, "Mayors of Pittsburgh," pp. 143–145.

52. Of the twenty oarsmen mentioned in the *Evening Telegraph,* 15 July 1876, only five could be identified in city directories. Their occupations were puddler, lathe sawyer, travel agent, pattern-maker, and nailer. Of the four boat club officials mentioned, only one, a house painter, could be identified. Of seven rowers mentioned in the *Evening Telegraph,* 12 July 1873, two were identified: one a glassblower, the other a laborer. The *Commercial Gazette,* 4 and 5 July 1887, mentioned twelve oarsmen, among whom were identified a moulder, a baker, a clerk, a candy-maker, and a riverman.

53. *NLT,* 19 December 1874; on the popularity of boating in Pittsburgh, see *Post,* 20 May 1863, 24 June 1867; *Gazette,* 4 July, 6 August, 11 September 1867; *NLT,* 10 July 1880; *Evening Telegraph,* 12 July 1883; *Commercial Gazette,* 15 November 1886; P. Smith, *Memory's Milestones,* p. 33; Lorant, *Pittsburgh,* p. 144; Siebert, "Old Bayardstown," p. 94.

54. On Hamill and Morris, information in city directories was used to supplement Beck, "Old Fifth Ward," pp. 123–124; Kelley, *American Rowing,* pp. 26–29; Crowther and Ruhl, *Rowing and Track,* pp. 149–150, 155–157, 196–198; *Post,* 22 May 1863; *NLT,* 22 April 1876.

55. City directories were used to locate names found in the company's *Constitution and By-Laws* (1861), Vigilant Fire Company Papers, CLP; see also *NLT,* 19 December 1874.

56. "Notes on the Big Fire of 1845," *WPHM* 27 (1944), pp. 88–89; Johnston, *Life,* pp. 209–211; Dawson, *Our Firemen,* pp. 211–212; *Post,* 12 May 1863; Ronald M. Zarychta, "Municipal Reorganization: The Pittsburgh Fire Department as a Case Study," *WPHM* 58 (1975), pp. 471–472.

57. *Post,* 6 July 1867; Dawson, *Our Firemen,* pp. 23–27, 57, 63, 113, 118; Evans, "Pittsburgh in 1845," p. 24; Mann, *Our Police,* p. 91; Allegheny Fire Department, *History of the Allegheny Fire Department* (n.p., n.d.), pp. 36, 47–48; Beck, "Old Fifth Ward," pp. 115–116; Johnston, *Life,* pp. 211–213. On bonuses to firemen, see Bank of Pittsburgh, *Souvenir, 1810–1896,* p. 52; Lorant, *Pittsburgh,* pp. 102, 108. On fire company rivalry and violence in other cities, see "The Old New York Volunteer Fire Department," *Harper's New Monthly Magazine,* January 1881, pp. 191–192; J. E. Hilary Skinner, *After the Storm; or Jonathan and His Neighbors in 1865–6* (London 1866), vol. 1, pp. 15–16; Bruce Laurie, "Fire Companies and Gangs in Southwark: The 1840s," in *The Peoples of Philadelphia: A History of Ethnic Groups and Lower-Class Life, 1790–1940,* ed. Allen F. Davis and Mark H. Haller (Philadelphia 1973), pp. 78–82.

58. Siebert, "Old Bayardstown," pp. 92–93; Dawson, *Our Firemen,* p. 34; Beck, "Old Fifth Ward," p. 120; Zarychta, "Municipal Reorganization," pp. 472–473; on Orange versus Green terror in the Strip district, see Victor A. Walsh, "Class, Culture, and Nationalism: The Irish Catholics of Pittsburgh, 1870–1883" (Unpub. manuscript), pp. 22–23.

59. Vigilant Fire Company, *Constitution and By-Laws,* pp. 14–16; Dawson, *Our Firemen,* pp. 25, 32, 53, 55, 61; Zarychta, "Municipal Reorganization," p. 478.

60. Dawson, *Our Firemen,* pp. 32, 61, 63, 120; Johnston, *Life,* p. 217; *NLT,* 19 December 1874.

61. Dawson, *Our Firemen,* p. 55; *Post,* 29 May 1863; *Gazette,* 6 August 1867; see invitations, programs, and clippings in Vigilant Fire Company Papers.

62. Daniel, "Sanitary Fair," pp. 159–160; Donald M. Goodfellow, "'Old Man Eloquent' Visits Pittsburgh," *WPHM* 28 (1945), pp. 102–107; Dawson, *Our Firemen,* p. 26; Johnston, *Life,* pp. 213–214.

63. *Post,* 14, 15, 18, 22, and 30 May, 2 and 4 June 1863.

64. Ibid., 12 May 1863; Dawson, *Our Firemen,* p. 53; Kerr, "Mayors of Pittsburgh," pp. 134–139; see list of sponsors and managers in program for annual ball, 3 December 1867, Vigilant Fire Company Papers, CLP; names were identified in city directories.

65. On the celebration of the Fourth of July in Pittsburgh, see *Evening Telegraph,* 12 July 1873, 15 June 1876; *Post,* 24 June, 6 July, 1867; Johnston, *Life,* pp. 213–214. Richard Realf is best remembered for his "Hymn to Pittsburgh" ("My father was mighty Vulcan . . . "), first published in *NLT,* 23 February 1878, and reprinted as the frontispiece to the first Pittsburgh Survey number of *Charities and the Commons,* 6 February 1909; see also Fleming, *History of Pittsburgh,* vol. 2, p. 616. A boat regatta was part of Fourth of July celebrations in Boston: Crowthwer and Ruhl, *Rowing and Track,* pp. 22–23; see also Skinner, *After the Storm,* pp. 1–13, and McNeill, *The Labor Movement,* p. 129, on lower class forms of celebration in other cities; see also below, Chapter 7, Note 35.

66. *Post,* 10 and 29 June 1863, 2 and 6 July 1867; *Christian Advocate,* 6 July 1867, 12 July 1877; *Gazette,* 6 July 1867; *NLT,* 3 July 1875, 1 and 8 July 1876, 3 July 1880, and especially 7 July 1877; *Commercial Gazette,* 2 July 1874, 5 July 1887.

67. *Christian Advocate,* 6 July 1882, 30 June 1887; see also Willard Glazier, *Peculiarities of American Cities* (Philadelphia 1886), p. 343. The plebeian Fourth contrasts sharply with the city centennial of November 25, 1858, perhaps the last demonstration of elite assertiveness in the realm of public celebration until the late 1880s. Commemorating the fact that "our city had been in the possession of the Anglo-Saxon race for an hundred years," the old elite strove for a degree of pomp and formality far greater than that associated with the customary Fourth of July celebration. See *Pittsburgh Centennial Keepsake* (Pittsburgh 1858); *Gazette,* 26 November 1858.

## Notes to Chapter 4

1. *NLT,* 24 November 1876 and 3 February 1877; the following account of the Murphy movement draws principally from W. H. Daniels, ed., *Temperance Reform and Its Great Reformers* (Chicago 1878), pp. 435–510; J. Samuel Vandersloot, *The True Path; or, The Murphy Movement and Gospel Temperance* (Chicago 1877), pp. 144–160, 222, 228–245; Earl C. Kaylor, "The Prohibition Movement in Pennsylvania, 1865–1920" (Ph.D. dissertation, Pennsylvania State University, 1963), pp. 222–255.

2. Two recent histories of Prohibition are Norman H. Clark, *Deliver Us From Evil: An Interpretation of American Prohibition* (New York 1976), and

Jack S. Blocker, Jr., *Retreat from Reform: The Prohibition Movement in the United States 1890–1913* (Westport, Conn. 1976); the latter is unsympathetic, the former surprisingly and sometimes perversely sympathetic to the movement. While Blocker is better on fissures within the temperance movement prior to the Eighteenth Amendment campaign, both he and Clark minimize the disjuncture between voluntary temperance and Prohibition, or between earlier and later movements. No American historian has produced a work to rival Brian Harrison's *Drink and the Victorians: The Temperance Question in England 1815–1872* (London 1971), a book which demonstrates with thoroughness and astonishing nuance the interaction of class and cultural determinants of temperance opinion. See also his "Religion and Recreation in Nineteenth-Century England," *Past and Present* 38 (1967), pp. 98–125. On working-class temperance in Germany, see James S. Roberts, "Drink and Industrial Work Discipline in Nineteenth-Century Germany," *Journal of Social History* 15 (1981), pp. 25–38. On the ante-bellum movement in Pittsburgh, see Lloyd L. Sponholtz, "Pittsburgh and Temperance, 1830–1854," *WPHM* 46 (1963), pp. 347–379; the first seven chapters of Kaylor, "Prohibition Movement," show the diversity of opinion within the post-bellum temperance movement in Pennsylvania. On the appeal of temperance to the working class, see Bruce Laurie, "'Nothing on Compulsion': Life Styles of Philadelphia Artisans, 1820–1850," *Labor History* 15 (1974), pp. 365–366; Paul Faler, "Cultural Aspects of the Industrial Revolution," ibid., pp. 390–392; Alan Dawley and Paul Faler, "Working-Class Culture and Politics in the Industrial Revolution: Sources of Loyalism and Rebellion," *Journal of Social History* 9 (1976), pp. 466–471. For a unique insight into one workingman's struggle with drink, see Neil L. Shumsky, "Frank Roney's San Francisco—His Diary: April, 1875–March, 1876," *Labor History* 17 (1976), pp. 245–264.

3. *Post,* 5 September 1887; Vandersloot, *True Path,* p. 240; Kaylor, "Prohibition Movement," pp. 235–236; Daniels, *Temperance Reform,* pp. 447–448, 466–467, 470–478, 480, 488; Baynham, "Pittsburgh Music," p. 145; "Twelve Days of Murphy Meetings," *The Chautauquan* (April 1886), p. 416.

4. Daniels, *Temperance Reform,* pp. 468, 480–482; Kaylor, "Prohibition Movement," pp. 234–235.

5. Daniels, *Temperance Reform,* pp. 446–447; Kaylor, "Prohibition Movement," pp. 236–239; Vandersloot, *True Path,* pp. 150–151, 222.

6. *NLT,* 12 December 1874, 6 February 1875; see also 4 December 1875, 1 and 29 July 1876, 1 and 29 January, 13 August 1881, 7 January 1882; Samuel Walker, "Terence V. Powderly, the Knights of Labor, and the Temperance Issue," *Societas* 5 (1975), pp. 280–292, insists that the Knights' leadership saw temperance simply as a tool of organization; Ronald M. Benson, "American Workers and Temperance Reform, 1866–1933" (Ph.D. dissertation, Notre Dame University, 1974), provides a survey of official attitudes to temperance within the labor movement and concludes that those attitudes were consistently positive.

7. AAISW, *Constitution* (Pittsburgh), pp. 28, 31 and *Revised Constitution* (Pittsburgh 1886), p. 36.

8. LA 300, *Report of Second National Convention* (Pittsburgh 1883), pp. 14, 21–22; LA 300, *Third Convention,* pp. 6, 13, 15–19, 23; LA 300, *Fourth Convention,* pp. 24, 27, 53; LA 300, *Report of Fifth National Convention* (Pittsburgh 1889), pp. 8–9.

9. *NLT,* 25 December 1875, 18 November 1876, 20 January, 7 July 1877, 24 January, 17 July 1880, 16 July 1881, 9 July 1887; *Peoples Monthly,* June, August, September 1871, March, April, May 1872; Kaylor, "Prohibition Movement," p. 235; Daniels, *Temperance Reform,* pp. 470–471; P. Smith, *Memory's Milestones,* p. 100; Fleming, *History of Pittsburgh,* vol. 2, p. 616.

10. U.S. Senate, *Labor and Capital,* vol. 1, pp. 1119, 1145, 1164; vol. 2, p. 8.

11. Victor A. Walsh, "Class, Culture, and Nationalism" pp. 145–151; Kaylor, "Prohibition Movement," pp. 38, 46–47, 236, 275–276; Henry George, "Labor in Pennsylvania," *North American Review,* March 1886, p. 276; *NLT,* 1 July 1876, 7 January 1882.

12. Montgomery, "Workers' Control," pp. 491–492; see also Soffer, "A Theory of Trade Union Development," pp. 141–163; and works by Dawley and Faler cited in Note 2 above.

13. *NLT,* 3 February, 3 March 1877; Daniels, *Temperance Reform,* p. 488.

14. For a thoughtful exploration of these and other themes, see Daniel T. Rodgers, *The Work Ethic in Industrial America, 1850–1920* (Chicago 1978); see also Montgomery, *Beyond Equality,* pp. 177ff, 390. For an early example of labor's use of this moralistic rhetoric in Pittsburgh politics, see *Gazette,* 26 March 1850.

15. For example, see *NLT,* 8 January and 30 April 1881; *Peoples Monthly,* June and July 1871.

16. Eric Foner, *Free Soil, Free Labor, Free Men: The Ideology of the Republican Party before the Civil War* (New York 1970), especially ch. 7; Michael F. Holt, *Forging a Majority: The Formation of the Republican Party in Pittsburgh, 1848–1860* (New Haven 1969); Paul J. Kleppner, "Lincoln and the Immigrant Vote: A Case of Religious Polarization," in *Ethnic Voters and the Election of Lincoln,* ed. Frederick C. Luebke (Lincoln, Neb. 1971), pp. 170–172.

17. *NLT,* 8 January 1881; U.S. Senate, *Labor and Capital,* vol. 1, p. 28; Walker, "Terence V. Powderly," pp. 290–292.

18. John Lukacs, "The Bourgeois Interior," *American Scholar* 39 (1970), pp. 616–630; for the use of this notion in interpreting American temperance, see Clark, *Deliver Us from Evil,* chs. 1 and 3.

19. *NLT,* 8 July 1886; *Peoples Monthly,* July 1871; AAISW, *Constitution* (Pittsburgh), p. 4.

20. *NLT,* 17 July 1877, 15 March 1879, 3 June, 17 and 24 July 1880, 8 January 1881, 7 January 1882; see also Betts, *Sporting Heritage,* p. 173; John P. Arnold and Frank Penman, *History of the Brewing Industry and Brewing Science in America* (Chicago 1933), p. 80.

21. Linda Schneider, "The Citizen Striker: Workers' Ideology in the Homestead Strike of 1892," *Labor History* 23 (1982), p. 63; *NLT,* 17 July 1877, 24 January 1880, 8 January, 19 July 1881, 28 January 1882; *Journal of United Labor* 19 September 1889; Shumsky, "Frank Roney," passim.

22. See Raymond Calkins, *Substitutes for the Saloon* (Boston 1901); Allen T. Burns, "Labor at Leisure—Sketch at First Hand," *The Commons,* April 1904, pp. 110–113. On the broader uses of the saloon, also see Bennett, "Iron Workers," pp. 115–116, 119–121, 124, 141–143; *NLT,* 3 September

1881; Jon M. Kingsdale, "The 'Poor Man's Club': Social Function of the Urban Working-Class Saloon," *American Quarterly*, 25 (1973), pp. 472–489.

23. *NLT,* 3 July 1875, 19 February, 1 and 8 April, 8 July 1876, 10 January 1880, 9, 16, and 24 July, 10 September 1887; *Post,* 5 September 1887; *Journal of United Labor,* 12 September 1889; Bennett, "Iron Workers," p. 132. On the tension between the union hall and the saloon, see Ware, *The Labor Movement,* p. 332.

24. *NLT,* 6 January 1877. On the meaning of citizenship and political involvement for nineteenth-century labor, a stimulating discussion can be found in Fink, "The Uses of Political Power," in Frisch and Walkowitz, ed., *Working-Class America.*

25. AAISW, *Constitution* (Pittsburgh), p. 4; John L. Butler, "History of the Knights of Labor Organization in Pennsylvania," in Pa. Statistics 1887, p. G.41; *NLT,* 19 December 1876, 17 February 1877; see also, Knights of Labor, Machinery Constructors of North America, NTA 198, *Constitution* (New York 1887), p. 5.

26. Bennett, "Iron Workers," pp. 141–143; *Commercial Gazette,* 7 November 1882; *Journal of United Labor,* 30 June 1888; Edwin M. Chamberlin, *The Sovereigns of Industry* (Boston 1875). On Burtt, see Montgomery, *Beyond Equality,* pp. 367, 389–392; *NLT,* 9 and 16 July, 6 August, 1881; *Commercial Gazette,* 6 July 1881; Beck, "Old Fifth Ward," p. 117.

27. *NLT,* 5 and 18 January 1884, as well as 27 February and 4 December 1875, 1 and 29 July, 9 December 1876, 23 July, 1 and 13 August 1881; *Journal of United Labor,* 19 September 1889.

28. *NLT,* 23 July 1881, 7 July 1883, 17 September, 29 October 1887; see also ibid., 17 July 1877; *Journal of United Labor,* 31 March, 19 May, 18 November 1888; Commons et al., *History of Labour,* vol. 2, pp. 352–353.

## Notes to Chapter 5

1. Macartney, *Right Here in Pittsburgh,* pp. 133–135, 142; Bruce, *1877,* pp. 304–305, 311; see Joseph J. Holmes, "The National Guard of Pennsylvania: Policeman of Industry, 1865–1905" (Ph.D. dissertation, University of Connecticut 1970), and also his "Decline of the Pennsylvania Militia, 1815–1870," *WPHM* 57 (1974), pp. 199–217.

2. Mann, *Our Police,* pp. 113, 139–140, 158–159, 164; Kerr, "Mayors of Pittsburgh," pp. 179–180, 185–188; *NLT,* 24 February 1877; Evans, *Oliver,* pp. 63–66; Wayne Lammie, "Political Attitudes of Small Pittsburgh Merchants in the Progressive Era" (Unpub. manuscript), pp. 21–23; Montgomery, *Beyond Equality,* p. 211. On the RGA, see below p. 73.

3. *NLT,* 15 January, 19 February, 29 July 1876, 9 July 1887; see also Knights of Labor, Machinery Constructors, *Constitution,* p. 3; *NLT,* 3 October 1874; Ware, *Labor Movement,* pp. 32–35; Commons et al., *History of Labour,* vol. 2, pp. 201–202.

4. *NLT,* 29 July, 18 November, 2 December 1876; Kerr, "Mayors of Pittsburgh," pp. 168–169, 180–183, 194; Lorant, *Pittsburgh,* pp. 193–196, 201, 204, 261, 264, 292–293, 475; see Lincoln Steffen's grudgingly admiring portrait of Magee in *The Shame of the Cities* (New York 1904), pp. 101–133;

also see Samuel P. Hays, "The Development of Pittsburgh," pp. 443–444, on the political significance of the small retailer in midcentury Pittsburgh.

5. K. Austin Kerr, "Labor–Management Cooperation: An 1897 Case," *Pennsylvania Magazine of History and Biography* 99 (1975), pp. 64–65; Commons,, et al., *History of Labour,* vol. 2, p. 468; *Iron Age,* 6 December 1888, p. 859; Harry C. Mavrinac, "Labor Organization in the Iron and Steel Industry in the Pittsburgh District, 1870–1890 . . . " (MA. thesis, University of Pittsburgh, 1956), pp. 40–43; Montgomery, *Beyond Equality,* pp. 209–211, 465; A. H. Kerr, "Mayors of Pittsburgh," p. 197, *NLT,* 29 July 1876; Gary Fink, ed., *Biographical Dictionary of American Labor Leaders* (Westport, Conn. 1974), pp. 172, 499; *Biographical Enclyclopedia of Pennsylvania* (Philadelphia 1874), pp. 394–395.

6. *Commercial Gazette,* 4 and 5 October 1887; city directories, 1880, 1890.

7. Zarychta, "Municipal Reorganization," pp. 471–486.

8. See Montgomery, *Beyond Equality,* pp. 208ff.

9. *NLT,* 8 April, 29 July, 18 November 1876, 17 December 1877, 19 July 1879, 5 January 1884, 9 July, 3 September, 26 November, 10 December 1887, 8 February 1890; *Journal of United Labor,* 14 February 1889; on the professionalization of politics, see Morton Keller, *Affairs of State: Public Life in Late Nineteenth Century America* (Cambridge 1977), ch. 7.

10. AAISW, *Souvenir of the Eleventh Annual Reunion* (Pittsburgh 1890), p. 30; *NLT,* 1 January 1881; Commons, et al., *History of Labour,* vol. 2, pp. 329–330; Foster, "Amalgamated Association," p. G.2; Fitch, *Steel Workers,* pp. 510–513. The tariff had long been a working-class issue in Pittsburgh; in the 1840s, Whigs promised workers that high tariffs would bring "TWO DOLLARS A DAY AND ROAST BEEF": Johnston, *Life,* p. 229.

11. Commons, et al., *History of Labour,* vol. 2, pp. 201–202; *Journal of United Labor,* 12 September 1889; *Commoner,* 11 February 1888; DA 3, *Proceedings of Second Quarterly Meeting* (Pittsburgh 1888), p. 61.

12. Cecilia F. Bucki, "The Evolution of Poor Relief Practices in Nineteenth-Century Pittsburgh" (Unpub. manuscript), pp. 27–30; A. H. Kerr, "Mayors of Pittsburgh," pp. 180, 185–187; city directories, 1870–1890; Walsh, "'A Fanatic Heart'," p. 197.

13. A. H. Kerr, "Mayors of Pittsburgh," pp. 195, 208–212, 216; *NLT,* 17 February 1877.

14. Steffens, *Shame of the Cities,* pp. 107–108; A. H. Kerr, "Mayors of Pittsburgh," pp. 180–182.

15. Commons, et al., *History of Labour,* vol. 2, p. 247; Bennett, "Iron Workers," pp. 271–292; Walsh, "'A Fanatic Heart'," pp. 198–199; Ware, *Labor Movement,* pp. 35, 42–45; *NLT,* 30 August 1879, 22 January, 5 and 26 February 1881, 14 January, 15 and 29 July, 19 August, 26 October 1882, 5 November 1887.

16. See letters to Powderly from Alexander Rankin, 4 October 1881, and from Armstrong, 22 March 1882, in Powderly Papers, reel 3; in the latter, Armstrong pleaded with Powderly not to "desert" the "cause." Also see Powderly, *Thirty Years of Labor,* pp. 142–149; Ware, *Labor Movement,* p. 357.

17. *NLT,* 10 July 1880; Knights of Labor, *Proceedings of Third General Assembly* (Chicago 1879), p. 62; Commons, et al., *History of Labour,* vol. 2, pp. 341–342.

18. *Commercial Gazette,* 6 November 1882; see also *NLT,* 26 February
1881. At the time, J. H. Burtt worked in Wheeling and was an official of
the Flint Glass Workers Union: John Ehmann and William J. Smith, "The
Flint Glass Workers," in Pa. Statistics 1888, pp. F.28–29; Knights of Labor,
*Proceedings of Second General Assembly* (St. Louis 1879), pp. 43–44, and
*Proceedings of Sixth General Assembly* (New York 1882), p. 267.
19. Bennett, "Iron Workers," pp. 291–292.
20. *Commercial Gazette,* 6 November 1882; Klein and Hoogenboom,
*History of Pennsylvania,* pp. 321–322; Fitch, *Steel Workers,* pp. 510–513.
21. *Commercial Gazette,* 15 November 1886.
22. A. H. Kerr, "Mayors of Pittsburgh," pp. 195–198.
23. *NLT,* 14 July 1879, 16 and 30 July 1881, 28 January 1882, 5 January
1884, 3 December 1887; see also Montgomery, *Beyond Equality,* p. 304,
and Powderly, *Thirty Years of Labor,* pp. 240–270.
24. *Commercial Gazette,* 5 September 1887; *NLT,* 5 January 1884, 9 July,
3 and 10 September, 26 November 1887, 8 February, 1 March 1890.
25. Commons, et al., *History of Labour,* vol. 2, pp. 328–415.
26. Stromquist, "Working Class Organization," pp. 25–48; Robinson,
*Amalgamated Association,* pp. 43–53, 105–111, 126–127; *NLT,* 10 September,
29 October, 26 November and 10 December 1887.
27. DA 3, *Second Quarterly Meeting,* p. 17; Knights of Labor, *Second
General Assembly,* pp. 70–73, 92, 244–246; *Proceedings of Eleventh General
Assembly* (Minneapolis 1887), p. 1281; *Proceedings of Thirteenth General
Assembly* (Atlanta 1889), pp. 17–18, 20–21; LA 300, *Fifth Convention,* pp.
13–63; Butler, "History of the Knights of Labor," p. G.38; letters to Powderly
from Fred Friedman, 4 May 1881, and James Campbell, 17 October 1881;
Davis, *American Glass Industry,* pp. 126–132; Ware, *Labor Movement,* pp.
194–200, 373; *NLT,* 1 June 1889 and 25 January 1890. Within a few years,
the Window Glass Workers Association decided that it made less sense to
try to control the Knights of Labor than to leave it, whereupon the Association abandoned the name LA 300 and became an independent trade
union.
28. *Commoner,* 11 November, 4 December 1887, 11 and 25 February
1888; Bernard J. Sauers, "A Political Process of Urban Growth," pp. 265–288.
29. *Commercial Gazette,* 15 and 20 October, 7 and 10 November 1887;
*Christian Advocate,* 2 and 30 June, 20 October, 3 and 10 November 1887,
as well as 28 September 1867, 7 January 1871, and 6 July 1882.
30. *NLT,* 12 and 26 November, 10 December 1887, 8 and 15 February
1890; Commons, et al., *History of Labour,* vol. 2, p. 468.
31. The following account of Armstrong's funeral and related ceremonies
draws on *NLT,* 8 and 15 October 1887; *Commercial Gazette,* 3, 4, and 5
October 1887.
32. *Commoner,* 16 November 1887; *Journal of United Labor,* 18 October
1888; *NLT,* 8 and 15 October 1887; DA 3, *Second Quarterly Meeting,* p.
24; *Commercial Gazette,* 6 November 1887, 2 July 1892; *Post,* 31 August,
10 November 1887. Compare the RGA with the anti-labor Allegheny Grocers'
Association, which was run by the president of a food processing company:
*Commercial Gazette,* 16 November 1886; city directory, 1890. On Grundy,
see city directories, 1860–1900; *NLT,* 1 and 15 April 1876, 10 January 1880,
12 March 1881, 29 December 1898; *Post,* 9 and 12 November 1897, 29

December 1898; Pennsylvania Secretary of State, *Smull's Legislative Handbook* (Harrisburg 1910), p. 514.

33. *Commercial Gazette,* 3 October 1887.

34. *Post,* 3 September 1887; *NLT,* 23 July, 17 September, 29 October, 19 and 26 November 1887; DA 3, *Second Quarterly Meeting,* p. 32; Robinson, *Amalgamated Association,* p. 43.

35. On the Guskys as friends of labor and philanthropists, see Arthur G. Burgoyne, *Homestead* (Pittsburgh 1893), pp. 233–234; Mavrinac, "Labor Organization," p. 50; *Commercial Gazette,* 24 June, 5 July, 5 September, 25 November 1887, 2 July 1892; *NLT,* 16 July 1887, 29 December 1898; *Post,* 25 December 1897; Pittsburgh Central High School, *Class Book of 1880,* pp. 140–143; *Biographical Album of Prominent Pennsylvanians* (Philadelphia 1888), vol. 1, pp. 443–444; and city directories 1880–1900.

36. Butler, "History of the Knights of Labor," pp. G.29–31; LA 300, *Third Convention,* p. 26; *NLT,* 3 December 1887.

37. The history of the Law and Order movement is well narrated in Kaylor, "Prohibition Movement," ch. 9; see also Pittsburgh Law and Order League, *Report* (Pittsburgh 1888).

38. Law and Order League, *Report,* pp. 3–6, 7, 9–10.

39. Ibid., pp. 34–36, 48–49.

40. *Post,* 5 November 1887; see also Kaylor, "Prohibition Movement," chs. 7–9.

41. *Post,* 31 August, 5 and 19 September 1887.

42. Law and Order League, *Report,* pp. 11, 18, 21–24, 27–28; Kaylor, "Prohibition Movement," pp. 298–301; *Post,* 7 and 11 November 1887; on Judge White see also *Minute Book,* 27 May 1889, WCTU (Wilkinsburg, Pa.) Records, AIS.

43. *NLT,* 4 January 1890, and also 31 August and 3 September 1887.

44. Ayers, "Pennsylvania Sunday Blue Laws," pp. 20–22, 26–27, 30–31, 44–45; Law and Order League, *Report,* pp. 43–44.

45. *Post,* 31 August, 3, 8, and 9 September 1887; see also *Commercial Gazette,* 6 July 1892; Law and Order League, *Report,* p. 29.

46. *Post,* 31 August, 3, 5, and 15 September, 21 October, 7 and 10 November 1887; *NLT,* 4 January 1890, and also 1, 8, and 15 June 1889; Kaylor, "Prohibition Movement," pp. 300–301; Law and Order League, *Report,* pp. 21–28; *Commercial Gazette,* 9 November 1882, 8 August 1887. As early as 1882, retail liquor and brewing interests had lined up behind the Democrats: see *Commercial Gazette,* 6 November 1882.

47. See, in Korson, ed., *Pennsylvania Songs and Legends,* pp. 432–433, a popular song inspired by the Pittsburgh Law and Order campaign and containing the following defiant refrain:

And the new license plan, it ain't worth a damn,

In Soho on Saturday night.

Evasion of blue laws and of Prohibition became a western Pennsylvania specialty and a point of honor among workingmen. See *NLT,* 13 June 1891; Bennett, "Iron Workers," p. 132; "Prohibition in Pennsylvania," *Survey,* 14 May 1921, pp. 198–199.

NOTES

## Notes to Chapter 6

1. For data on the growth of Pittsburgh, see U.S. Census 1910, vol. 10, pp. 925–932, and U.S. Census 1920, vol. 1, pp. 586–587. For further data, detailed descriptions, and photographs, see Fleming, *History of Pittsburgh*, vol. 2; James M. Swank, *Progressive Pennsylvania* (Philadelphia 1908); *Art Works of Pittsburgh* (Pittsburgh, 1893); "The City of Pittsburgh," pp. 49–57; Glazier, *Peculiarities of American Cities*, pp. 332–347; *A Visit to the States*, pp. 340–350; Kitson, "Iron and Steel Industries of America," pp. 629–632; Beatrice Webb, *American Diary, 1898*, ed. David A. Shannon (Madison, Wis., 1963), pp. 87–88. Also useful are Roy Lubove, ed., *Pittsburgh* (New York 1976), a collection of contemporaneous comments and descriptions, including some of those cited above; Roy Stryker and Mel Seidenberg, eds., *A Pittsburgh Album 1758–1958* (Pittsburgh 1959), a good collection of captioned illustrations and photographs; Lorant, *Pittsburgh*, chs. 5–7; Roy Lubove, *Twentieth-Century Pittsburgh: Government, Business, and Environmental Change* (New York 1969), chs. 1–4.

2. See Warren, *American Steel*, pp. 134–138; Brody, *Steelworkers in America*, ch. 6; Tarr, *Transportation*, p. 24; *Iron Age*, 13 December 1888; Kitson, "Iron and Steel Industries of America," pp. 631–632; "The City of Pittsburgh," p. 203; Scoville, *Revolution in Glassmaking*, p. 27.

3. U.S. Census 1880, vol. 18, p. 863; see also George H. Thurston, *Pittsburgh and Allegheny in the Centennial Year* (Pittsburgh 1876), pp. 13–14; P. Smith, *Memory's Milestones*, pp. 14–15; and Annie C. Miller, *Chronicles of Families, Houses and Estates of Pittsburgh and Its Environs* (Pittsburgh 1927).

4. Tarr, *Transportation*, pp. 17–27; Robert J. Jucha, "Anatomy of a Streetcar Suburb: A Development History of Shadyside, 1852–1916," *WPHM* 62 (1979), pp. 301–320; see also Joan Miller, "The Early Historical Development of Hazelwood" (Unpub. manuscript); Ted C. Soens, "A Community in Transition: Hazelwood—1890–1905" (Unpub. manuscript); William J. Rampon, "The Historical Geography of Swissvale, Pennsylvania" (M.A. thesis, University of Oklahoma, 1959); Sven Hammar, "Wilkinsburg and Edgewood: Commuter Suburbs" (Unpub. manuscript).

5. Tarr, *Transportation*, pp. 21–26, 193ff; Evans, *Oliver*, pp. 299–301; *Post*, 10 November 1897.

6. Paul U. Kellogg, ed., *The Pittsburgh Survey*, 6 vols. (New York 1909–1914).

7. See John F. McClymer, "The Pittsburgh Survey, 1907–1914: Forging an Ideology in the Steel District," *Pennsylvania History* 41 (1974), pp. 169–188; Samuel P. Hays, "Introduction" to the reprint of Margaret Byington's *Homestead: The Households of a Mill Town* (Pittsburgh 1974; originally published in 1910 as volume 4 of the Survey); Edward T. Devine, "Results of the Pittsburgh Survey," *American Journal of Sociology* 14 (1909), pp. 660–664; J. T. Holdsworth, *Report of the Economic Survey of Pittsburgh* (Pittsburgh 1912).

8. *NLT*, 9 July 1887.

9. Fritz, *Autobiography*, p. 33; *Peoples Monthly*, July 1871, p. 20; Brody, *Steelworkers in America*, chs. 3 and 4; Katherine Stone, "The Origins of

*150*

Job Structures in the Steel Industry," *Review of Radical Political Economics* 6 (1974), pp. 61–97; Bennett, "Iron Workers," ch. 2.

10. Brody, *Steelworkers in America,* ch. 1; Stone, "Origins," pp. 63–65; Fitch, *Steel Workers,* pp. 26–29.

11. P. Davis, *American Glass Industry,* ch. 8; "The Passing of the National Window Glass Workers," pp. 4–5; Scoville, *Revolution in Glassmaking,* pp. 13, 27–29.

12. Livesay, *Carnegie,* pp. 77–80; Evans, *Oliver,* pp. 100–107; Nelson, *Managers and Workers,* pp. 38–41; Brody, *Steelworkers in America,* pp. 7–17.

13. Robinson, *Amalgamated Association,* pp. 124–128; Stromquist, "Working Class Organization," pp. 38, 41–46; *Iron Age,* 13 September 1888.

14. *Iron Age,* 2 August 1888; also 5, 12, and 19 July, 16 and 30 August 1888.

15. Ibid., 26 July, 9 and 23 August 1888.

16. U.S. Bureau of Labor, *Bulletin* 1 (1895), p. 16.

17. Stromquist, "Working Class Organization," pp. 25–48.

18. Brody, *Steelworkers in America,* pp. 11, 50–52; Mavrinac, "Labor Organization," pp. 54–56; Robinson, *Amalgamated Association,* pp. 125–126; Fitch, *Steel Workers,* pp. 95–97.

19. On the role of skilled workers in the organization of industrial workers in Europe and America, see "The Skilled Worker and Working-Class Protest," Special Issue of *Social Science History* 4 (Winter 1980); see also David Montgomery, *Workers' Control in America: Studies in the History of Work, Technology and Labor Struggles* (New York 1979), pp. 106–108.

20. The best account of Carnegie's and Frick's motives and methods in regard to the Homestead struggle can be found in Joseph F. Wall, *Andrew Carnegie* (New York 1970), ch. 16; see also Burgoyne, *Homestead.* Our knowledge of the lives of Homestead's workers and of their community remains more limited, but it will be greatly enhanced when Paul Krause completes his dissertation, "Homestead Reconsidered: Labor Insurgency in the Gilded Age" (Duke University). Mr. Krause has kindly shared some of his findings and observations with me.

21. Fitch, *Steel Workers,* pp. 139–141, 154–161; Brody, *Steelworkers in America,* pp. 43–48; Stone, "Origins," pp. 68–69.

22. Livesay, *Carnegie,* pp. 85, 110–111; see also Brody, *Steelworkers in America,* pp. 18–19; Bennett, "Iron Workers," p. 39; U.S. Census 1890, vol. 6, pt. 1, pp. 574–575; U.S. Census 1910, vol. 10, p. 930, and also vol. 8, p. 111.

23. Brody, *Steelworkers in America,* p. 107; Stone, "Origins," pp. 69–75; Fitch, *Steel Workers,* pp. 182–191; see also Nelson, *Managers and Workers,* pp. 52–54.

24. U.S. Census 1860, vol. 3, pp. 296–297; U.S. Census 1870, vol. 1, p. 768; U.S. Census 1880, *Compendium,* pp. 1390–1391; U.S. Census 1910, vol. 1, pp. 448, 1051, 1076–1077, and vol. 4, pp. 590–592. Lorant, *Pittsburgh,* pp. 101–102; Kleinberg, "Technology's Stepdaughters," pp. 25–29; Nelson, *Managers and Workers,* pp. 84–85. Kellogg, ed., *Wage-Earning Pittsburgh,* Byington, *Homestead,* and Fitch, *Steel Workers,* provide the fullest picture of immigrant life in western Pennsylvania. Also invaluable is Thomas Bell's,

*Out of This Furnace* (Pittsburgh 1976), a novel based on the lives of the author's Slovak immigrant ancestors and originally published in 1941.

25. U.S. Senate, *Labor and Capital,* vol. 1, p. 1139; Kellogg, ed., *Wage-Earning Pittsburgh,* p. 41; see also the observation of Thomas I. Miller, manager of the Atlas mill, that "the iron and steel men," i.e., the skilled workers, were "native labor," in U.S. Senate, *Labor and Capital,* vol. 2, p. 21; see also Charles R. Walker, *Steel: The Diary of a Furnace Worker* (Boston 1922), p. 107.

26. Kellogg, ed., *Wage-Earning Pittsburgh,* p. 45; Kellogg, ed., *Pittsburgh District,* pp. 15–21, 227.

27. John Bodnar et al., "Migration, Kinship, and Urban Adjustment: Blacks and Poles in Pittsburgh, 1900–1930," *Journal of American History* 66 (1979), pp. 548–565.

28. M. Martina Abbott, *A City Parish Grows and Changes* (Washington 1953).

29. Kellog, ed., *Wage-Earning Pittsburgh,* pp. 33–60; Fitch, *Steel Workers,* pp. 142–149.

30. Bodnar et al., "Migration," pp. 560–562; Josephine McIlvain, "Twelve Blocks: A Study of One Segment of Pittsburgh's South Side, 1880–1915," *WPHM* 60 (1977), pp. 367–370; Kleinberg, "Technology's Stepdaughters," p. 36. Single and double family dwellings were the most common types within Pittsburgh's very tight housing market. The Survey estimated that only 10 percent of the population lived in multiple family dwellings: Kellogg, ed., *Pittsburgh District,* pp. 118–123; see also Lubove, *Twentieth-Century Pittsburgh,* pp. 28–40, and also ch. 4.

31. Kellog, ed., *Wage-Earning Pittsburgh,* pp. 38–39.

32. Fitch, *Steel Workers,* p. 147.

33. Abbott, *City Parish,* pp. 45–46.

34. Kellogg, ed., *Wage-Earning Pittsburgh,* pp. 97–110, 121, 160, 424–436 and *Pittsburgh District,* pp. 124–130; Bodnar et al., "Migration," pp. 559–560; see also Beck, "Old Fifth Ward," p. 122; Siebert, "Old Bayardstown," p. 174.

35. Byington, *Homestead,* pp. 133, 164; Fitch, *Steel Workers,* pp. 147–149; Kellogg, ed., *Wage-Earning Pittsburgh,* pp. 40, 56ff and *Pittsburgh District,* pp. 244–245; *Post,* 29 June 1898. On the Croat community in Pittsburgh, see George J. Prpić, "The Croatian Immigrants in Pittsburgh," in *The Ethnic Experience in Pennsylvania,* ed. Bodnar (Lewisburg, Pa. 1973), pp. 273–281.

36. *Post,* 9 September 1887. On unemployment in iron and steel, see Byington, *Homestead,* pp. 42–43, 134; Nelson, *Managers and Workers,* pp. 86–87.

37. Brody, *Steelworkers in America,* pp. 62–68, 173–174; Gerald G. Eggert, *Steelmasters and Labor Reform, 1886–1923* (Pittsburgh 1981), pp. 33–40; Fitch, *Steel Workers,* pp. 133–136.

38. Robert A. Woods, "Pittsburgh: An Interpretation of Its Growth," *Charities and the Commons,* 2 January 1909, p. 531; U.S. Senate, *Labor and Capital,* vol. 1, p. 1166; see also Fitch, *Steel Workers,* pp. 214–220; Brody, *Steelworkers in America,* ch. 6.

39. Kerr, "Labor-Management Cooperation," pp. 45–71; *Post,* 9 through 11 November 1897.

40. Burgoyne, *Homestead,* chs. 18–20; *NLT,* 6 and 13 October, 3 and 10 November 1898.

41. See Robert H. Wiebe, *The Search for Order 1877–1920* (New York 1967). On "unrestricted capital," see Fitch, *Steel Workers,* ch. 15. On the significance of Homestead, see Livesay, *Carnegie,* pp. 142–144; LA 300, *Sixth Convention* (Pittsburgh 1892), p. 19; *NLT,* 6 October 1898.

42. John N. Ingham, "A Strike in the Progressive Era: McKees Rocks, 1909," *Pennsylvania Magazine of History and Biography* 90 (1966), pp. 353–377; Paul U. Kellogg, "The McKees Rocks Strike," *Survey,* 7 August 1909, pp. 656–665; Fitch, *Steel Workers,* pp. 237–238; Brody, *Steelworkers in America,* ch. 8; Hessen, *Steel Titan,* pp. 194–210; Eggert, *Steelmasters and Labor Reform,* pp. 42–55. On the "new unionism" see Montgomery, *Workers' Control in America,* ch. 4.

43. Brody, *Steelworkers in America,* chs. 8 and 13; Eggert, *Steelmasters and Labor Reform,* chs. 2–4.

44. Pittsburgh Chamber of Commerce, *Pittsburgh the Powerful* (Pittsburgh 1907); see also Kellogg, ed., *Pittsburgh District,* pp. 19–27, 54, 59, 490–491; Lubove, *Twentieth-Century Pittsburgh,* pp. 6–9.

## Notes to Chapter 7

1. *Christian Advocate,* 6 January 1881.

2. Moorhead, *Whirling Spindle,* pp. 233, 256. On new elite architectural tastes, see James D. VanTrump, "The Romanesque Revival in Pittsburgh," *Journal of the Society of Architectural Historians* 16 (1957), pp. 22–28; Montgomery Schuyler, "The Building of Pittsburgh," *Architectural Record* 30 (1911), pp. 229ff; see also illustrations in Pittsburgh Chamber, *Pittsburgh the Powerful,* pp. 65 ff.

3. Pittsburgh Chamber, *Pittsburgh the Powerful,* pp. 208, 270–271; Bakewell, "Pittsburgh Fifty Years Ago," pp. 7–8; Kleinberg, "Technology's Stepdaughters," Chapter 4.

4. Moorhead, *Whirling Spindle,* pp. 265–269; Samuel J. Fisher, *Our Suburb* (Pittsburgh, n.d.), pp. 71–72; *Commercial Gazette,* 16 November, 8 December 1886, 24 June, 2 July, 15 October 1887; *Post,* 15 May 1898.

5. Fleming, *History of Pittsburgh,* vol. 2, pp. 603–607.

6. See Baynham, "Pittsburgh Music," passim; on the austerity of Pittsburgh church music at midcentury, see Johnston, *Life,* pp. 110, 162, 167–171; Pittsburgh newspapers regularly announced and reported concerts of church music as well as other performances; for example, see *Commercial Gazette,* 6 November 1882, 24 June, 15 October 1887; *Post,* 6 and 24 December 1905; see also the following manuscript collections in CLP: Pittsburgh Gounod Club, Records; Pittsburgh Music Programs, 1875–1937; Carl Retter, Music Scrapbook, 1875–1886; Charles C. Mellor, Musical Scrapbook; Anna B. C. McDonald, Pittsburgh Music Programs and Clippings, 1870–1877.

7. Fleming, *History of Pittsburgh,* vol. 2, p. 627; in CLP see the selection of early art exhibition catalogs and the Agnes Way Scrapbook and clippings; *Commercial Gazette,* 6 and 7 November 1882, 16 November 1886, 25 November 1887; especially useful were Wilkins, *Art in Nineteenth-Century Pittsburgh,* Introduction and pp. 22–23, 30–31, 37–40.

8. Details and quotations from Pittsburgh Board of Trade, *The East End* (Pittsburgh 1907), unpaginated.

9. Fisher, *Our Suburb,* pp. 8–12, 38–44, 48; on pastoralism, see Jucha, "Shadyside," p. 304; Warner, *Streetcar Suburbs,* pp. 11ff.

10. Moorhead, *Whirling Spindle,* pp. 268, 270; also, Pittsburgh Chamber, *Pittsburgh the Powerful,* pp. 73–78; Stryker and Seidenberg, eds., *Pittsburgh Album,* p. 42; Robert A. Woods, "A City Coming to Itself," *Charities and the Commons,* 6 February 1909, pp. 789–792.

11. *Commercial Gazette,* 16 November, 8 December 1886, 9 and 10 November 1887; Moorhead, *Whirling Spindle,* pp. 270–271; Fleming, *History of Pittsburgh,* vol. 2, pp. 603–607; Pittsburgh Chamber of Commerce, "Old Organizations in Pittsburgh" (Unpub. manuscript), pp. 19–20.

12. Evans, *Oliver,* p. 302; *Post,* 9 and 10 November, 21 and 25 December 1897, 6 December, 18–24 December 1905; *NLT,* 23 December 1915; see also Fisher, *Our Suburb,* pp. 39, 74; Pittsburgh Central High School, *Class Book of 1880,* p. 111.

13. Ingham, "The American Urban Upper Class," pp. 70–75; see also Joseph F. Rishel, "The Founding Families of Allegheny County" (Ph.D. dissertation, University of Pittsburgh, 1975), p. 205.

14. Evans, *Oliver,* p. 302; Lowrie, "Pittsburgh Stage," pp. 134–225, in particular, pp. 155–160; see also Margaret C. Golden, "Directory of Theater Buildings in Pittsburgh since Earliest Times" (M.A. thesis, Carnegie Institute of Technology, 1953), and Dorothea B. Gardner, "History of the Nixon Theater, Pittsburgh, Pennsylvania" (Ph.D. dissertation, University of Pittsburgh, 1959); also Bakewell, "Pittsburgh Fifty Years Ago," pp. 7–8. On the rise of theatrical syndicates see "The Great Theatrical Syndicate," *Leslie's Monthly Magazine,* October 1904, pp. 582–592, and November 1904, pp. 31–42; see also *Post,* 24 November 1905.

15. The following paragraphs on the Exposition are based on *NLT,* 8 and 29 July 1876, 20 August, 3 September 1881, 11 November 1915; *Christian Advocate,* 19 July 1877; *Commercial Gazette,* 22 November 1886, 1 October 1887; Bakewell, "Pittsburgh Fifty Years Ago," pp. 7–8; and Baynham, "Pittsburgh Music," p. 134; on Smythe, city directories for the years 1870–1890 were also consulted.

16. John Higham, "The Reorientation of American Culture in the 1890s," in *Writing American History* (Bloomington, Ind. 1970), pp. 73–102.

17. *Outing,* April 1884, p. 63; Guy Lewis, "The Muscular Christianity Movement," *Journal of Health, Physical Education and Recreation* 37 (1966), pp. 28, 42; John A. Lucas, "A Prelude to the Rise of Sport: Ante-Bellum America, 1850–1860," *Quest* (1968), pp. 50–57; Betts, *America's Sporting Heritage,* pp. 91–92; see also *Leslie's Monthly Magazine,* September 1904, p. 492; *Commercial Gazette,* 16 November 1886.

18. Higham, "Reorientation of American Culture," pp. 94ff; see also Eugen Weber, "Gymnastics and Sports in *Fin-de-Siècle* France: Opium of the Classes?" *American Historical Review* 76 (1971), pp. 70–77; Christopher Lasch, "The Moral and Intellectual Rehabilitation of the Ruling Class," in *The World of Nations* (New York, 1973), pp. 80–102. On the tension between aristocratic and plebeian models of life and on the question of the organized release of instinctual energy, see William James's remarkable essays of the year 1899, "The Gospel of Relaxation" and "What Makes Life Significant?"

published together in *Talks to Teachers on Psychology: and to Students on Some of Life's Ideals* (New York 1899); see also Theodore Roosevelt, *The Strenuous Life: Essays and Addresses* (New York 1900).

19. Fisher, *Our Suburb*, pp. 70–72; Fleming, *History of Pittsburgh*, vol. 2, pp. 604–607; *Commercial Gazette*, 4 and 5 July, 14 and 25 November 1887, 5 July 1892; *Post*, 9 November 1897; on the nationwide proliferation of golf clubs see *Outing*, May 1899, pp. 129–142, June 1899, pp. 260–268, July 1899, pp. 354–365, August 1899, pp. 443–457.

20. Richard Harmond, "Progress and Flight: An Interpretation of the American Cycle Craze of the 1890s," *Journal of Social History* 5 (1971–1972), pp. 235–257; Betts, *America's Sporting Heritage*, p. 152; *Outing*, May 1884, p. 154, July 1899, p. 429; *Commercial Gazette*, 2 and 5 July 1887, 5 July 1892; *Post*, 12 and 19 June 1898; the careers of the Banker brothers were traced in the 1880 and 1890 city directories.

21. Pittsburgh Central High School, *Class Book of 1880*, pp. 8–9, 107–110; also see pp. 30–37, 44, 65–69, 71–72, 84–95, 185; *Commercial Gazette*, 31 May, 5 July 1892.

22. *Commercial Gazette*, 5 July 1892; on the cult of strenuosity among college men in the late nineteenth century, see Joseph F. Kett, *Rites of Passage: Adolescence in America 1790 to the Present* (New York 1977), especially ch. 7.

23. *Post*, 25 December 1897 and 15 May 1898.

24. *Commercial Gazette*, 25 November 1887, 31 May 1892; *Post*, 9 November 1897; J. Thomas Jable, "The Birth of Professional Football: Pittsburgh Athletic Clubs Ring in Professionals in 1892," *WPHM*, 62 (1979), pp. 131–147; Betts, *America's Sporting Heritage*, p. 127; C. Smith, *Pittsburgh Sports Hall of Fame*, pp. 13, 75, 84–85; see *NLT*, 14 November 1915, for report of Pitt versus Washington and Jefferson game at Forbes Field, a contest that drew 30,000 spectators.

25. See Hays, "Development of Pittsburgh," pp. 431–448; Fleming, *History of Pittsburgh*, vol. 2, pp. 636–637; Golden, "Theater Buildings," p. 4; Pittsburgh Board of Trade, *East End*, passim; on the Free Dispensary, see Kleinberg, "Technology's Stepdaughters," pp. 150–151, and city directory, 1900.

26. See Note 10, above; also Kellogg, ed., *Pittsburgh District*, pp. 18–19, 28–30.

27. CLP, *Fifth Annual Report* (Pittsburgh 1901), p. 73; CLP, *First Annual Report* (Pittsburgh 1897), p. 33; *Post*, 24 December 1905; see also Byington, *Homestead*, pp. 258–260, on organ recitals at the Homestead library.

28. CLP, *Fifth Annual Report*, pp. 73–74; CLP, *Sixth Annual Report* (Pittsburgh 1902), pp. 69–70.

29. *Pittsburgh Centennial Keepsake* (Pittsburgh 1858), p. 2.

30. Glazier, *Peculiarities of American Cities*, pp. 344–345; Evans, *Oliver*, p. 70; A. H. Kerr, "Mayors of Pittsburgh," p. 158. On the development of Pittsburgh's parks, see Howard B. Stewart, ed., *Historical Data: Pittsburgh Public Parks* (Pittsburgh 1943); Barbara Judd, "Edward Bigelow: Creator of Pittsburgh's Arcadian Parks," *WPHM* 58 (1975), pp. 53–68; see also Holdsworth, *Report of the Economic Survey*, pp. 177–184; Lubove, *Twentieth-Century Pittsburgh*, pp. 51ff.

31. Johnston, *Life,* pp. 107–112, 119–120, 123, 127–128, 133, 284–296; Sarepta Kussart, "The Early History of the Fifteenth Ward of the City of Pittsburgh" (Unpub. manuscript), p. 50; Beck, "The Old Fifth Ward," p. 116; P. Smith, *Memory's Milestones,* pp. 14–15; *NLT,* 24 July 1880; *Gazette,* 18 July 1867; *Post,* 21 June 1867, 31 August, 1 September 1887; *Peoples Monthly,* February 1872.

32. On the ideology of the park movement, see Robert Lewis, "Frontier and Civilization in the Thought of Frederick Law Olmsted," *American Quarterly* 29 (1977), pp. 385–403; see also Roy Rosenzweig, "Middle-Class Parks and Working-Class Play: The Struggle over Recreational Space in Worcester, Massachusetts, 1870–1910," *Radical History Review* 21 (1979), pp. 31–48.

33. The next two paragraphs draw on Stewart, *Pittsburgh Public Parks,* pp. 4–5, 15–16, 23; Judd, "Edward Bigelow," passim.

34. Charles M. Robinson, "Civic Improvement Posssibilities of Pittsburgh," *Charities and the Commons,* 6 February 1909, pp. 823–824. See also Lawrence A. Finfer, "Leisure as Social Work in the Urban Community: The Progressive Recreation Movement, 1890–1920" (Ph.D. dissertation, Michigan State University 1974), for an enlightening discussion of this entire subject.

35. Lewis, "Frontier and Civilization," p. 403. On late nineteenth-century July Fourth celebrations in America, see Glazier, *Peculiarities of American Cities,* pp. 332–347; Skinner, *After the Storm,* pp. 1–13; Edward H. Rogers, *Reasons for Believing that the People Will Use Leisure Wisely* (Boston 1866), p. 4; see also above, Chapter 3, Note 65.

36. *Gazette,* 6 July 1867; *Post,* 6 July 1867; *Peoples Monthly,* June 1871, p. 1; *Commercial Gazette,* 31 May 1892; *Christian Advocate,* 3 June 1871, 6 July 1882, 30 June 1887.

37. *NLT,* 1 July 1876.

38. *NLT,* 8 July 1876, 7 January 1877, 3 and 10 July 1880; *Christian Advocate,* 12 July 1877; *Commercial Gazette,* 2, 4, and 5 July 1887, 2 July 1892.

39. *Commercial Gazette,* 5 July 1887; *NLT,* 9 and 16 July 1887; DA 3, *Second Quarterly Meeting,* p. 24.

40. *Commercial Gazette,* 5 July 1887; and city directories 1880 and 1890 to identify organizers.

41. See Judd, "Edward Biggelow," passim; *Commercial Gazette,* 2 and 5 July 1892.

42. *Commercial Gazette,* 5 July 1892. On Marshall, see *Biographical Encyclopedia of Pennsylvania,* pp. 657–658; *Peoples Monthly,* 6 June 1871, p. 1; U.S. Senate, *Labor and Capital,* vol. 1, p. 1164.

43. *Commercial Gazette,* 5 July 1892; see also *Post,* 19 and 20 June 1898.

44. *Commercial Gazette,* 5 September 1887, 1, 2, and 15 September 1892; *NLT,* 23 July, 3, 5, and 10 September 1887; *Post,* 3 September 1887; Stromquist, "Working Class Organization," pp. 19–22.

45. Frances J. Olcott, *The Public Library a Social Force in Pittsburgh* (Pittsburgh 1910), pp. 16, 22. Olcott's study for the Survey was also published in Kellogg, ed., *Pittsburgh District,* pp. 325–366.

46. Byington, *Homestead,* pp. 255–256.

47. Ibid., p. 259.

48. Olcott, *Public Library,* pp. 3–10; on "outreach," see Harris, "Four Stages of Cultural Growth: The American City," p. 39.

49. Olcott, *Public Library,* pp. 13, 18–21; Byington, *Homestead,* pp. 263, 266–270.

50. On the playground movement in Pittsburgh, see Beulah Kennard, "The Playgrounds of Pittsburgh," in *Pittsburgh District,* ed. Kellogg, pp. 306–324; see also Byington, *Homestead,* pp. 120–121; Lubove, *Twentieth-Century Pittsburgh,* pp. 50 ff.

51. Kennard, "Playgrounds of Pittsburgh," p. 310.

52. Ibid., p. 311; Byington, *Homestead,* p. 121; for the national context, see Finfer, "Leisure as Social Work," ch. 3.

53. Joseph Lee, "Sunday Play," *The Playground,* October 1910, p. 226; Richard C. Cabot, "The Soul of Play," *The Playground,* December 1910, p. 287; see also George W. Knox, "Recreation and the Higher Life," *The Playground,* December 1910, pp. 293–296.

54. Woods, "A City Coming to Itself," pp. 793–796; see also Robinson, "Civic Improvement," p. 824; Judd, "Edward Bigelow," p. 64.

55. Kennard, "Playgrounds of Pittsburgh," p. 313; Robinson, "Civic Improvement," p. 816; Kellogg, ed., *Pittsburgh District,* p. 36.

56. Olcott, *Public Library,* pp. 13, 15, 18.

57. Byington, *Homestead,* pp. 257ff.

58. Olcott, *Public Library,* p. 12; Fitch, pp. 203–204; LA 300, *Sixth Convention,* p. 19; the pastor of St. Peter and Paul Catholic Church in Pittsburgh condemned Carnegie's philanthropy in terms almost identical to those of the glassworkers: Theodore P. Sturm, "The Social Gospel in the Methodist Churches of Pittsburgh, 1865–1920" (Ph.D. dissertation, West Virginia University, 1971), p. 246.

59. *NLT,* 12 January 1884, 9 July 1887, 11 and 25 January, 15 February 1890; Livesay, *Carnegie,* pp. 131ff.

60. Carnegie Free Library of Allegheny, *First Annual Report* (Pittsburgh 1891), passim; Kellogg, ed., *Pittsburgh District,* p. 325n.; *NLT,* 11 January 1890.

61. On welfare capitalism, see Nelson, *Managers and Workers,* ch. 6; Brody, *Steelworkers in America,* ch. 8; Fitch, *Steel Workers,* pp. 211ff. For provocative discussion of the nature of authority and control in the industrial milieu, see Richard Sennett, *Authority* (New York 1980). On Lowell, see Thomas Dublin, *Women at Work: The Transformation of Work and Community in Lowell, Massachusetts, 1826–1860* (New York 1979), and Thomas Bender, *Toward an Urban Vision: Ideas and Institutions in Nineteenth-Century America* (Lexington, Ky., 1975).

62. Nelson, *Managers and Workers,* p. 102; Robert C. Alberts, *The Good Provider: H. J. Heinz and His 57 Varieties* (New York 1973), especially ch. 10; Elizabeth B. Butler, *Women and the Trades, Pittsburgh 1907–1908* (New York 1909), pp. 314–315; Kellogg, ed., *Wage-Earning Pittsburgh,* pp. 219, 224, 229, 231, 236, 250, 255, 258–259.

63. Alberts, *Good Provider,* pp. 137ff.

64. Butler, *Women and the Trades,* p. 315; see a very similar critique of corporate "charity" in Pa. Statistics 1887, p. 7B.

65. For a brilliant discussion of a "popular form of *laissez faire*" in a different context, see Harrison, "Religion and Recreation in Nineteenth-Century England," pp. 115ff.

66. Butler, *Women and the Trades,* pp. 324–326, 329–330; Kellogg, ed., *Pittsburgh District,* pp. 36–37; C. Smith, *Pittsburgh Sports Hall of Fame,* p. 51.

67. Butler, *Women and the Trades,* pp. 326–327, 316–317; Kellogg, ed., *Wage-Earning Pittsburgh,* pp. 453–454; CLP, *Seventh Annual Report* (Pittsburgh, 1903), p. 21.

68. "The Limits of Religion," *Survey,* 18 June 1921, pp. 393–394.

69. Leroy Scott, "Little Jim Park," *Charities and the Commons,* 6 February 1909, pp. 911–912. Along with the rest of Painter's Row, the park was demolished by the U.S. Steel Corporation even before the Survey was completed. Scott's report was not published with the summary volumes.

70. This expression is used by Gareth Stedman Jones in "Class Expression versus Social Control? A Critique of Recent Trends in the Social History of 'Leisure.'" *History Workshop* 4 (1977), p. 163.

### Notes to Chapter 8

1. Peter Burke, *Popular Culture in Early Modern Europe* (New York 1978), p. 244.

2. "The Great Theatrical Syndicate," October 1904, pp. 581–592, and November 1904, pp. 31–42; Eilsler, *Stage Memories,* pp. 106–107.

3. See Lowrie, "Pittsburgh Stage," pp. 155ff.

4. Nye, *Unembarrassed Muse,* pp. 170ff; Harris "Four Stages of Cultural Growth," pp. 40–41.

5. *NLT,* 11 November 1915; *Post,* 24 December 1905; Lowrie, "Pittsburgh Stage," pp. 170–174; Golden, "Theater Buildings," p. 4; Fleming, *History of Pittsburgh,* vol. 2, pp. 636–637. On the early history of film, see Robert Sklar, *Movie-Made America: A Cultural History of American Movies* (New York 1975), chs. 1 and 2.

6. Butler, *Women and the Trades,* pp. 333, 324; Byington, *Homestead,* pp. 110–111; Kellogg, ed., *Wage-Earning Pittsburgh,* p. 373, 414–15; by 1917, even the WCTU had come to "recognize the great influence of moving pictures for good or evil:" Records of the WCTU, Wilkinsburg, Pa., box 2, folder 12, AIS. In *Mass Entertainments: The Origins of a Modern Industry* (Adelaide, Australia 1960), p. 18, Asa Briggs notes that "the cinema did not so much divert an older audience from other kinds of entertainment as create an enormous new one." See also Mary K. Simkhovitch, *The City Worker's World* (New York 1917), pp. 122–134.

7. Pittsburgh Board of Trade, *East End;* Byington, *Homestead,* pp. 30–31, 110–115; Butler, *Women and the Trades,* p. 333; Fitch, *Steel Workers,* p. 177.

8. Crowther and Ruhl, *Rowing and Track,* pp. 160, 199–202; Kelley, *American Rowing,* pp. 25, 267–271; Somers, *Sports in New Orleans,* pp. 140, 151–158; *Commercial Gazette,* 27 July 1887.

9. Thomas M. Croak, "The Professionalization of Prizefighting: Pittsburgh at the Turn of the Century," *WPHM* 62 (1979), pp. 333–343; *Commoner,*

4 and 25 February, 17 March 1888; see also Betts, *America's Sporting Heritage,* pp. 166ff; Al-Tony Gilmore, *Bad Nigger! The National Impact of Jack Johnson* (Port Washington, N.Y. 1975). On the role of ethnicity in boxing (as contrasted with baseball), see Steven A. Reiss, *Touching Base: Professional Baseball and American Culture in the Progressive Era* (Westport, Conn. 1980), pp. 184–198.

10. *Commoner,* 6 November 1887, 10 March, 5 May 1888; C. Smith, *Pittsburgh Sports Hall of Fame,* pp. 14–24; Benswanger, "Professional Baseball in Pittsburgh," pp. 11–13; Lieb, *Pittsburgh Pirates,* pp. 26–50; Fleming, *History of Pittsburgh,* vol. 2, p. 606. For a provocative and thoughtful answer to the question, "Why did baseball become our national game?" see Allen Guttmann, *From Ritual to Record: The Nature of Modern Sports* (New York 1977), ch. 4.

11. Lieb, *Pittsburgh Pirates,* pp. 23, 26–27, 33. In *Touching Base,* p. 33, Reiss properly notes—though he exaggerates the significance of—the fact that ticket prices and schedules restricted working-class spectatorship.

12. *Commercial Gazette,* 8 October 1887.

13. Ibid., 14 and 15 October 1887; Lieb, *Pittsburgh Pirates,* pp. 17–18; Betts, *America's Sporting Heritage,* pp. 121–123. For a view of baseball as democratizing and Americanizing, see George Hibbard, "The Heiress' Love Story," *Leslie's Monthly Magazine,* October 1904, pp. 607–613.

14. *Post,* 9, 18, and 19 October 1909; Betts, *America's Sporting Heritage,* p. 119; C. Smith, *Pittsburgh Sports Hall of Fame,* p. 24; also Reiss, *Touching Base,* pp. 62–63, 76, 97, 133. A cartoon in *NLT,* 21 October 1915, suggested that Pittsburghers were far more interested in "World Series Scores" than in European "War Scores."

15. On "politics as a safety valve," see Alan Dawley, *Class and Community: The Industrial Revolution in Lynn* (Cambridge, Mass. 1976), pp. 214–219, 236–241.

16. Joseph R. Gusfield, "The Sociological Reality of America: An Essay on Mass Culture," in Herbert J. Gans, et al., eds., *On the Making of Americans: Essays in Honor of David Reisman* (Philadelphia 1979), pp. 41–62. On ritual and drama in working-class sport in Britain, see William J. Baker, "The Making of a Working-Class Football Culture in Victorian England," *Journal of Social History,* 13 (1979), pp. 241–251.

17. J. Thomas Jable, "Sport, Amusement, and Pennsylvania Blue Laws, 1682–1973" (Ph.D. dissertation, Pennsylvania State University, 1974), chs. 4–6; Ayers, "Pennsylvania Sunday Blue Laws," pp. 32, 47, 50ff; Reiss, *Touching Base,* pp. 133, 137; John A. Lucas, "The Unholy Experiment—Professional Baseball's Struggle against Pennsylvania Sunday Blue Laws, 1926–1934," *Pennsylvania History* 38 (1971), pp. 163–175; "Prohibition in Pennsylvania," pp. 198–199; see also *Journal of United Labor,* 12 and 19 September, 14 November 1889.

18. Paul Wild, "Recreation in Rochdale, 1900–40," in J. Clarke et al., eds., *Working-Class Culture: Studies in History and Theory* (New York 1979), p. 143.

19. Briggs, *Mass Entertainments,* p. 18; for a perceptive though highly mechanistic interpretation of the shaping of audiences and consumers, see Stuart Ewen, *Captains of Consciousness: Advertising and the Social Roots of the Consumer Culture* (New York 1976).

## Notes to Chapter 9

1. The epigraph is from an interview conducted by David Saposs, quoted in David Brody, *Labor in Crisis: The Steel Strike of 1919* (Philadelphia: 1965), p. 157. On the events of 1919, in addition to Brody's indispensible book, see the two reports of the Interchurch World Movement: *Report on the Steel Strike of 1919* (New York 1920), and *Public Opinion and the Steel Strike* (New York 1921).

2. See, for example, John Bodnar, et al., *Lives of Their Own: Blacks, Italians, and Poles in Pittsburgh, 1900-1960* (Urbana, Ill. 1982), ch. 5, on increasing rates of residential persistence, and ch. 6, on increasing home-ownership.

3. On the Magee-Flinn machine in the early twentieth-century see Kerr, "Mayors of Pittsburgh," pp. 211ff; Lorant, *Pittsburgh*, pp. 261-266; Klein and Hoogenboom, *History of Pennsylvania*, pp. 326-329, 371, 375, 378, 382-383; William S. Vare, *My Forty Years in Politics* (Philadelphia 1933), pp. 121-122; Matthew S. Quay, *Pennsylvania Politics* (Philadelphia 1901), pp. 113-116, 149; Steffens, *The Shame of the Cities*, pp. 101-133; Charles E. Russell, "What Are You Going to Do about It? 2. Graft as an Expert Trade in Pittsburgh," *Cosmopolitan Magazine*, August 1910, pp. 283-292; Albert Jay Nock, "What a Few Men Did in Pittsburg," *American Magazine*, August 1910, pp. 808-818.

4. Samuel P. Hays, "The Politics of Reform in Municipal Government in the Progressive Era," *Pacific Northwest Quarterly* 55 (1964), pp. 157-169, presents the classic statement of the view that reformers were essentially elitist. For a recent critique of this and a generation of similar writing, see the review esssay by Terrence J. McDonald, "Putting Politics Back into the History of the American City," *American Quarterly* 34 (1982), pp. 200-209.

5. On Guthrie and the reformers, see Fleming, *History of Pittsburgh*, vol. 2, pp. 848-851; Lubove, *Twentieth-Century Pittsburgh*, chs. 2 and 3; Charles R. Woodruff, "Guthrie of Pittsburgh," *The World To-Day*, November 1909, pp. 1171-1173; *Post*, 12 November 1897, 6 December 1905; Pennsylvania Secretary of State, *Smull's Legislative Handbook*, p. 523; see the contributions of Pittsburgh reformers George Guthrie, Oliver McClintock, Edwin Z. Smith, and C.E. Rumsey to several meetings of the Conference for Good City Government (CGCG): CGCG, *Proceedings* (1896), pp 28-29, 146-161; CGCG, *Proceedings* (1898), pp. 257-266; CGCG, *Proceedings* (1901), pp. 133-151; Kellogg, ed., *Pittsburgh District*, pp. 21-27, 44-60; also see Notes 3 and 4, above.

6. Frank Wing, "Thirty-Five Years of Typhoid," in Kellogg, ed., *Pittsburgh District*, pp. 63-86; Woodruff, "Guthrie of Pittsburgh," pp. 1171-1172.

7. Michael Nash, *Conflict and Accommodation: Coal Miners, Steel Workers, and Socialism, 1890-1920* (Westport, Conn. 1982), pp. 114-118. See also Fitch, *Steel Workers*, pp. 17, 216, 235-236; Kellogg, ed., *Wage-Earning Pittsburgh*, p. 30, 56-57; *NLT*, 18 May 1916; Walker, *Steel*, pp. 99-100, 129. In *Strangers in the Land: Patterns of American Nativism 1860-1925* (New York 1963), p. 189, John Higham notes: "Never [had] the political parties made greater efforts to curry favor among the immigrants than in the election of 1912." See also *NLT*, 29 August, 15 September 1912, 18 November 1915.

8. See above, Chapter 8, Note 15.

9. Brody, *Labor in Crisis,* ch. 2. On the growth of "urban liberalism" and of political attitudes more favorable to immigrants and, to a degree, to organized labor, see John D. Buenker, *Urban Liberalism and Progressive Reform* (New York 1973); Eugene M. Tobin, "Direct Action and Conscience: The 1913 Paterson Strike as Example of the Relationship between Labor Radicals and Liberals," *Labor History* 20 (1979), pp 73–88; see also David A. Hollinger, "Ethnic Diversity, Cosmopolitanism, and the Emergence of the American Liberal Intelligentsia," *American Quarterly* 28 (1975), pp. 133–151.

10. William Z. Foster, *The Great Strike and Its Lessons* (New York 1920), p. 17.

11. Interchurch World Movement, *Public Opinion,* pp. 119, 183–185, and also pp. 117, 145, 238; see also Brody, *Labor in Crisis,* pp. 148–149.

# BIBLIOGRAPHY

## I. SOURCE MATERIALS

*A. Manuscript Collections*

Abbreviations:
AIS Archives of Industrial Society, University of Pittsburgh
CLP Carnegie Library of Pittsburgh
HSWP Historical Society of Western Pennsylvania
Calvin and S. Jarvis Adams Papers. HSWP.
Joseph Albree Papers. HSWP.
Albert J. and James P. Barr Papers. HSWP.
Breck's Battery, Pennsylvania National Guard, Records. HSWP.
George L. Hailman Family Papers. HSWP.
Jones and Laughlin Corporation Papers. AIS.
Anna B. Colville McDonald Collection. CLP.
William Martin Papers. AIS.
Charles C. Mellor Musical Scrapbook. CLP.
Oliver Iron and Steel Company Papers. AIS.
A. B. Palmer Papers. HSWP.
Pittsburgh Fire Department, Engine Company No. 14 Records. HSWP.
Pittsburgh Gounod Club Records. CLP.
Pittsburgh Music Programs, 1875–1957. CLP.
Pittsburgh Theatre Programs, 1868–1909. CLP.
Terence V. Powderly Papers. Catholic University of America. Microfilm
    copy in University of Pittsburgh Library.
Carl Retter Music Scrapbook. CLP.
Frank Semple Papers. HSWP.
Shakespeare Reading Club Programs. HSWP.
W. D. Slease Papers. HSWP.
Vigilant Fire Company Papers. CLP.
Agnes Way Scapbook. CLP.
Women's Christian Temperance Union, Wilkinsburg, Pa., Records. AIS.

*B. Government Publications*

Allegheny (Pennsylvania) Fire Department. *History of the Allegheny Fire Department.* N.p., n.d.
Pennsylvania Bureau of Industrial Statistics. *Annual Report* 1 (1872–1873). Harrisburg, Pa., 1873.
———. *Annual Report* 3 (1874–1875). Harrisburg, Pa., 1875.
———. *Annual Report* 4 (1875–1876). Harrisburg, Pa., 1876.
———. *Annual Report* 5 (1876–1877). Harrisburg, Pa., 1877.
———. *Annual Report* 8 (1879–1880). Harrisburg, Pa., 1880.
———. *Annual Report* 9 (1880–1881). Harrisburg, Pa., 1881.
———. *Annual Report* 15 (1887). Harrisburg, Pa., 1887.
———. *Annual Report* 16 (1888). Harrisburg, Pa., 1888.
Pennsylvania General Assembly. *Report of the Committee Appointed to Investigate the Railroad Riots in July, 1877.* Harrisburg, Pa., 1878.
Pennsylvania Secretary of State. *Smull's Legislative Handbook and Manual of the State of Pennsylvania.* Harrisburg, Pa., 1910.
U.S. Bureau of the Census. *Eighth Census* (1860). 4 vols. Washington, D.C., 1864–1866.
Vol. 1: Population.
Vol. 2: Manufactures.
———. *Ninth Census* (1870). 3 vols. Washington, D.C., 1872.
Vol. 1: Population, Part 1.
Vol. 3: Wealth and Industry.
———. *Tenth Census* (1880). 22 vols. Washington, D.C., 1883–1888.
Vol. 1: Population.
Vol. 2: Manufactures.
Vol. 3: Agriculture.
Vol. 15: Mining Industries.
Vol. 18: Social Statistics of Cities, Part 1.
*Compendium.*
U.S. Bureau of the Census. *Eleventh Census* (1890). 15 vols. Washington, D.C., 1892–1897.
Vol. 1: Population, Parts 1 and 2.
Vol. 6: Manufacturing Industries, Parts 1 and 2.
Vol. 7: Mineral Industries.
———. *Twelfth Census* (1900). 10 vols. Washington, D.C., 1900–1901.
Vol. 1: Population, Part 1.
Vol. 2: Population, Part 2.
Vol. 7: Manufacturers, Part 1.
———. *Thirteenth Census* (1910). 11 vols. Washington, D.C., 1912–1914.
Vol. 1: Population, Part 1.
Vol. 4: Population, Part 4.
Vol. 8: Manufacturers, Part 1.
Vol. 9: Manufactures, Part 2.
Vol. 10: Manufactures, Part 3.
———. *Fourteenth Census* (1920). 13 vols. Washington, D.C., 1921–1923.
Vol. 1: Population, Part 1.
Vol. 4: Population, Part 4.
Vol. 9: Manufacturers, Part 2.

U.S. Bureau of Labor. *Bulletin* 1. Washington, D.C., 1895.
U.S. Senate, Committee on Education and Labor. *Report upon the Relations between Labor and Capital.* 4 vols. Washington, D.C., 1885.

C. *Proceedings, Reports, Organizational Records*

Amalgamated Association of Iron and Steel Workers. *Constitution, By-Laws and Rules of Order.* Columbus: Paul and Thrall, 1876.
————. *Constitution, By-Laws and Rules of Order.* Pittsburgh: National Labor Tribune Printing, 1876.
————. *Proceedings of the Fourth Convention,* Pittsburgh, 1879.
————. *Revised Constitution.* Pittsburgh, 1886.
————. *Souvenir of the Eleventh Annual Reunion.* Pittsburgh, 1890.
Anti-Saloon League, Allegheny County. *First Annual Report.* Pittsburgh, 1904.
Bank of Pittsburgh. *Souvenir, 1810–1896.* Pittsburgh, 1896.
Carnegie Free Library of Allegheny. *First Annual Report.* Pittsburgh, 1891.
Carnegie Library of Pittsburgh. *First Annual Report.* Pittsburgh, 1897.
————. *Fifth Annual Report.* Pittsburgh, 1901.
————. *Sixth Annual Report.* Pittsburgh,, 1902.
————. *Seventh Annual Report.* Pittsburgh, 1903.
Conference for Good City Government. *Proceedings.* 1896.
————. *Proceedings.* 1898.
————. *Proceedings.* 1901.
Kankakee Sporting Club. *Constitution and By-Laws.* Pittsburgh, 1872.
Knights of Labor. District Assembly 3. *Proceedings of the Second Quarterly Meeting.* Pittsburgh, 1888.
Knights of Labor. General Assembly. *Proceedings of the General Assembly.* Reading, Pa., 1878.
————. *Proceedings of the Second General Assembly.* St. Louis, 1879.
————. *Proceedings of the Third General Assembly.* Chicago, 1879.
————. *Proceedings of the Fourth General Assembly.* Pittsburgh, 1880.
————. *Proceedings of the Fifth General Assembly.* Detroit, 1881.
————. *Proceedings of the Sixth General Assembly.* New York, 1882.
————. *Proceedings of the Seventh General Assembly.* Cincinnati, 1883.
————. *Proceedings of the Eighth General Assembly.* Philadelphia, 1884.
————. *Proceedings of the Special Session of the General Assembly.* Cleveland, 1886.
————. *Proceedings of the Tenth General Assembly.* Richmond, 1886.
————. *Proceedings of the Eleventh General Assembly.* Minneapolis, 1887.
————. *Proceedings of the Thirteenth General Assembly.* Atlanta, 1889.
Knights of Labor. Local Assembly 300, Window Glass Workers Association. *Report of the Second National Convention.* Pittsburgh, 1883.
————. *Report of the Third National Convention.* Pittsburgh, 1884.
————. *Report of the Fourth National Convention.* Pittsburgh, 1886.
————. *Report of the Fifth National Convention.* Pittsburgh, 1889.
————. *Report of the Sixth National Convention.* Pittsburgh, 1892.
Knights of Labor. National Trade Assembly 198, Machinery Constructors' Association of North America. *Constitution.* New York, 1887.
Pittsburgh Association for the Improvement of the Poor. *Fifth Annual Report.* Pittsburgh, 1880.

————. *Sixth Annual Report.* Pittsburgh, 1881.
————. *Eighth Annual Report.* Pittsburgh, 1883.
Pittsburgh Law and Order League. *Report.* Pittsburgh: Johnston, 1888.
*Sportsmen's Association of Cheat Mountain.* Pittsburgh, 1889.
Sportsmen's Association of Western Pennsylvania. *Charter of Incorporation and By-Laws.* Pittsburgh, 1882.

*D. Reference Works*

*Art Works of Pittsburgh.* Pittsburgh: Parish, 1893.
*Atlas of the Cities of Pittsburgh and Allegheny.* Philadelphia: G. M. Hopkins, 1882.
*A Biographical Album of Prominent Pennsylvanians.* First Series. 3 vols. Philadelphia: The American Biographical Publishing Company, 1888.
*The Biographical Encyclopedia of Pennsylvania of the Nineteenth Century.* Philadelphia: Galaxy Publishing, 1874.
*Directory of Pittsburgh and Allegheny Cities.* Pittsburgh: Diffenbacher, 1860.
*Directory of Pittsburgh and Allegheny Cities.* Pittsburgh: Diffenbacher, 1870.
*Directory of Pittsburgh and Allegheny Cities.* Pittsburgh: Diffenbacher, 1880.
*Directory of Pittsburgh and Allegheny Cities.* Pittsburgh: Diffenbacher, 1890.
*Directory of Pittsburgh and Allegheny Cities.* Pittsburgh: Diffenbacher, 1900.
*Directory of Pittsburgh and Allegheny Cities.* Pittsburgh: Diffenbacher, 1905.
*Pittsburgh as It Is.* Pittsburgh: Haven, 1857.
*Pittsburgh Directory, 1908.* Pittsburgh: Polk and Dudley, 1908.
Thurston, George Henry. *Pittsburgh and Allegheny in the Centennial Year.* Pittsburgh: Anderson, 1876.
*Who's Who in Pennsylvania.* New York: Hamersly, 1904.

*E. Autobiographies, Memoirs, Reminiscences*

Bakewell, Mary E. "Pittsburgh Fifty Years Ago as I Recall It." *Western Pennsylvania Historical Magazine* 30 (March-June 1947):1–8.
Beck, James A. "The Old Fifth Ward of Pittsburgh." *Western Pennsylvania Historical Magazine* 28 (September-December 1945):111–126.
Carnegie, Andrew. *Autobiography of Andrew Carnegie.* Boston: Houghton Mifflin, 1920.
Davis, James J. *The Iron Puddler: My Life in the Rolling Mills and What Came of It.* Indianapolis: Bobbs-Merrill, 1922.
Ellsler, John A. *The Stage Memories of John A. Ellsler.* Cleveland: The Rowfant Club, 1950.
Fisher, Samuel J. *Our Suburb.* Pittsburgh: The Crescent Press, n.d.
Fritz, John. *The Autobiography of John Fritz.* New York: Wiley, 1912.
Henderson, George. "A Country Boy Begins Life in Pittsburgh." *Western Pennsylvania Historical Magazine* 3 (January 1920): 9–20.
Johnston, William G. *Life and Reminiscences from Birth to Manhood.* New York: Knickerbocker Press, 1901.
Macartney, Clarence E. *Right Here in Pittsburgh.* Pittsburgh: Gibson Press, 1937.
Miller, Annie C. *Chronicles of Families, Houses and Estates of Pittsburgh and Its Environs.* Pittsburgh: n.p., 1927.

BIBLIOGRAPHY

Moorehead, Elizabeth. *Whirling Spindle: The Story of a Pittsburgh Family.* Pittsburgh: University of Pittsburgh Press, 1942.

Nevin, Adelaide Mellier, comp. *Social Mirror: Character Sketch of the Women of Pittsburgh and Vicinity.* Pittsburgh: T. W. Nevin, 1888.

Parke, John E. *Recollections of Seventy Years and Historiccal Gleanings of Allegheny, Pennsylvania.* Boston: Rand-Avery, 1886.

Pittsburgh Central High School. *Class Book of 1880.* Pittsburgh: Murdoch, Kerr, 1906.

Powderly, Terence V. *Thirty Years of Labor 1859-1889.* Philadelphia, 1890; reprint, New York: Kelley, 1967.

Russell, Charles, Lord of Killowen. *Dairy of a Visit to the United States of America in the Year 1883.* New York: The U.S. Catholic Historical Society, 1910.

Siebert, P. W. "Old Bayardstown." *Western Pennsylvania Historical Magazine* 9 (April and July 1926): 90-103, 169-187.

Smith, Percy Frazer. *Memory's Milestones: Reminiscences of Twenty Years of a Busy Life in Pittsburgh.* Pittsburgh: Murdoch, Kerr, 1918.

Vare, William S. *My Forty Years in Politics.* Philadelphia: Roland Swain, 1933.

Walker, Charles Rumford. *Steel: The Diary of a Furnace Worker.* Boston: Atlantic Monthly Press, 1922.

Webb, Beatrice. *Beatrice Webb's American Diary, 1898.* Edited by David A. Shannon. Madison: University of Wisconsin Press, 1963.


*F. Books, Articles, Pamphlets by Contemporaries*

Ashworth, John H. *The Helper and American Trade Unions.* Baltimore: The Johns Hopkins Press, 1915.

Bridge, James Howard. *The Inside History of the Carnegie Steel Company: A Romance of Millions.* New York: Aldine, 1903.

Burgoyne, Arthur G. *Homestead: A Complete History of the Struggle between the Carnegie Steel Company and the Amalgamated Association of Iron and Steel Workers.* Pittsburgh: Rathorne, 1893.

Burns, Allen T. "Labor at Leisure—Sketch at First Hand." *The Commons,* April 1904, pp. 110-113.

Butler, Elizabeth B. *Women and the Trades, Pittsburgh, 1907-1908.* (Vol. 1 of *The Pittsburgh Survey,* ed. Paul U. Kellogg.) New York: Russell Sage Foundation, 1909.

Byington, Margaret F. *Homestead: The Households of a Mill Town.* (Vol. 4 of *The Pittsburgh Survey,* ed. Paul U. Kellogg.) New York: Russell Sage Foundation, 1910; reprint by the University of Pittsburgh Center for International Studies, 1974, with a new introduction by Samuel P. Hays.

Cabot, Richard C. "The Soul of Play." *The Playground,* December 1910, pp. 285-292.

Calkins, Raymond. *Substitutes for the Saloon.* Boston: Houghton Mifflin, 1901.

Campbell, James. "The Window-Glass Blowers' Association." In Pennsylvania Bureau of Industrial Statistics, *Annual Report* 16 (1888), pp. F30-37.

Chamberlin, Edwin M. *The Sovereigns of Industry.* Boston: Lee and Shepherd, 1875.

"City of Pittsburgh." *Harper's Weekly,* 27 February 1892, pp. 202–205.

"The City of Pittsburgh." *Harper's New Monthly Magazine,* December 1880, pp. 49–68.

Crowther, Samuel, and Ruhl, Arthur. *Rowing and Track Athletics.* New York: Macmillan, 1905.

Daniels, W. H., ed. *Temperance Reform and Its Great Reformers.* Chicago: Hichcock and Walden, 1879.

Dawson, Charles T. *Our Firemen: The History of the Pittsburgh Fire Department from the Village Period until the Present Time.* Pittsburgh: Pittsburgh Commercial Gazette, 1889.

Devine, Edward T. "Results of the Pittsburgh Survey." *American Journal of Sociology* 14 (March 1909): 660–664.

Eastman, Crystal. *Work Accidents and the Law.* (Vol. 2 of *The Pittsburgh Survey,* ed. Paul U. Kellogg.) New York: Russell Sage Foundation, 1910.

Edwards, Richard Henry. *Popular Amusements.* Studies in American Social Conditions, no. 8. New York: Association Press, 1915.

Ehman, John, and Smith, William J. "The Flint Glass Workers." In Pennsylvania Bureau of Industrial Statistics, *Annual Report* 16 (1888), pp. F1–30.

Fitch, John A. *The Steel Workers.* (Vol. 3 of *The Pittsburgh Survey,* ed. Paul U. Kellogg.) New York: Russell Sage Foundation, 1910.

Fleming, George T. *History of Pittsburgh and Environs.* 3 vols. New York and Chicago: American Historical Society, 1922.

Foster, Charles G. "The Amalgamated Association of Iron and Steel Workers." In Pennsylvania Bureau of Industrial Statistics, *Annual Report* 15 (1887), pp. G1–27.

Foster, William Z. *The Great Steel Strike and Its Lessons.* New York: Huebsch, 1920.

"The Fourth of July." *Outlook,* 19 July 1913, pp. 596–597.

Glazier, Willard. *Peculiarities of American Cities.* Philadelphia: Hubbard, 1886.

George, Henry. "Labor in Pennsylvania." *North American Review,* March 1886, pp. 268–277.

Godfrey, A. H. "Glorious Fourth Awheel." *Outing,* July 1899, pp. 379–385.

"The Great Theatrical Syndicate." *Leslie's Monthly Magazine,* October 1904, pp. 581–592, and November 1904, pp. 31–42.

Hamsun, Knut. *The Cultural Life of Modern America.* Translated by Barbara Gordon Morgridge. Cambridge: Harvard University Press, 1969; originally published in Copenhagen, 1889.

Hard, William. "Making Steel and Killing Men." *Everybody's,* November 1907, pp. 579–591.

Hartt, Rollin Lynde. *The People at Play: Excursions in the Humor and Philosophy of Population Amusements.* Boston and New York: Houghton Mifflin, 1909.

Hibbard, George. "The Heiress' Love Story." *Leslie's Monthly Magazine,* October 1904, pp. 607–613.

Holdsworth, J. T. *Report of the Economic Survey of Pittsburgh.* Pittsburgh: Pittsburgh Department of Supplies, 1912.

Interchurch World Movement, Commission of Inquiry. *Public Opinion and the Steel Strike.* New York: Harcourt, Brace, 1921.

———. *Report on the Steel Strike of 1919.* New York: Harcourt, Brace, 1920.

James, William. *Talks to Teachers on Psychology: and to Students on Some of Life's Ideals.* New York: Holt, 1900.

Keeler, Ralph, and Fenn, Harry. "The Taking of Pittsburgh." *Every Saturday.*
"Part I: The March," 4 March 1871, pp. 198–199.
"Part II: The Reconnaissance," 11 March 1871, p. 238.
"Part III: Before the Works," 18 March 1871, pp. 262–263.
"Part IV: Among the Inhabitants," 25 March 1871, pp. 272–275.

Kellogg, Paul U. "The McKees Rocks Strike," *Survey,* 7 August 1909, pp. 656–665.

———. ed. *The Pittsburgh Survey.* 6 vols. New York: Russell Sage Foundation, 1909–1914.

Vol. 1: *Women and the Trades: Pittsburgh, 1907–1908,* by Elizabeth B. Butler, 1909.

Vol. 2: *Work Accidents and the Law,* by Crystal Eastman, 1910.

Vol. 3: *The Steel Workers,* by John Fitch, 1910.

Vol. 4: *Homestead: The Households of a Mill Town,* by Margaret F. Byington, 1910.

Vol. 5: *The Pittsburgh District Civic Frontage,* 1914.

Vol. 6: *Wage-Earning Pittsburgh,* 1914.

Kitson, James. "Iron and Steel Industries of America: Notes on the Visit of the British Iron and Steel Institute to the United States, 1890," *Contemporary Review,* May 1891, pp. 625–641.

Knox, George William. "Recreation and the Higher Life," *The Playground,* December 1910, pp. 293–296.

Lee, Joseph. "Sunday Play." *The Playground,* October 1910, pp. 221–232.

"The Limits of Religion." *Survey,* 18 June 1921, pp. 393–394.

McNeill, George E., ed. *The Labor Movement: The Problem of Today.* New York: Hazen, 1887.

Mann, Henry, ed. *Our Police: A History of the Pittsburgh Police Force: Under Town and City.* Pittsburgh: Pittsburgh Commercial Gazette, 1889.

Martin, Edward W. *The History of the Great Riots.* Philadelphia: National Publishing, 1877.

Nock, Albert Jay. "What a Few Men Did in Pittsburgh: A True Detective Story of To-day." *American Magazine,* August 1910, pp. 808–818.

Olcott, Frances J. *The Public Library as a Social Force in Pittsburgh.* Pittsburgh: Carnegie Library, 1910.

"The Old New York Volunteer Fire Department." *Harper's New Monthly Magazine,* January 1881, pp. 191–208.

Oppenheim, James. "The Hired City." *American Magazine,* May 1910, pp. 33–40.

Parton, James. "Pittsburg." *Atlantic Monthly,* January 1868, pp. 17–36.

"Pittsburgh." *Harper's Weekly,* February 1871, pp. 144–147.

Pittsburgh Board of Trade. *The East End.* Pittsburgh, 1907.

*Pittsburgh Centennial Keepsake.* Pittsburgh, 1858.

Pittsburgh Chamber of Commerce. *The Insurrection among the Railway Employees of the United States, and the Losses in Pittsburgh Resulting Therefrom, in July 1877* . . . . Pittsburgh: Stevenson, 1877.

——— . *Pittsburgh the Powerful.* Pittsburgh: Industry Publishing, 1907.

*The Pittsburgh District Civic Frontage.* (Vol. 5 of *The Pittsburgh Survey,* ed. Paul U. Kellogg.) New York: Russell Sage Foundation, 1914.

"Prohibition in Pennsylvania." *Survey,* 14 May 1921, pp. 198–199.

Quay, Matthew Stanley. *Pennsylvania Politics: The Campaign of 1900 as Set Forth in the Speeches of Hon. Matthew Stanley Quay.* Philadelphia: Campbell, 1901.

Robinson, Charles Mulford. "Civil Improvement Possibilities of Pittsburgh." *Charities and the Commons,* 6 February 1909, pp. 801–826.

Robinson, Jesse S. *The Amalgamated Association of Iron, Steel and Tin Workers.* Baltimore: Johns Hopkins University Press, 1920.

Rogers, Edward H. *Reasons for Believing that the People Will Use Leisure Wisely; with a Statement of the Character of the Eight-Hour Movement. By a Workingman.* Boston: Voice Printing and Publishing, 1866.

Roosevelt, Theodore. *The Strenuous Life: Essays and Addresses.* New York: Century, 1900.

Russell, Charles Edward. "What Are You Going to Do about It? 2. Graft as an Expert Trade in Pittsburgh." *Cosmopolitan Magazine,* August 1910, pp. 283–292.

Schuyler, Montgomery. "The Building of Pittsburgh." *Architectural Record* 30 (September 1911): 204–282.

Scott, Leroy. "Little Jim Park." *Charities and the Commons,* 6 February 1909, pp. 911–912.

Simkhovitch, Mary Kingsbury. *The City Worker's World in America.* New York: Macmillan, 1917.

Skinner, J. E. Hilary. *After the Storm; or Jonathan and His Neighbors in 1865-6.* 2 vols. London: Richard Bentley, 1866.

Steffens, Lincoln. *The Shame of the Cities.* New York: McClure, Phillips, 1904.

Swank, James M. *History of the Manufacture of Iron in All Ages and Particularly in the United States from Colonial Times to 1891.* Philadelphia, 1892; reprint, New York: Burt Franklin, n.d.

——— . *Progressive Pennsylvania.* Philadelphia: Lippincott, 1908.

Trollope, Anthony. *North America.* New York: Knopf, 1951; originally published in 1862.

"Twelve Days of Murphy Meetings," *The Chautauquan,* April 1886, p. 416.

Vandersloot, J. Samuel. *The True Path; or, the Murphy Movement and Gospel Temperance.* Chicago: Fairbanks, 1878.

*A Visit to the States: A Reprint of Letters from the Special Correspondent of the Times.* First Series. London: George Edward Wright, 1887.

Vivian, Henry H. *Notes of a Tour in America.* London: Stanford, 1878.

*Wage-Earning Pittsburgh.* (Vol. 6 of *The Pittsburgh Survey,* ed. Paul U. Kellogg.) New York: Russell Sage Foundation, 1914.

Woodruff, Clinton Rogers, "Guthrie of Pittsburgh," *The World To-day,* November 1909, pp. 1171–1173.

Woods, Robert A. "A City Coming to Itself." *Charities and the Commons,* 6 February 1909, pp. 785–800.

BIBLIOGRAPHY

————. "Pittsburgh: An Interpretation of Its Growth." *Charities and the Commons*, 2 January 1909, pp. 525–533.

F. *Periodicals Frequently Consulted*

Published in Pittsburgh:
*The Christian Advocate.* 1867–1890.
*The Commercial Gazette.* 1877–1901.
*The Commoner.* 1887–1888.
*The Evening Telegraph.* 1873–1883.
*The Gazette.* 1850–1877.
*The Index.* 1901.
*Iron Age.* 1887–1889.
*National Labor Tribune,* 1873–1921.
*Peoples Monthly.* 1871–1875.
*The Post.* 1863–1921.
Other:
*The Journal of United Labor.* Philadelphia. 1887–1889.
*Outing.* New York. 1882–1899.


## II. SECONDARY MATERIALS

A. *Dissertations and Other Unpublished Manuscripts*

Ayers, Phyllis Laverne. "The History of Pennsylvania Sunday Blue Laws." M.A. thesis, University of Pittsburgh, 1952.
Baynham, Edward Gladstone. "A History of Pittsburgh Music, 1758–1958." Typescript, 1970. Carnegie Library of Pittsburgh.
Bennett, John William. "Iron Workers in Woods Run and Johnstown: The Union Era 1865–1895." Ph.D. dissertation, University of Pittsburgh, 1977.
Benson, Ronald M. "American Workers and Temperance Reform, 1866–1933." Ph.D. dissertation, Notre Dame University, 1974.
Burki, Cecilia F. "The Evolution of Poor Relief Practices in Nineteenth-Century Pittsburgh." Seminar paper, University of Pittsburgh History Dept., 1977.
Caye, James, Jr. "Violence in the Nineteenth Century Community: The Roundhouse Riot, Pittsburgh, 1877." Seminar paper, University of Pittsburgh History Dept., 1969.
Finfer, Lawrence A. "Leisure as Social Work in the Urban Community: The Progressive Recreation Movement, 1890–1920." Ph.D. dissertation, Michigan State University, 1974.
Gardner, Dorothea B. "History of the Nixon Theater, Pittsburgh, Pennsylvania." Ph.D. dissertation, University of Pittsburgh, 1959.
Golden, Margaret C. "Directory of Theater Buildings in Use in Pittsburgh, Pennsylvania, since Earliest Times." M.A. thesis, Carnegie Institute of Technology, 1953.
Hammer, Sven. "Wilkinsburg and Edgewood: Commuter Suburbs." Seminar paper, Carnegie-Mellon University History Dept., 1968.

Holmes, Joseph J. "The National Guard of Pennsylvania: Policeman of Industry, 1865–1905." Ph.D. dissertation, University of Connecticut, 1970.

Jable, J. Thomas. "Sport, Amusements, and Pennsylvania's Blue Laws, 1682–1973." Ph.D. dissertation, Pennsylvania State University, 1974.

Kaylor, Earl Clifford. "The Prohibition Movement in Pennsylvania, 1865–1920." Ph.D. dissertation, Pennsylvania State University, 1963.

Kerr, Allen Humphreys. "The Mayors and Recorders of Pittsburgh, 1816–1952: Their Lives and Somewhat of Their Times." Typescript, n.d. Historical Society of Western Pennsylvania.

Kleinberg, Susan. "Technology's Stepdaughters: The Impact of Industrialization upon Working Class Women, Pittsburgh, 1865–1890." Ph.D. dissertation, University of Pittsburgh, 1973.

Krause, Paul. "Homestead Reconsidered: Labor Insurgency in the Gilded Age." Ph.D. dissertation, Duke University (in progress).

Kussart, Sarepta. "The Early History of the Fifteenth Ward of the City of Pittsburgh." Typescript, 1925. Carnegie Library of Pittsburgh.

Lammie, Wayne. "Political Attitudes of Small Pittsburgh Merchants in the Progressive Era." Seminar Paper, University of Pittsburgh History Dept., 1961.

Lowrie, James Allison. "A History of the Pittsburgh Stage, 1861–1891." Ph.D. dissertation, University of Pittsburgh, 1943.

Mavrinac, Harry Charles. "Labor Organization in the Iron and Steel Industry in the Pittsburgh District, 1870–1890, with Special Reference to William Martin." M.A. thesis, University of Pittsburgh, 1956.

Miller, Joan. "The Early Historical Development of Hazelwood." Seminar paper, University of Pittsburgh History Dept., 1967.

Pittsburgh Chamber of Commerce. "Old Organizations in Pittsburgh." Typescript, 1929. Carnegie Library of Pittsburgh.

Rampon, William Jennings. "The Historical Geography of Swissvale, Pennsylvania." M.A. thesis, University of Oklahoma, 1959.

Rishel, Joseph F. "The Founding Families of Allegheny County: Examination of Nineteenth Century Elite Continuity." Ph.D. dissertation, University of Pittsburgh, 1975.

Soens, Ted C. "A Community in Transition: Hazelwood—1890–1905." Seminar paper, Carnegie-Mellon University History Dept., 1969.

Stromquist, Shelton. "Working Class Organization and Industrial Change in Pittsburgh, 1860–1890." Seminar paper, University of Pittsburgh History Dept., 1973.

Sturm, Theodore Paul. "The Social Gospel in the Methodist Churches of Pittsburgh, 1865–1920." Ph.D. dissertation, West Virginia University, 1971.

Walsh, Victor A. "Class, Culture, and Nationalism: The Irish Catholics of Pittsburgh, 1870–1883." Seminar paper, University of Pittsburgh History Dept., 1976.

BIBLIOGRAPHY

B. *Published Works*

1. *Books*

Abbot, M. Martina. *A City Parish Grows and Changes.* Washington, D.C.: The Catholic University of America Press, 1953.

Alberts, Robert C. *The Good Provider: H. J. Heinz and His 57 Varieties.* New York: Houghton Mifflin, 1973.

Andrews, J. Cutler. *Pittsburgh's Post-Gazette: "The First Newspaper West of the Alleghenies."* Boston: Chapman and Grimes, 1936.

Arnold, John P., and Penman, Frank. *History of the Brewing Industry and Brewing Science in America.* Chicago: Peterson, 1933.

*Art in Nineteenth-Century Pittsburgh, An Exhibition Catalog.* Introductory essay by David Wilkins. Pittsburgh: University of Pittsburgh, 1977.

Bell, Thomas. *Out of this Furnace.* Pittsburgh: University of Pittsburgh Press, 1976.

Bender, Thomas. *Toward an Urban Vision: Ideas and Institutions in Nineteenth-Century America.* Lexington: University Press of Kentucky, 1975.

Betts, John Rickard. *America's Sporting Heritage: 1850–1950.* Reading, Mass.: Addison-Wesley, 1974.

Blocker, Jack S. *Retreat from Reform: The Prohibition Movement in the United States, 1890–1913.* Westport, Conn.: Greenwood Press, 1976.

Brody, David. *Labor in Crisis: The Steel Strike of 1919.* Philadelphia: Lippincott, 1965.

———. *Steelworkers in America: The Nonunion Era.* Cambridge: Harvard University Press, 1960.

Bruce, Robert V. *1877: Year of Violence.* Indianapolis: Bobbs-Merrill, 1959.

Buenker, John D. *Urban Liberalism and Progressive Reform.* New York: Scribner's, 1973.

Burke, Peter. *Popular Culture in Early Modern Europe.* New York: Harper and Row, 1978.

Chambers, Bruce W. *The World of David Gilmour Blythe (1815–1865).* Washington, D.C.: Smithsonian Institution Press, 1980.

Clark, Norman H. *Deliver Us from Evil: An Interpretation of American Prohibition.* New York: Norton, 1976.

Clarke, J., Critcher, C., and Johnson, R., eds. *Working-Class Culture: Studies in History and Theory.* New York: St. Martin's Press,, 1979.

Commons, John R., et al. *History of Labour in the United States.* 4 vols. New York: Macmillan, 1918–1935.

Davis, Natalie Zemon. *Society and Culture in Early Modern France.* Stanford, Calif.: Stanford University Press, 1975.

Davis, Pearce. *The Development of the American Glass Industry.* Cambridge: Harvard University Press, 1949.

Dawley, Alan. *Class and Community: The Industrial Revolution in Lynn.* Cambridge: Harvard University Press, 1976.

Dublin, Thomas. *Women at Work: The Transformation of Work and Community in Lowell, Massachusetts, 1826–1860.* New York: Columbia University Press, 1979.

Eggert, Gerald G. *Steelmasters and Labor Reform, 1886–1923.* Pittsburgh: University of Pittsburgh Press, 1981.

172

Ewen, Stuart. *Captains of Consciousness: Advertising and the Social Roots of the Consumer Culture.* New York: McGraw-Hill, 1976.

Fink, Gary, ed. *Biographical Dictionary of American Labor Leaders.* Westport, Conn.: Greenwood Press, 1974.

Foner, Eric. *Free Soil, Free Labor, Free Men: The Ideology of the Republican Party before the Civil War.* New York: Oxford University Press, 1970.

Frisch, Michael H., and Walkowitz, Daniel J., eds. *Working-Class America: Essays on Labor, Community, and American Society.* Urbana: University of Illinois Press, 1983.

Gans, Herbert J., Glazer, Nathan, Gusfield, Joseph R., and Jencks, Christopher, eds. *On the Making of Americans: Essays in Honor of David Riesman.* Philadelphia: University of Pennsylvania Press, 1979.

Gilmore, Al-Tony. *Bad Nigger! The National Impact of Jack Johnson.* Port Washington, N.Y.: Kennikat Press, 1975.

Grimsted, David. *Melodrama Unveiled: American Theater and Culture, 1800–1850.* Chicago: University of Chicago Press, 1968.

Gutman, Herbert G. *Work, Culture, and Society in Industrializing America: Essays in American Working-Class and Social History.* New York: Random House, Vintage Books, 1977.

Guttman, Allen. *From Ritual to Record: The Nature of Modern Sports.* New York: Columbia University Press, 1977.

Harrison, Brian. *Drink and the Victorians: The Temperance Question in England 1815–1872.* London: Faber and Faber, 1971.

Hessen, Robert. *Steel Titan: The Life of Charles M. Schwab.* New York: Oxford University Press, 1975.

Higham, John. *Strangers in the Land: Patterns of American Nativism 1860–1925.* New York: Atheneum, 1963.

———. *Writing American History: Essays on Modern Scholarship.* Bloomington: University of Indiana Press, 1970.

Hobsbawm, Eric J. *Labouring Men: Studies in the History of Labour.* New York: Basic Books, 1964.

Holt, Michael Fitzgibbon. *Forging a Majority: The Formation of the Republican Party in Pittsburgh 1848–1860.* New Haven: Yale University Press, 1969.

Keller, Morton. *Affairs of State: Public Life in Late Nineteenth Century America.* Cambridge: Harvard University Press, 1977.

Kelley, Robert F. *American Rowing: Its Background and Traditions.* New York: Putnam's, 1932.

Kett, Joseph F. *Rites of Passage: Adolescence in America 1790 to the Present.* New York: Basic Books, 1977.

Klein, Philip S., and Hoogenboom, Ari. *A History of Pennsylvania.* New York: McGraw-Hill, 1973.

Korson, George, ed. *Pennsylvania Songs and Legends.* Philadelphia: University of Pennsylvania Press, 1949.

Krout, John Allen. *Annals of American Sport.* Vol. 15 of *The Pageant of America.* New Haven: Yale University Press, 1929.

Lieb, Frederick G. *The Pittsburgh Pirates.* New York: Putnam's, 1948.

Livesay, Harold C. *Andrew Carnegie and the Rise of Big Business.* Boston: Little, Brown, 1975.

Long, Clarence D. *Wages and Earnings in the United States 1860–1890.* Princeton: Princeton University Press, 1960.

Lorant, Stefan. *Pittsburgh: The Story of an American City.* Garden City, N.Y.: Doubleday, 1964.

Lubove, Roy, ed. *Pittsburgh.* Documentary History of American Cities Series, ed. Tamara K. Hareven and Stephen Thernstrom. New York: Franklin Watts, 1976.

———. *Twentieth-Century Pittsburgh: Government, Business, and Environmental Change.* New York: Wiley, 1969.

Miller, Dorothy. *The Life and Work of David G. Blythe.* Pittsburgh: University of Pittsburgh Press, 1950.

Montgomery, David. *Beyond Equality: Labor and the Radical Republicans, 1862–1872.* New York: Random House, Vintage Books, 1967.

———. *Workers' Control in America: Studies in the History of Work, Technology and Labor Struggles.* New York: Cambridge University Press, 1979.

Nash, Michael. *Conflict and Accommodation: Coal Miners, Steel Workers, and Socialism, 1890–1920.* Westport, Conn.: Greenwood Press, 1982.

Nelson, Daniel. *Managers and Workers: Origins of the New Factory System in the United States 1880–1920.* Madison: University of Wisconsin Press, 1975.

Nye, Russell. *The Unembarrassed Muse: The Popular Arts in America.* New York: Dial Press, 1970.

Palmer, Brian D. *A Culture of Conflict: Skilled Workers and Industrial Capitalism in Hamilton, Ontario, 1860–1914.* Montreal: McGill–Queens University Press, 1979.

Pollard, Sidney. *Genesis of Modern Management: A Study of the Industrial Revolution in Great Britain.* London: Edward Arnold, 1965.

Reiss, Steven A. *Touching Base: Professional Baseball and American Culture in the Progressive Era.* Westport, Conn.: Greenwood Press, 1980.

Rodgers, Daniel T. *The Work Ethic in Industrial America, 1850–1920.* Chicago: University of Chicago Press, 1978.

Rose, William Ganson: *Cleveland: The Making of a City.* Cleveland: World Publishing, 1950.

Scott, Joan Wallach. *The Glassworkers of Carmaux: French Craftsmen and Political Action in a Nineteenth-Century City.* Cambridge: Harvard University Press, 1974.

Scoville, Warren C. *Revolution in Glassmaking: Entrepreneurship and Technological Change in the American Industry, 1880–1920.* Cambridge: Harvard University Press, 1948.

Sennett, Richard. *Authority.* New York: Knopf, 1980.

Sklar, Robert. *Movie-Made America: A Cultural History of American Movies.* New York: Random House, Vintage Books, 1975.

Smith, Chet. *Pittsburgh and Western Pennsylvania Sports Hall of Fame.* Pittsburgh: Wolfson, 1969.

Somers, Dale A. *The Rise of Sports in New Orleans, 1850–1900.* Baton Rouge: Louisiana State University Press, 1972.

Stedman Jones, Gareth. *Outcast London: A Study in the Relationship Between Classes in Victorian Society.* London: Oxford University Press, 1971.

Stewart, Howard B., ed. *Historical Data: Pittsburgh Public Parks.* Pittsburgh: Greater Pittsburgh Parks Association, 1943.

Stryker, Roy, and Seidenberg, Mel. *The Pittsburgh Album, 1758–1958.* Pittsburgh: Pittsburgh Post-Gazette, 1959.

Tarr, Joel A. *Transportation Innovation and Changing Spatial Patterns: Pittsburgh, 1850–1910.* Pittsburgh: Transportation Research Institute, Carnegie-Mellon University, 1972.

Temin, Peter. *Iron and Steel in Nineteenth-Century America: An Economic Inquiry.* Cambridge: MIT Press, 1964.

Thompson, E. P. *The Making of the English Working Class.* New York: Random House, Vintage Press, 1963.

Walkowitz, Daniel J. *Worker City, Company Town: Iron- and Cotton-Worker Protest in Troy and Cohoes, New York, 1855–1884.* Urbana: University of Illinois Press, 1978.

Wall, Joseph Frazier. *Andrew Carnegie.* New York: Oxford University Press, 1970.

Ware, Norman J. *The Labor Movement in the United States 1860–1895: A Study in Democracy.* New York: Appleton, 1929.

Warner, Sam Bass. *The Private City: Philadelphia in Three Periods of Its Growth.* Philadelphia: University of Pennsylvania Press, 1968.

———. *Streetcar Suburbs: The Process of Growth in Boston 1870–1900.* Cambridge: Harvard University Press and MIT Press, 1962.

Warren, Kenneth. *The American Steel Industry, 1850–1970: A Geographical Interpretation.* London: Clarendon Press, Oxford University Press, 1973.

Watillon, Leon. *The Knights of Labor in Belgium.* Translated by Frederic Myers. Los Angeles: Institute of Industrial Relations, University of California, 1959.

Wiebe, Robert A. *The Search for Order, 1877–1920.* New York: Hill and Wang, 1967.

## 2. Articles

Alt, John. "Beyond Class: The Decline of Industrial Labor and Leisure." *Telos* 28 (Summer 1976):55–80.

Anchor, Robert. "History and Play: Johan Huizinga and His Critics." *History and Theory* 17 (1978):63–93.

Baker, Robert P. "Labor History, Social Science, and the Concept of the Working Class." *Labor History* 14 (Winter 1973):98–105.

Baker, William J. "The Making of a Working-Class Football Culture in Victorian England." *Journal of Social History* 13 (Winter 1979):241–251.

Benswanger, William E. "Professional Baseball in Pittsburgh." *Western Pennsylvania Historical Magazine* 30 (March-June 1947):9–14.

Birdsall, William C. "The Problem of Structure in the Knights of Labor." *Industrial and Labor Relations Review* 6 (July 1953):532–546.

Bodnar, John, Weber, Michael, and Simon, Roger. "Migration, Kinship, and Urban Adjustment: Blacks and Poles in Pittsburgh, 1900–1930." *Journal of American History* 66 (December 1979):548–565.

Cohn, William H. "Popular Culture and Social History." *Journal of Popular Culture* 11 (Summer 1977):167–179.

Croak, Thomas M. "The Professionalization of Prizefighting: Pittsburgh at the Turn of the Century." *Western Pennsylvania Historical Magazine* 62 (October 1972):333–343.

Cumbler, John. "The City and Community: The Impact of Urban Forces on Working Class Behavior." *Journal of Urban History* 3 (August 1977):427–442.

————. "Labor, Capital, and Community: The Struggle for Power." *Labor History* 15 (Summer 1974):395–415.

Daniel, Dorothy. "The Sanitary Fair." *Western Pennsylvania Historical Magazine* 41 (Summer 1958):145–162.

Dawley, Alan, and Faler, Paul. "Working-Class Culture and Politics in the Industrial Revolution: Sources of Loyalism and Rebellion." *Journal of Social History* 9 (June 1976):466–480.

Evans, Henry Oliver. "Life in Pittsburgh in 1845." *Western Pennsylvania Historical Magazine* 28 (March-June 1945):20–25.

Faler, Paul. "Cultural Aspects of the Industrial Revolution." *Labor History* 15 (Summer 1974):367–394.

Fink, Leon. "Class Conflict in the Gilded Age: The Figure and the Phantom." *Radical History Review* 3 (Fall-Winter 1975):56–73.

Garlock, Jonathan. "The Knights of Labor Data-Bank." *Historical Methods Newsletter* 6 (September 1973):150–160.

Goodfellow, Donald M. "Centenary of a Pittsburgh Library." *Western Pennsylvania Historical Magazine* 31 (March-June 1948):21–25.

————. "'Old Man Eloquent' Visits Pittsburgh." *Western Pennsylvania Historical Magazine* 28 (September-December 1945):99–110.

Gutman, Herbert. "The Workers' Search for Power." In *The Gilded Age,* pp. 31–54. Revised edition, edited by H. Wayne Morgan. Syracuse: Syracuse University Press, 1970.

Harmond, Richard. "Progress and Flight: An Interpretation of the American Cycle Craze in the 1890s." *Journal of Social History* 5 (Winter 1971–1972):235–257.

Harris, Neil. "Four Stages of Cultural Growth: The American City." *Indiana Historical Society Lectures, 1971–1972: History and the Role of the City in American Life,* pp. 24–49. Indianapolis: Indiana Historical Society, 1972.

Harrison, Brian. "Religion and Recreation in Nineteenth-Century England." *Past and Present* 38 (December 1967):98–125.

Hays, Samuel P. "The Changing Political Structure of the City in Industrial America." *Journal of Urban History* 1 (November 1974):6–38.

————. "The Development of Pittsburgh as a Social Order." *Western Pennsylvania Historical Magazine* 57 (October 1974):431–448.

————. "The Politics of Reform in Municipal Government in the Progressive Era." *Pacific Northwest Quarterly* 55 (October 1964):157–169.

Heale, M. J. "From City Fathers to Social Critics: Humanitarianism and Government in New York, 1790–1860." *Journal of American History* 63 (June 1976):21–41.

Hollinger, David A. "Ethnic Diversity, Cosmopolitanism, and the Emergence of the American Liberal Intelligentsia." *American Quarterly* 28 (Summer 1975):133–151.

Holmes, Joseph J. "The Decline of the Pennsylvania Militia, 1815–1870." *Western Pennsylvania Historical Magazine* 57 (April 1974):199–217.
Holt, James. "Trade Unionism in the British and U.S. Steel Industries, 1880–1914: A Comparative Study." *Labor History* 18 (Winter 1977):5–35.
Ingham, John N. "The American Urban Upper Class: Cosmopolitans or Locals?" *Journal of Urban History* 2 (November 1975):67–87.
———. "Rags to Riches Revisited: The Effect of City Size and Related Factors on the Recruitment of Business Leaders." *Journal of American History* 63 (December 1976):615–637.
———. "A Strike in the Progressive Era: McKees Rocks, 1909." *Pennsylvania Magazine of History and Biography* 90 (July 1966):353–377.
Jable, J. Thomas. "The Birth of Professional Football: Pittsburgh Athletic Clubs Ring in Professionals in 1892." *Western Pennsylvania Historical Magazine* 62 (April 1979):131–147.
Jucha, Robert J. "Anatomy of a Streetcar Suburb: A Development History of Shadyside, 1852–1916." *Western Pennsylvania Historical Magazine* 62 (October 1979):301–320.
Judd, Barbara. "Edward Bigelow: Creator of Pittsburgh's Arcadian Parks." *Western Pennsylvania Historical Magazine* 58 (January 1975):53–68.
Kerr, K. Austin. "Labor-Management Cooperation: An 1897 Case." *Pennsylvania Magazine of History and Biography* 99 (January 1975):45–71.
———. "Organizing for Reform: The Anti-Saloon League and Innovation in Politics." *American Quarterly* 32 (Spring 1980):37–53.
Kingsdale, Jon M. "The 'Poor Man's Club': Social Functions of the Urban Working-Class Saloon." *American Quarterly* 25 (October 1973):472–489.
Kleppner, Paul J. "Lincoln and the Immigrant Vote: A Case of Religious Polarization." In *Ethnic Voters and the Election of Lincoln.* Edited by Frederick C. Luebke. Lincoln: University of Nebraska Press, 1971.
Krueger, Thomas A. "American Labor Historiography, Old and New: A Review Essay." *Journal of Social History* 4 (Spring 1971):277–285.
Laurie, Bruce. "Fire Companies and Gangs in Southwark: The 1840s." In *The Peoples of Philadelphia: A History of Ethnic Groups and Lower-Class Life, 1790–1940,* pp. 71–87. Edited by Allen F. Davis and Mark H. Haller. Philadelphia: Temple University Press, 1973.
———. "'Nothing on Compulsion': Life Styles of Philadelphia Artisans, 1820–1850." *Labor History* 15 (Summer 1974):237–266.
Laurie, Bruce, Hershberg,, Theodore, and Alter, George. "Immigrants and Industry: The Philadelphia Experience, 1850–1880." *Journal of Social History* 9 (1975):219–248.
Lewis, Guy. "The Muscular Christianity Movement." *Journal of Health, Physical Education and Recreation* 37 (May 1966):27–42.
Lewis, Robert. "Frontier and Civilization in the Thought of Frederick Law Olmsted." *American Quarterly* 29 (Fall 1977):385–403.
Lucas, John A. "A Prelude to the Rise of Sport: Ante-Bellum America, 1850–1860." *Quest* 11 (December 1968):50–57.
———. "The Unholy Experiment—Professional Baseball's Struggle against Pennsylvania's Sunday Blue Laws, 1926–1934." *Pennsylvania History* 38 (April 1971):163–175.
Lukacs, John. "The Bourgeois Interior." *American Scholar* 39 (Autumn 1970), pp. 616–630.

Lyons, William E. "Populism in Pennslyvania, 1892–1901." *Pennsylvania History* 32 (Spring 1965):49–65.

McClymer, John F. "The Pittsburgh Survey, 1907–1914: Forging an Ideology in the Steel District." *Pennsylvania History* 41 (April 1974):169–188.

McDonald, Terrence J. "Putting Politics Back into the History of the American City," Review Essay. *American Quarterly* 34 (Summer 1982):200–209.

McIlvain, Josephine. "Twelve Blocks: A Study of One Segment of Pittsburgh's South Side, 1880–1915." *Western Pennsylvania Historical Magzine* 60 (October 1977):351–370.

Meyerhuber, Carl I., Jr. "Black Valley: Pennsylvania's Alle–Kiski and the Great Strike of 1919." *Western Pennsylvania Historical Magazine* 62 (July 1979):251–265.

Montgomery, David. "Strikes in Nineteenth-Century America." *Social Science History* 4 (Winter 1980):81–104.

———. "Workers' Control of Machine Production in the Nineteenth Century." *Labor History* 17 (Fall 1976):485–509.

"Notes on the Big Fire of 1845." *Western Pennsylvania Historical Magazine* 27 (March-June 1944):86–94.

O'Connor, John, Jr. "David Gilmour Blythe, Artist." *Western Pennsylvania Historical Magazine* 27 (March-June 1944):29–36.

"The Passing of the National Window Glass Workers." *Monthly Labour Review* 29 (October 1929):1–16.

Powell, Elwin H. "The Evolution of the American City and the Emergence of Anomie: A Culture Case Study of Buffalo, New York, 1810–1910." *British Journal of Sociology* 13 (June 1962):156–168.

Prpić, George J. "The Croatian Immigrants in Pittsburgh." In *The Ethnic Experience in Pennsylvania*. Edited by John E. Bodnar. Lewisburg, Pa.: Bucknell University Press, 1973.

Roberts, James S. "Drink and Industrial Work Discipline in Nineteenth-Century Germany." *Journal of Social History* 15 (Fall 1981):25–38.

Rodgers, Daniel T. "Tradition, Modernity, and the American Industrial Worker: Reflections and Critique." *Journal of Interdisciplinary History* 7 (Spring 1977):655–681.

Rosenzweig, Roy. "Middle-Class Parks and Working-Class Play: The Struggle over Recreational Space in Worcester, Massachusetts, 1870–1910." *Radical History Review* 21 (Fall 1979):31–48.

Sauers, Bernard J. "A Political Process of Urban Growth: Consolidation of the South Side with the City of Pittsburgh, 1872." *Pennsylvania History* 41 (July 1974):265–288.

Schneider, Linda. "The Citizen Striker: Workers' Ideology in the Homestead Strike of 1892." *Labor History* 23 (Winter 1982):47–66.

Sewell, William H., Jr. "Social Change and the Rise of Working-Class Politics in Nineteenth-Century Marseilles." *Past and Present* 65 (November 1974):75–109.

Shumsky, Neil L. "Frank Roney's San Francisco—His Diary: April, 1875–March 1876." *Labor History* 17 (Spring 1976):245–264.

"The Skilled Worker and Working-Class Protest." Special Issue of *Social Science History* 4 (Winter 1980).

Soffer, Benson. "A Theory of Trade Union Development: The Role of the 'Autonomous' Workman." *Labor History* 1 (Spring 1960):141–163.

Sponholtz, Lloyd L. "Pittsburgh and Temperance, 1830–1854." *Western Pennsylvania Historical Magazine* 46 (October 1963):347–379.

Stedman Jones, Gareth. "Class Expression versus Social Control? A Critique of Recent Trends in the Social History of 'Leisure.'" *History Workshop* 4 (Autumn 1977):163–170.

———. "Working-Class Culture and Working-Class Politics in London, 1870–1900; Notes on the Remaking of a Working Class." *Journal of Social History* 7 (Summer 1974):460–508.

Stone, Katherine. "The Origins of Job Structures in the Steel Industry." *Review of Radical Political Economics* 6 (Summer 1974):61–97.

Story Ronald. "Class and Culture in Boston: The Atheneum, 1807–1860." *American Quarterly* 27 (May 1975):178–199.

Thompson, E. P. "Eighteenth-Century English Society: Class Struggle Without Class?" *Social History* 3 (May 1978):133–166.

———. "Patrician Society, Plebeian Culture." *Journal of Social History* 7 (Summer 1974):382–405.

Tobin, Eugene M. "Direct Action and Conscience: The 1913 Paterson Strike as Example of the Relationship between Labor Radicals and Liberals." *Labor History* 20 (Winter 1979):73–88.

Van Trump, James D. "The Romanesque Revival in Pittsburgh." *Journal of the Society of Architectural Historians* 16 (October 1957):22–28.

Walker, Samuel. "Terence V. Powderly, the Knights of Labor, and the Temperance Issue." *Societas* 5 (Autumn 1975):279–294.

Walsh, Victor A. "'A Fanatic Heart': The Cause of Irish-American Nationalism in Pittsburgh during the Gilded Age." *Journal of Social History* 15 (Winter 1981):187–204.

Weber, Eugen. "Gymnastics and Sports in *Fin-de-Siècle* France: Opium of the Classes?" *American Historical Review* 76 (February 1971):70–98.

Zarychta, Ronald M. "Municipal Reorganization: The Pittsburgh Fire Department as a Case Study." *Western Pennsylvania Historical Magazine* 58 (October 1975):471–486.

# Index

Allegheny City, 32, 41, 82; elite
residents of, 33, 99, 104, 106,
116–117; labor politics in, 28, 68, 69,
111, 116–117
Amalgamated Association of Iron and
Steel Workers, 8, 13, 14–15, 28;
conflicts within, 22, 85; decline of,
83–89, 92–94; exclusivity of, 26,
70–71, 74, 87, 89, 92, 94; founding
of, 25–26 (*see also* Sons of Vulcan);
and Knights of Labor, 26, 60, 70–72,
74–75; and politics, 64–67, 72, 93–95;
and temperance, 53–55, 58. *See also*
Craftsmen, industrial; Iron and steel
industry; Strikes, incidence of
Amateurs: in the arts, 35–36, 39, 97–98,
117; in sports, 36, 43–47, 102–104,
123, 125
American Federation of Labor, 14, 66,
70
"Americanization," 91–92, 116, 119,
125–126, 127–131. *See also*
Immigrants, south and east European:
socialization of
Amusement parks, 75–76, 111, 122
Armstrong, Thomas A.: and Civil War
veterans, 24–25, 28–29, 69, 73 (*see
also* Veterans); and Greenback-Labor
Party, 28–29, 68–69, 68 n. 16 (*see
also* Republicanism); and 1877 strike,
8; funeral of, 72–74; and *National
Labor Tribune*, 28–29, 70; and
temperance, 58–60, 73–74 (*see also*
Temperance movement, and labor)

Art: cosmopolitan, 97, 98, 100 (*see also*
Cosmopolitanism); plebeian, 37–38,
38 n. 28, 101 (*see also* Plebeian
culture)
Athletic clubs, 104, 105, 123. *See also*
Sports, elite; "Strenuous life"
"Autonomous workman," 11. *See also*
Craftsmen, industrial

Baseball: elite condemnation of, 44 n.
49, 124; popularity of, 44, 124–125,
124 n. 11 and n. 13, 131;
professionalization of, 123–125. *See
also* Sports
Bigelow, Edward, 107–111, 128, 131
Blackmore, James, 25, 44
Blacks: portrayed in theater, 41; seek
work in steel mills, 88, 89, 91
Blocker, Jack S., Jr., 52 n. 2
Blythe, David, 37–38
Boat clubs: membership of, 44–45, 45
n. 52; passing of, 123; popularity of,
49–50, 50 n. 65, 64, 66
Bourgeois culture: early constraints
upon, 31 n. 2, 34–37, 35 n. 18, 50 n.
67; later transformation of, 96–107.
*See also* Plebeian culture
"Bourgeois interior," 57
Boxing, 43, 123. *See also* Sports
Braddock (Pa.), 81, 86
Briggs, Asa, 2, 122 n. 6, 126
Brody, David, 2–3, 88, 91
Brokaw, Nate, 64, 76
Brown, J. O., 63, 76
Burke, Peter, 2, 120

*181*

Transportation, role in development of Pittsburgh of, 5–6, 9–11, 32–33, 80–82
Typhoid fever, in Pittsburgh, 128–129

Union halls, as centers of sociability, 39, 58–60, 64, 120. *See also* Craftsmen, industrial; Plebeian culture; Saloons
United States Senate: Stanley Committee, 94; *Report on Labor and Capital,* 16–17, 37 n. 26, 54 (*see also* Layton, Robert)
United States Steel Corporation, 92, 94, 119. *See also* Carnegie, Andrew; Iron and steel industry
University of Pittsburgh, 34, 103–104, 105
Unskilled workers. *See* Craftsmen, industrial: and less-skilled workers; Steelworkers

Vaudeville. *See* Theater
Veterans: and baseball, 44, 123; in politics, 24–25, 28–29, 65, 67, 69, 73 (*see also* Civil War, effect on workers; Republicanism)

"Walking city," 32–33. *See also* Pittsburgh: physical growth of; Suburbs
Warner, Glenn S., 104
Warner, Sam Bass, 3, 33 n. 7
Water supply, an issue in Pittsburgh politics, 71, 128–129
Welfare capitalism, 94–95, 116–119. *See also* Carnegie, Andrew: promotes cultural reform
Western University. *See* University of Pittsburgh

White, J. W. F., 77, 124
White-collar workers, 16; growth in number of, 87–88; and Knights of Labor, 74; and leisure, 36, 45–46, 102, 118, 121; suburbanization of, 82
Wiehe, William, 54, 73
Wilkins, David G., 38 n. 28
Wilson, Woodrow, and labor, 129–130
Window Glass Workers Association (Local Assembly 300): condemns Carnegie, 116; and Knights of Labor, 27–28, 70–72, 71 n. 27; and politics, 28, 67, 71–72, 93; power of, 15, 27, 60, 71, 84; and temperance, 53–55. *See also* Glass industry; Knights of Labor
Women, and bourgeois culture, 35–36, 57–58, 98, 100, 102, 114, 116, 118; and mass culture, 122; and plebeian culture, 37, 39, 41, 42–43, 57–58; and welfare capitalism, 117–118
Women's Christian Temperance Union, 77, 122 n. 6. *See also* Temperance movement
Working-class consciousness, 2–3, 8; and work, 20–21; and labor movement, 23, 26, 28; and citizenship, 28–30; and mass culture, 125–126. *See also* Plebeian culture; Republicanism; Temperance movement, and labor
*Workman's and Soldier's Advocate,* 24–25. *See also* Armstrong, Thomas A.
World War I, effect on workers, 126 n. 18, 127–131. *See also* Civil War: effect on workers

Young Men's Christian Association, 47, 113, 118–119